W9-DGS-588

The Making of the 20th Century

This series of specially commissioned titles focuses attention on significant and often controversial events and themes of world history in the present century. Each book provides sufficient narrative and explanation for the newcomer to the subject while offering, for more advanced study, detailed source-references and bibliographies, together with interpretation and reassessment in the light of recent scholarship.

In the choice of subjects there is a balance between breadth in some spheres and detail in others; between the essentially political and matters economic or social. The series cannot be a comprehensive account of everything that has happened in the twentieth century, but it provides a guide to recent research and explains something of the times of extraordinary change and complexity in which we live. It is directed in the main to students of contemporary history and international relations, but includes titles which are of direct relevance to courses in economics, sociology, politics and geography.

The Making of the 20th Century

The Versailles Settlement
Peacemaking in Paris, 1919

Alan Sharp

St. Martin's Press   New York

22731179

© Alan Sharp 1991

All rights reserved. For information, write:
Scholarly and Reference Division,
St. Martin's Press, Inc., 175 Fifth Avenue,
New York, NY 10010

First published in the United States of America in 1991

Printed in Hong Kong

ISBN 0–312–06049–1 cloth
ISBN 0–312–05579–X paper

Library Cataloging-in-Publication Data
Sharp, Alan.
The Versailles settlement : peacemaking in Paris, 1919 / Alan
Sharp.
p.   cm. — (The Making of the 20th century)
Includes bibliographical references and index.
ISBN 0–312–06049–1. — ISBN 0–312–05579–X (pbk.)
1. Paris Peace Conference (1919–1920) 2. World War, 1914–1918—
Peace. 3. World War, 1914–1918—Reparations. I. Title.
II. Series.
D644.S478   1991
940.3′142—dc20   90–22402
                                                           CIP

D
644
.S478
1991

The publishers have tried to trace all copyright holders, but in any case where they
may have failed will be pleased to make the necessary arrangements at the first
opportunity.

Contents

HOLY SPIRIT LIBRARY

92 1551

List of Maps

Foreword

My family and friends have been kind enough, on our French holidays, to indulge and share my enthusiasm for detours to visit those poignant reminders of the terrible cost of the First World War, the battlefield graveyards so beautifully tended and maintained. When the peace conference met it was with the hope that the settlement which would follow would justify this sacrifice and prevent any repetition of such a tragedy. Sadly, the next war was even more costly. This book seeks to explain how the peacemakers saw their task and how they hoped to achieve their ends. The greatest pleasure in completing it, apart from a profound sense of relief, comes from the opportunity to offer my thanks to the many people who have helped me. Unfortunately my father died whilst it was nearing completion. I wish that he could have seen it published as a small repayment for the love and support he and my mother have given me.

Two people, R. H. D. Young of Alleyn's School and Professor Ron Fryer of the University of Nottingham, taught me more about history than any one else, which is high praise for I have had some excellent teachers. Rather belatedly I offer them my thanks. I am also grateful to colleagues at the University of Ulster, in particular Ken Ward, Antony Alcock, Dave Eastwood, Steve Ickringill, Keith Jeffery, Ray Pearson, Dennis Smith, and two former colleagues, David Johnson and Steve Spackman, for their comments, ideas and toleration in the course of many discussions, some more heated than others. Even more tolerant have been the heads of department I have been fortunate to serve, Bill Wallace, Peter Roebuck and Tom Fraser, all of whom have been generous with their assistance. Gillian Coward, photographer extraordinaire, has been a tower of strength, not merely in her help with the maps and the cover. I have inflicted the ideas, and more lately the draft, of this study on several generations of undergraduates and postgraduates on our part-time MA programme and admire their fortitude. I have also gained much as a tutor on some of the imaginative history courses produced by Arthur Marwick and his colleagues at the Open University. I offer my thanks and appreciation to them, and to colleagues and students at more summer schools and tutorials than I care to remember.

John Grenville, Ruth Henig and Erik Goldstein have been kind enough to read and comment on sections of this book and have saved me from error on several occasions, whilst Wendy Simpson cast her eagle eye over the proofs. I am especially indebted to Tony Lentin whose encouragement, painstaking attention to detail and enthusiastic support for the project were crucial to its completion. I offer them all both my sincere gratitude for the improvements they have made, and a minority share in the responsibility for any remaining mistakes.

The University of Ulster granted a period of study leave. The Faculty of Humanities research fund and the British Academy gave financial assistance. The University Library was diligent in pursuing the obscure texts I requested, whilst Vanessa Graham has proved remarkably calm as deadlines passed. Relatives and friends, strategically scattered near libraries, have provided shelter and solace on various research trips. I hope that those responsible will recognise themselves and accept my thanks.

My greatest debt, however, is to my family and especially to my wife Jen, without whose friendship and patience nothing would have been possible. She had grown used to being a cricket, bridge and student sports widow, but to discover a word-processor amongst her rivals came as something of a shock. I am relieved to return the machine to David and Louise for more serious business. I dedicate this book to them.

University of Ulster at Coleraine   **ALAN SHARP**

The Peacemakers

DAVID LLOYD GEORGE (1863–1945). Liberal prime minister of a Coalition government dominated numerically by his Conservative allies. Dexterous, devious and not devoted to the truth except in the titles of his books: the 'Welsh Wizard'.

ARTHUR JAMES BALFOUR (1848–1930). Conservative foreign secretary. Philosopher and politician, an ex-prime minister not noted for his incisive decision-making. 'Cette vieille fille' (old woman), according to Clemenceau.

WILLIAM HUGHES (1864–1951). Australian prime minister, also Welsh. Deaf, determined and difficult.

JAN CHRISTIAN SMUTS (1870–1950). South African defence minister, Boer War opponent turned admirer of the British Empire, a member of the British War Cabinet and Imperial War Cabinet. Persuasive and clever. 'Slimme Jannie' (Crafty Jan).

PHILIP KERR (1882–1940). Lloyd George's private secretary and *confidant* who played a major role in the British delegation. This was often resented by both politicians and diplomats.

FRANCE

GEORGES CLEMENCEAU (1841–1929). Prime minister and President of the Peace Conference. A formidable politician with a wicked sense of humour and a caustic tongue who kept files on his opponents. Survivor of several duels: the 'Tiger'.

STEPHEN PICHON (1857–1933). Foreign minister, a close friend of Clemenceau's but, according to the latter, one of the geese who saved the Capitol. Perhaps symbolically he had to vacate his office in the *Quai d'Orsay* to accommodate the peacemakers.

ANDRÉ TARDIEU (1876–1945). Diplomat, politician and journalist. Held no ministerial post during the conference but was Clemenceau's closest adviser, especially during the Rhineland and Saar negotiations.

ITALY

VITTORIO EMANUELE ORLANDO (1860–1952). Liberal prime minister from an academic background who had been a professor of Constitutional Law in his native Sicily. A man of progressive views but rather out of his depth in Paris.

SIDNEY SONNINO (1847–1922). Conservative foreign minister whose views were often at odds with those of Orlando. His mother was Scots but he was an admirer of Germany though he judged that the *Entente* had more to offer. He was one of the principal negotiators of the 1915 Treaty of London which brought Italy into the war against Germany.

THE UNITED STATES

WOODROW WILSON (1856–1922). Democratic President since 1912. Like Orlando moved from an academic background (professor and President of Princeton) into politics via the governorship of New Jersey. Always likely to disappoint his admirers whose expectations presupposed powers and policies beyond his mortal capacities.

ROBERT LANSING (1864–1928). Secretary of State but, in common with his fellow foreign ministers, rather a marginal figure at the conference. An international lawyer whose analytical and practical though rather limited mind was not entirely in tune with that of Wilson.

EDWARD MANDELL HOUSE (1858–1938). Influential in launching and guiding Wilson's early political career, he emerged as an important diplomatic channel during the war. Genial, able and well-liked, his strength and his weakness was his tendency to compromise. A political 'fixer' who looked for the deals despite his unimpeachable personal integrity.

1 The Old World Falls Apart

In January 1919 the plenipotentiaries and delegates of over thirty Allied and Associated states assembled in Paris for a conference whose task was to restore European and world peace after the most ruinous and devastating war in the history of mankind to date. At its height there were more than a thousand diplomats and statesmen in Paris, far eclipsing any earlier peacemaking assembly in both its size and the extent of its responsibilities. The outbreak of a second major European war in 1939 suggests that they failed to create a lasting peace but, as Gerhard Schulz points out: 'There is a serious lack of logic in all verdicts passed on the peace treaty which ignore the fact that the pre-war policies could not prevent war and which fail to appreciate the essential continuity of the pre-war period, the war, peace-time and the era of revision.' Although none of the leaders of 1914 had planned to start a war which would last for over four years and consume millions of men and vast amounts of treasure, the fact remains that the Paris conference was only necessary because, whether through miscalculation or design, a war between the great powers had taken place. In other words, the world of 1914 was one in which there were sufficient problems of a sufficient magnitude to convince at least some of the leaders of the major powers that a war, albeit a short and successful one, was necessary to the continued great power status and future prosperity of their states. It was thus not an ideal world, seductive though it must have appeared to those who suffered its bloody demise.[1]

THE SHIFTING BALANCE OF POWER

Central to its problems was a painful and complex process of readjustment of the European balance of power. In 1898 Lord Salisbury said: 'You may roughly divide the nations of all the world as the living and the dying . . . the weak states are becoming weaker and the strong states are becoming stronger . . . the living nations will gradually encroach on the territory of the dying and the seeds and causes of conflict among civilised nations will speedily appear.' The Foreign Office took on the air of a doctor's waiting room as ambassadors anxiously sought Salisbury's prognosis for their state, but in the broader view his speech does encapsulate the social Darwinism of the time, with its emphasis on expansion or decay, conceptualising international relations as a struggle. Its anticipation of an increase in the volume and complexity of problems facing the world at the turn of the century is also typical, even if Salisbury remained more optimistic about the prospects than many of his younger colleagues. Population changes, the rise and decline of political systems and the expansion or contraction of economies all suggested that there would be a reordering of the European and world league tables, and possibly maps, so that they coincided more accurately with the realities of power.[2]

Such a process did not necessarily mean that a major war was inevitable – there had been almost a century without a general war when the crisis of July 1914 exploded – but Europe in the new century was full of unpleasant ideas about ultimate tests and blood sacrifices. Contemporaries wrote in increasingly fatalistic tones about the prospect of war. They did so partly because of the intellectual climate of the period, partly because having little idea of what a modern war between industrialised nations would entail, they still saw war as an acceptable, if extreme, part of diplomatic strategy. They felt also that certain problems were reaching an acute stage precisely at the same time as industrial, economic, social and political changes on an unprecedented scale were occurring. Imperialism, nationalism, the decay of the Chinese and Ottoman empires and the question of who would inherit their possessions and influence, were coupled with the need to readjust the internal structures of states to take account of urbanisation and the arrival of mass electorates.

The development of Germany after her unification in 1871 suggested that she had no reason to fear that she would be placed among the dying. This was especially marked in the years between 1890 and 1913. Her population increased from 49 to 66 millions, the annual output of her coal mines grew from 89 to 277 million tons, whilst her steel production of 17.6 million tons in 1913 was greater than the combined totals of Britain, France and Russia. In 1870 Britain had produced twice as much steel and three-and-a-half times as much coal as Germany, yet by 1913 the steel position had been reversed and she produced only slightly more coal (292 million tons). In chemical and electrical goods Germany led the world, and her young, vigorous and rapidly expanding population was well-educated, providing intelligent recruits for her industries and powerful armies.[3]

Germany's rise was set in the context of a world previously dominated, both industrially and in terms of imperial possessions and influence, by Britain, but the situation was more complex than a simple head-to-head challenge for supremacy. The world in 1900 was getting both smaller and larger; smaller in terms of communications and speed of travel, larger in terms of the number of important powers and hence the complexity of international problems. If Germany was overtaking Britain in the production and consumption of energy, both were left far behind by the rapid development of the United States, though this was obscured by the fact that much of America's productivity was absorbed internally and had not yet been unleashed upon the world. In the Far East, Japan announced her coming presence with victories over China in 1894–5 and, more surprisingly, over Russia in 1904–5.

Russia had a larger population than the combined totals of Germany, Austria-Hungary and Britain, the next three most populous states of Europe, but it was spread over a vast area, nearly one-sixth of the earth's surface. Rapidly industrialising, Russia had frightened her nineteenth-century rivals by her sheer potential for future domination, though this potential was probably unrealisable at that time given her size and the available communications technology. In 1914, however, the Tsarist system was threatened by a resurgent opposition, coming to terms with its defeat after the early successes of the 1905 revolution. Historians are divided as to the fate of the empire if war had not come in 1914, some arguing that the regime was incapable of reform and adaptation, others asserting that there was nothing inevitable about a revolution which occurred only after three years of titanic struggle. There can be no doubt that a major factor affecting the attitude of German decision-makers in 1914 was their assessment of the future effects of Russian strategic railway plans and military reforms, which they judged would greatly enhance her capabilities.[4]

Great Britain had enjoyed an amazing expansion of power and wealth in the nineteenth century, and her empire of 12 million square miles meant that Victoria in her last year ruled a quarter of the world's population, but Britain faced the new century with less confidence. She thought of herself as a world and imperial power,

4   THE VERSAILLES SETTLEMENT

but the Boer War had revealed startling deficiencies in the health and education of her people, and in the strength of her armed forces. It had also shown her to be diplomatically isolated and her South African discomfiture was relished by jealous rivals. In an age of rapid technological advance and an increasing vogue for aspiring powers to possess navies, it was becoming progressively more difficult for Britain to maintain her traditional naval superiority, though she made successful efforts to do so. Her industrial growth was slower than any of her main rivals although her economy was still very powerful, and supported by her 'invisible' earnings from shipping, banking, insurance and the dividends from her substantial overseas investments. A new generation of rulers believed that Salisbury's confident, perhaps complacent, style of diplomacy was outmoded and that a more active policy was required, though many were sufficiently muddled to believe that Britain could enter agreements with other powers and yet still retain her traditional 'free hand' in foreign policy.[5]

Some of the other powers had far more reason for concern about the future. Italy's position was always in doubt; lacking both the numbers and the resources, she was either the greatest of the lesser powers, or the least of the great powers, a perpetual striver for promotion or struggler against relegation. Austria-Hungary was a great power, but her respectable population of 52 million and impressive industrial growth rate were undermined by her internal problems as other national groups aspired to the same privileges as the Germans and Magyars within the empire. Beset on all sides by potential enemies, she depended increasingly upon her major ally, Germany, to sustain her pretensions as a player in the top league. In France the nineteenth century had seen a steady relative decline in her power since 1815, when she had the largest population in Europe apart from Russia. For reasons which have never entirely been explained, the French population of 28 million in 1800 had reached only 39 million by 1914, at a time when her rivals were doubling, sometimes tripling theirs. Her industrial capacity was far behind that of Britain, less than half that of Germany, and was overtaken in the last years of peace by Russia. She was finding it increasingly difficult to sustain an army commensurate with her pretensions, needing to conscript over 80 per cent of her available young men to do so.[6]

The question which the other European great powers faced was whether there was sufficient adjustment available for the existing system to absorb the new Germany without destroying itself. This depended upon whether the role Germany saw for herself could be made compatible with the degree of power and influence the other states were prepared to concede, but the difficulties were exacerbated by their perception that Germany herself did not really know what she wanted. This left Germany always aggrieved, feeling that the other powers were working against her and that they wished to threaten her. Her attempts to remedy the situation, which tended to appear clumsy and bullying to her neighbours, seemed only to make matters worse. Her rapid development from an agricultural economy with a mainly rural population in 1870 to the industrial giant of 1900 was not only alarming to her neighbours, particularly France, but it also imposed a heavy strain on the traditional ruling elite, the *Junkers*, the great Prussian landlords. Faced by an expansion of the army and the machinery of government which outstripped the number of *Junkers* available to fill the posts traditionally theirs, and with the challenge of an urban working class organised by the German Social Democratic Party (SPD), the biggest socialist party in Europe, the structures established by Bismarck, precisely to ensure *Junker* domination, now seemed under severe threat. Their attempts to maintain their status and power in the face of industrialisation, urbanisation and the collapse of a deferential society have been seen by some historians as the key to understanding the erratic and aggressive foreign policy pursued by Germany in the early twentieth century. Thus, both internally and externally, the transformation of Germany posed a challenge to the existing system.[7]

NATIONALISM, IMPERIALISM AND ALLIANCES

The success of Germany acted as a powerful spur to nationalism across Europe, but especially in those eastern and central areas where the authority of the Ottoman and Austro-Hungarian empires was waning. Vienna watched the increasingly rapid decline of Turkish power with great misgivings, seeing the mantle of the 'sick man' about to be passed to the Habsburgs. Franz Josef resisted fiercely any attempt to satisfy the demands of the subject nationalities for some form of autonomy within the empire, and those demands grew in intensity. It was ironic that the hopes of those who sought autonomy and a federal structure for the empire rested on the

victim of Sarajevo, Franz Ferdinand. Elsewhere governments encouraged patriotism and nationalism in schools and through semi-
official or voluntary movements and thus ensured that international
relations would be conducted under the gaze of an increasingly
vociferous and intense populace, gaining their simplified version of
events from the new mass-circulation press.[8]

The expansion of Europe into Africa and Asia in the last quarter
of the nineteenth century presaged that curious mixture of short-
term optimism and long-term pessimism which was to be characteristic of the 1914 crisis. Driven by a powerful mixture of arrogance
and doubt, many of the European powers began formally annexing
territories and regions which they had either ignored or previously
been content to dominate at a distance. As a contribution to a
readjustment of the European balance imperialism was a failure, it
was Britain which attained the lion's share of over 4 million square
miles and 66 million people, leaving the others to pick at the scraps
and adding to Germany's frustration. The contribution of imperialism to the outbreak of the war has been much debated. Did imperialism prevent an earlier confrontation in the 1890s, or merely
postpone it, ensuring that when war did come it would be on a much
larger and wider scale? The paradox that the powers whose imperial
interests were most likely to clash actually fought on the same side in
1914 may be set against the idea that, whilst many imperial confron-
tations had been, or were in the process of being, amicably resolved
by 1914, the clashes which they had occasioned and the manner of
their resolution formed part of a wider 'crisis slide' which led to
war.[9]

This idea suggests that it was the accumulation and rapid se-
quence of problems which tipped the balance from peace to war in
the early twentieth century. Each problem alone could be solved,
but each solution reduced the options available for future solutions,
whilst the perceptions of success or failure retained by the participants acted as an important element in their approach to later
crises, narrowing their choices down to war or unlimited defeat.
Some German decision-makers, for example, perceived the outcome
of the 1911 Moroccan crisis as a humiliating failure and were not
prepared to retreat from the 1914 confrontation. The Russians
believed that they had no option but to support Serbia in 1914,
otherwise their claim to be the protector of Slav powers, already
seriously dented by events in 1908–9 and 1912–13, would be

exposed as hollow. Thus, although it was eventually to be the perennial Eastern Question which precipitated the war, there were many other factors contributing to a fatal lack of flexibility in July 1914.[10]

Not the least of these was the loss of that fluidity in the relationships between the great powers which had been so characteristic of the early nineteenth century. Here Bismarck's legacy of an alliance structure was particularly important. Fearing that the empire which he had forged in war would be destroyed if Europe became involved in a new major conflict, Bismarck directed his efforts after 1871 at preventing the most likely trigger of a new war, an Austrian-Russian clash in the Balkans. His policy of interposing Germany between Austria-Hungary and Russia was successful in the short term, but hardly viable as a long-term solution, and his successors were unable to escape from the logic of Bismarck's closer relationship with Austria-Hungary after the 1879 alliance. When Italy joined in 1881 this became the Triple Alliance. Russia was left to drift into the orbit of France, whose permanent enmity Bismarck had ensured by his annexation of Alsace-Lorraine. The Franco-Russian Dual Alliance of 1893/4, which confronted the Triple Alliance, was initially partially directed against Britain, with whom both France and Russia had imperial differences and who, at that time, was working more closely with the Triple Alliance. The gradual realignment of Britain with her traditional rivals, France and Russia, against the powers with which she had traditionally cooperated, Austria and Germany, completed a process by which Germany perceived herself to be encircled and beset by jealous and hostile powers.[11]

Feeling the need for support in the Far East, where the Japanese defeat of China in 1894–5 threatened to precipitate a scramble for China so soon after the scramble for Africa, Britain's first instinct was to turn to Germany. Two attempts to form an Anglo-German alliance failed in 1898 and 1901 and thereafter the two powers drifted apart, with Britain forming an alliance with Japan in 1902, and seeking to reduce her potential areas of friction first with the United States, and then, more significantly, with France in 1904, and with Russia in 1907. Both these *ententes* were arrangements which fell far short of alliances, but both in her own eyes and in the eyes of her fellow powers, Britain came to be more and more closely associated with the Dual Alliance. Germany's attempts to put pressure on Britain rebounded. Her decision to construct a powerful

navy made excellent sense from the point of view of internal politics
– it guaranteed the jobs and profits of the Ruhr and naval dockyard
workers and magnates, provided opportunities for the aspiring
middle class to become officers, and furnished post-Bismarckian
Germany with a prestigious symbol of her new, non-Prussian,
identity – but in international terms it was disastrous. Her attempts
to prise the Anglo-French *Entente* apart during the 1905 and 1911
Moroccan crises were entirely counter-productive, driving Britain to
plan military and naval arrangements with the French which,
though not committing her to participate in a Franco-German war,
did colour Britain's attitude to international problems.[12]

THE OUTBREAK OF WAR

Thus relationships between the great powers became increasingly,
though never entirely, set around the two alliance systems, with
Britain aligned with France and Russia. When the frailty of the
Ottoman hold on its remaining European possessions was exposed
after 1912, the structures which had conducted international relations since Vienna proved incapable of managing the resulting
crises. This was not immediately obvious, since Britain and Germany cooperated well during the London Conference of 1913 to
establish a new order in the Balkans. The partnership was not
renewed, as Grey hoped it might be, during the July crisis following
the assassination of Arch-Duke Franz Ferdinand, the heir to the
Austro-Hungarian empire, at Sarajevo in Bosnia, on 28 June 1914.
Grey could not assemble a new conference, and he could prevail
neither upon Berlin to restrain Vienna, intent upon destroying
Serbia, nor upon the French to restrain the Russians, determined
not to abandon her.

Close to the end of their tether, and rapidly running out of ideas,
the Austrians were ready to contemplate an heroic, death-or-glory,
solution to their nationalist difficulties by a spectacular victory
against Serbia, seen as the fount of Slav nationalism within the
empire. Yet aware of Russia's likely response, the emperor, Franz
Josef, sought the approval of Germany before issuing a challenge to
Serbia. On 5 July, in what has been termed the 'blank cheque',
Germany transformed Bismarck's defensive alliance with Austria-
Hungary into an offensive alliance which placed control firmly in
Austrian hands. Why she should have done this has been a matter of

endless historical debate, but the most plausible explanation suggests a curious combination of short-term optimism, coupled with a long-term pessimism hard to justify in view of Germany's economic and industrial potential. German decision-makers seem to have perceived that they must make a bid for world power very soon, or miss their opportunity for ever. If so, 1914 was a good time, since French and Russian military reforms would make them more formidable opponents before long, and Austria-Hungary was an asset of dwindling value, whilst German forces were well-prepared and ready to execute the Schlieffen plan, which apparently promised complete success against both France and Russia in six months.[13]

Thus the Germans provided the link which transformed what might have been the Third Balkan War into the Great War. Austria-Hungary declared war on Serbia on 28 July, and thereafter orders for mobilisation and counter-mobilisation spread the conflict across Europe as the alliance systems sprang into action. Germany declared war on Russia on 1 August and on France on 3 August, invading Belgium on 4 August. The British cabinet, previously divided as to whether or not they should support France, now largely united around the call to assist 'Gallant Little Belgium'. When Germany refused to comply with her demand to evacuate Belgian territory forthwith, Britain declared war at midnight on 4 August. On 6 August Austria-Hungary declared war on Russia, and on 12 August Britain and France declared war on Austria-Hungary. Of the European great powers only Italy, which declared her neutrality on 3 August, remained aloof.

WAR AIMS AND WARTIME DEVELOPMENTS

Much of the debate about 1914 has centred on the question of whether policy formulated after the war began may be seen as evidence of pre-war aims and ambitions. Thus, did Bethmann-Hollweg's September programme, which demanded widespread annexations and German spheres of influence after a successful war, reveal the true motives of Germany in July 1914, or was it a hastily produced document created only under the pressure of a war which Germany seemed imminently about to win? The answer seems to be that both propositions have an element of truth; war aims did correspond, in part to pre-war ambitions and grievances, like the Russian desire for the Straits or the French wish to regain Alsace-

Lorraine, whilst others grew with the war itself, like the rapid British decision that the German colonies must be forfeit. On the Allied side there were ambitious programmes, though the British and French in particular tended to be able to find more acceptable ways of expressing their aims, from an American point of view, than did the Central Powers. The extent to which either side was prepared to compromise its aims was never really put to the test because there was no point during the war at which both sides felt prepared for serious discussions. Either one side, normally the Germans, felt that victory was in their grasp, or the other side felt at too serious a disadvantage at any particular moment, though they retained hopes that the future would improve their bargaining power. Thus the war continued until one side collapsed.[14]

Edwin Montagu, the secretary of state for India, satirised the expansion of war aims in a splendid passage which has an element of truth to it:

And then there is the rounded Lord Curzon, who for historical reasons of which he alone is master, geographical considerations which he has peculiarly studied, finds, reluctantly, much against his will, with very grave doubts, that it would be dangerous if any country in the world was left to itself, if any country in the world was left to the control of any other country but ourselves, and we must go there, as I have heard him say, 'for diplomatic, economic, strategic and telegraphic reasons.' So we go on. It is fatal to let the French here. It is appalling to think even of ourselves as mandatories there. The idea of an American fleet in the Mediterranean is unspeakably horrid.

It was a caricature, but, despite all the apparent reluctance, the British and French empires did expand considerably in the next few years, and the rivalry which this would cause played its part in the peace conference.[15]

It may be convenient here to summarise, briefly, the changing fortunes and personnel of the war. With the failure of the Schlieffen plan in the west, and the great German defensive victory of Tannenberg in the east, the optimistic expectations of rapid victory faded on both sides, and the search for new allies became an increasing priority. The Central Powers gained the Ottoman empire in October 1914 and Bulgaria in September 1915. The *Entente* wooed Italy in April 1915 and Rumania in August 1916, while Greece finally joined them in July 1917. All these manoeuvrings involved detailed negotiations and the making or implying of promises which would later have to be met. Both sides played for rising stakes, using the double-edged weapon of nationalism in the hope of creating problems in the enemy's multinational empires: the *Entente* in the Balkans, Poland and Arabia; the Central Powers in Russian Poland, India and Ireland. In 1915 Serbia was defeated and the remnants of her armies forced to flee to Corfu, whilst Rumania was crushed in 1917, seeking an armistice in December. Potentially more disastrous from an *Entente* viewpoint was the final demise of Russia in the winter of 1917–18 and the signature of a separate peace between Germany and the Soviets at Brest-Litovsk on 3 March 1918. These setbacks raised interesting complications in the event of an *Entente* victory. Were the wartime deals still valid?

The great prize was, however, the United States, and much of the propaganda and diplomatic activity of both sides was directed towards persuading her of the rightness of their respective causes. President Woodrow Wilson's high-minded neutrality and demands for statements of war aims were irksome to the warring nations of Europe but they could not afford to ignore the possibility of American participation. Declaring that America was 'too proud to fight', Wilson won a second term in 1916 on a promise of continuing neutrality, but this was short-lived. The unlimited German submarine campaign of early 1917 and their attempts to involve Mexico in any war between themselves and America, revealed by British intelligence in the 'Zimmermann Telegram' of 16 January 1917, drove Wilson to seek an American declaration of war on Germany from Congress on 2 April 1917. On 6 April the United States declared war on Germany, and after the failure of attempts to conclude a separate peace with Austria-Hungary, she declared war on the empire on 7 December 1917. In both cases Wilson insisted that the United States would not join an alliance with the *Entente*, but would instead be an 'Associated Power' with corresponding freedom of action. Lloyd George flattered Wilson, telling him that America's vital role would not be in the war but at the peace table. 'The President's presence at the peace conference is necessary for the proper organization of the world which must follow peace. . . . If he sits in the conference . . . he will exert the greatest influence that any man has ever exerted in expressing the moral value of free government.' It was a notion which was put to the test sooner than either man imagined.[16]

THE COLLAPSE OF THE CENTRAL POWERS

The war ended almost as suddenly and unexpectedly as it had begun. 1917 and the early part of 1918 had driven the Allies to desperation, but their recovery was rapid and decisive; by the late summer of 1918 they anticipated victory, probably in 1919. Each of the major powers had initiated studies of their peace aims but the sudden collapse of the Central Powers caught them by surprise. The first hint came in September when Austria-Hungary made preliminary soundings about an armistice, then on 29 September, Bulgaria accepted an Allied armistice, leaving the Ottomans hopelessly exposed. On 30 October the Turks signed an armistice amounting to a surrender. Most dramatically on 4 October the German government appealed to President Wilson of the United States to negotiate a peace settlement on the basis of his Fourteen Points.[17]

On 5 October 1918 the Allied leaders had gathered in Paris for a meeting of the Supreme War Council to discuss the Balkan situation. The French interception of the German request changed the agenda. The Germans had approached Wilson alone but the Allied premiers established rapidly their general requirements for an armistice, referring the detailed military problems to their experts. By 8 October, Ferdinand Foch, the supreme Allied commander, had compiled a list of demands that amounted, militarily, to an unconditional surrender by Germany. It was not until 8 October that Wilson told the European leaders of the German request and sent the text of his reply. In this he demanded a German acceptance of not only the Fourteen Points but also his subsequent addresses, a German evacuation of occupied territory and an assurance that the German government represented its people and not merely the military elite. On 9 October the Supreme War Council considered these communications. Clemenceau and Lloyd George had already fallen out, significantly over the Middle East – Robert Cecil wrote to his cousin, Arthur Balfour, the foreign secretary, that 'the two spat at one another like angry cats' – but they were united in their resentment at the German approach to the most junior, in length of service, of her principal opponents. Clemenceau wanted to ignore Wilson's negotiations until the Germans approached the Allies but Lloyd George persuaded his colleagues to respond for two reasons.

THE OLD WORLD FALLS APART

He feared that silence might commit them to Wilson's peace plans without any reservations and he was anxious that Wilson alone might not obtain adequate military conditions for an armistice, perhaps allowing Germany time to regroup and fight on. These points were communicated to Wilson on 9 October and he was asked to send a trusted representative to Europe to maintain contact in a rapidly developing situation.[18]

Wilson responded by sending his friend and confidant, Colonel Edward House, as his personal envoy on 14 October. His reply to the second German note, received that day, showed a much stiffer attitude. The German note of 12 October accepted Wilson's conditions of 8 October and assured him that their government was representative. Wilson's reply on 14 October stressed that the military terms of an armistice were a matter for the Allied experts but would ensure Allied superiority. He demanded the cessation of the systematic destruction of evacuated territory and of submarine warfare and further proof that arbitrary government in Germany was at an end. The third German note, on 20 October, induced Wilson to recommend his European friends to consider an armistice.[19] He had shown himself a tough negotiator but he still had to persuade his friends to accept his programme. 'Have you ever been asked by President Wilson whether you accept the Fourteen Points?' caustically enquired Clemenceau, 'I have not been asked.' 'I have not been asked either', replied Lloyd George. Their resentment was doubtless increased by the realisation that they had little choice but to accept.[20]

WILSON'S PROGRAMME FOR THE PEACE OF THE WORLD

Wilson had captured the imagination of liberals throughout the warring nations and had achieved a moral domination of the Allied powers which was backed by American economic strength and growing military and naval might. Ironically Wilson had nearly cancelled the Fourteen Points speech which he made to Congress on 8 January 1918 because he felt Lloyd George's speech to the Trades Union Congress in London on 5 January had anticipated most of his major objectives.[21] There were indeed striking similarities of tone and content but it was Wilson and not Lloyd George who seemed to articulate the growing need for aims and objectives of a sufficiently high moral standing to justify the suffering and sacrifices of the past three and a half years of war. Wilson expanded his programme in a series of major speeches throughout 1918: the 'Four Principles' on 11 February, the 'Four Ends' on 4 July, and the 'Five Particulars' on 27 September. Clemenceau mocked the inflationary pressures on idealistic programmes since the time of Moses ('the good Lord Himself required only ten points') but the rapturous reception accorded Wilson by intellectual elites and vast crowds alike on his arrival in Europe in December 1918 bears testimony to the excitement his programme caused.[22]

It has been argued that there are three basic answers to the question of why there are wars: the nature of man; the nature of the state; and the nature of the international system. Since Wilson was an unrepentant Gladstonian liberal with a fundamental belief in the perfectability of mankind, he saw the first possible cause as, in fact, the central element in his cure for the evil of war. His underlying philosophy was that man was good and the collective free expression of the will of men would be a beneficial force. An informed, rational and impartial public would restrain governments from wild and violent actions and unreasonable demands. Hence his reliance on the linked ideas of national self-determination and democracy, and their extension into international relations through the League of Nations. With their belief in free trade, the freedom of the seas, and the reduction of armaments 'to the lowest point consistent with domestic safety' the Fourteen Points exuded liberal philosophy and values.[23]

Many liberals blamed the outbreak of war in 1914 on the secret machinations of the 'old diplomacy'. The new Wilsonian diplomacy was to 'proceed always frankly and in the public view' to reach 'open covenants of peace openly arrived at'. For the oppressed nationalities of the multinational, autocratic Austro-Hungarian and Ottoman empires Wilson prescribed 'the freest opportunity of autonomous development'. The invaded territories of Belgium, France, Rumania, Serbia and Montenegro were to be 'evacuated and restored', Alsace and Lorraine were to be returned to France and an independent Poland re-established with 'free and secure access to the sea'. Russia was to be left to discover her own solutions to her own problems whilst the 'international anarchy' of the pre-1914 period was to be tackled by 'a general association of nations . . . formed under specific covenants for the purpose of affording mutual guarantees of political independence and territorial integrity to great and small states alike'.[24]

Even more important than the specific content of the Points was their high moral tone and this was emphasised by Wilson's later and supplementary pronouncements which stressed the rejection of old and failed methods. 'Peoples and provinces are not to be bartered about from sovereignty to sovereignty as if they were mere chattels and pawns in a game.' There should be 'no special, selfish economic combinations' and 'no leagues or alliances or special covenants . . . within . . . the league of nations'. 'Every arbitrary power anywhere that can separately, secretly and of its single choice disturb the peace of the world' must be 'destroyed or reduced to impotence'. The overriding and central idea, however, was that: 'The impartial justice to be meted out must involve no discrimination between those to whom we wish to be just and those to whom we do not wish to be just.'[25]

As a statement of general principles and as a clarion call to liberals throughout Europe who retained a belief in the essentially progressive nature of historical development, Wilson's speeches could hardly be bettered. Whether they could be translated into a practicable settlement or whether he had set an impossible agenda remained to be seen but it was to this programme that the Germans had appealed. Wilson had now to persuade his European friends to accept his manifesto and Colonel House set about this task when he arrived in Europe on 26 October.

THE PRE-ARMISTICE AGREEMENT

The British disliked the American idea of the freedom of the seas, fearing that they would lose their power to blockade an enemy and destroy his trade. They hoped to establish that the 'free, open-minded and absolutely impartial adjustment of colonial claims' under Wilson's fifth point referred only to the enemy colonies. They were also anxious to see demands for reparations and the trial of war criminals included in any settlement and it was not easy to discern these elements in Wilson's speeches. The French wanted much more specific guarantees of security than the Wilsonian league and also sought reparations. The Italians were nervous of Wilson's formula for the readjustment of their frontiers 'along clearly recognisable lines of nationality', fearing that this formula would not entitle them to the territories they wished to claim.

In fact during the pre-armistice negotiations in the Supreme War

Council from 29 October until 4 November, House was able to establish, with relatively little opposition, the majority of Wilson's programme as the basis of the forthcoming settlement. The Italian objections were largely ignored whilst Wilson accepted that, by the restoration of occupied territory, he meant that Germany should pay for all the civilian damage she had caused by her aggression 'on land, by sea and from the air'. The French were more concerned at this stage with establishing an overwhelming position against Germany in the practical terms of the armistice than in discussing abstract points of principle and thus the major difficulty arose over the freedom of the seas.[26] Here a potentially disastrous Anglo-American confrontation loomed. Lloyd George wished to enter a formal reservation against Wilson's second point whilst House and the president seemed adamant that the principle must stand. House made a veiled threat of a separate peace; Lloyd George countered with a promise to outbuild America in a new naval arms race but eventually, and characteristically, House compromised. He accepted a reservation against the freedom of the seas in the pre-armistice agreement in return for Lloyd George's written assurance that the matter could be discussed at the peace conference. In fact it never was but Lloyd George had conceded more than Castlereagh, who a century earlier had refused to contemplate any discussion of the question.[27]

THE ARMISTICE

The pre-armistice agreement was embodied in the note sent to Germany on 5 November by the American secretary of state Robert Lansing. It incorporated the caveat about the freedom of the seas and the agreed gloss on reparations. On 8 November the Germans sought the Allied military and naval terms for an armistice. Lloyd George thought them so harsh that Germany would reject them but, although deeply shocked, the Germans perceived their military position as hopeless. On 9 November the Kaiser abdicated, Ebert became Chancellor and Scheidemann proclaimed the Republic. At 5 a.m. on 11 November Germany signed the armistice and six hours later fighting on the Western Front ceased.[28]

In practical terms the armistice was a German surrender. In the west she had to evacuate all invaded territory, including Alsace-Lorraine, within 15 days. Within 31 days she must withdraw 40 kilometres beyond the right bank of the Rhine. The Allies would then occupy the left bank of the Rhine and three bridgeheads 30 kilometres deep on the right bank with the remaining evacuated territory on the right bank forming a neutral zone. The Germans were to leave all installations, property and communications undamaged and to abandon, intact, all military equipment which they could not evacuate in time. In the east, although all former Rumanian, Turkish and Austro-Hungarian territory was to be evacuated immediately, German troops occupying Russian territories were to stand fast until required to withdraw by the Allies. Crippling surrenders of artillery, machine guns and aircraft were designed to prevent any continuation of the war whilst the naval terms demanded the surrender of all German submarines and the majority of her surface fleet for internment. The Allied blockade of Germany continued. Nonetheless the Germans had not surrendered unconditionally but on the promise of a Wilsonian peace. How effective a safeguard this was remained uncertain.[29]

The victors had more tangible grounds for optimism. The French believed that the armistice terms brought them the realities of power in return for some very vague commitments. House took the opposite view, believing that he had committed the Europeans to Wilson's principles. Lloyd George had perhaps the most reason for satisfaction. Despite his fears, the Germans had agreed to the armistice terms, destroying Germany's naval power and with it her colonial threat to the British empire. On many issues he shared Wilson's ideas. House's admission that it was possible to 'establish almost any point that anyone wished against Germany' from Wilson's speeches, tended to confirm British suspicions that his ideals had not yet been translated into practical proposals. Thus, with skilled diplomacy, Wilson's unformed ideas could be moulded to Britain's advantage.[30]

CONCLUSION

By the time it ended in 1918 the war had solved few of the problems which had created it. It had, in some cases, dramatically changed their form and increased their complexity, and it had added to their number. Its length and intensity produced an unpromising atmosphere in which to attempt to resolve these accumulated difficulties. Germany had provided the central dilemma before 1914 and she was to continue to do so, with her neighbours seeking security from her ambition and disagreeing as to her future place in the rebuilt system. With her colonies all captured and her fleet interned at Scapa Flow, Germany seemed no longer a colonial or naval threat, but little else was resolved. The nationalities problem which had plagued the old eastern and central European empires re-emerged in a startling new form, whilst the Eastern Question was still being put. In addition there was the matter of who would meet the bill for the war and the question of reordering international relations in such a way as to make a repetition of 1914 remote. The wartime promises made by the Allies, the collapse of four empires under the strains of war and defeat, together with the threat of revolution, added further intriguing prospects to the forthcoming process of peacemaking. Their victory had, however, given them the possibility of proposing, perhaps imposing, their solutions to all these problems.

2 The Paris Peace Conference

THE exasperated academic's suggestion that '*ad hoc ad nauseam*' should be the motto adopted by his university could be equally applied to the Paris Peace Conference of 1919. 'No matter how hard you try, you cannot imagine the shambles, the chaos, the incoherence, the ignorance here. Nobody knows anything because everything is happening behind the scenes', wrote the veteran French diplomat, Paul Cambon, voicing the feelings of many other frustrated professionals in Paris, whilst Arthur Balfour remarked: 'At this Conference all important business is transacted in the intervals of other business.' Contemporary and historical accounts of the conference have shared an emphasis on the haphazard conduct of affairs and the lack of any clearly defined and effective decision-making machinery before the emergence of the Council of Four in late March 1919. Then, in the space of six weeks, many of the major decisions were taken, leaving the conference open to the paradoxical charge that it had been both too slow and too swift in evolving a settlement for the problems of the Great War.[1]

This chapter has two main linked objectives. It seeks to analyse the organisation of peacemaking in its various stages and to indicate a chronology of the most important decisions within that organisational framework. Such an approach divides the subject into four phases: the period from October 1918 until the conference proper opened in January 1919, which was dominated by the wartime agencies such as the Supreme War Council, supplemented by meetings of Allied leaders and their representatives; the early stages of the conference itself when, with the exception of the negotiations about the League of Nations, the Council of Ten was the main forum of discussion and decision-making; the period from mid-March until the end of June when the Council of Four became the major decision-making body, with its work concentrated into two bursts of activity, from late March to early May and again in early June; and finally the residue of the peacemaking process from July 1919 until July 1923, during which responsibilities were uncertainly divided between governments and a variety of inter-Allied agencies.

FROM ARMISTICE TO PEACE CONFERENCE

In the two months following the armistice the initiative which
Wilson had gained in October passed to the French. This was
because they tried to suggest answers to a series of difficult questions. There must now be a peace conference but where would it be
held? How would it be organised? Who should attend? Was a state
like Brazil, whose belligerency against Germany had been purely
technical, to be accorded the same status, in the new age of Wilsonian diplomacy, as France or the United States? How quickly could
and should the conference meet? Should there be a rapid settlement
of the questions at issue with Germany and then a more leisurely
consideration of the wider problems resulting from the war with,
perhaps, ex-enemy and ex-neutral states in attendance? Contemporary diplomatic shorthand differentiated these two phases (not
strictly accurately) by the terms peace conference and peace congress, thinking in the context of 1814–15 and the Treaty of Paris
and the Congress of Vienna. If this occurred would the conference
phase see a settlement negotiated between the Allies and Germany
or one imposed, without consultation, by the former on the latter?

Even though there was a two-month delay, several of these
questions remained unanswered when the conference opened in
Paris on 18 January 1919. The choice of Paris became inevitable
when Wilson abandoned his support for the Swiss city preferred by
Lloyd George and House. Wilson feared the possibility of revolutionary developments in Switzerland which, he cabled, was 'satu-
rated with every kind of poisonous element and open to every hostile
element in Europe'. On 9 November House accepted Paris and
Lloyd George, isolated in his opposition, was eventually and grudgingly, forced to acquiesce. This was, in some ways, very sensible.
The conference would require an enormous amount of accommodation and a massive bureaucratic and technical infrastructure and
Paris could supply these needs. There was, however, the problem of
the probable atmosphere of a city and a state that had suffered
terribly during the war. Neither was Clemenceau's choice of Versailles as the site for the signature of the eventual treaty likely to
soothe German sensibilities or calm the fears of those anxious about
French designs.[2]

The venue was decided but confusion still surrounded most of the
other points about the organisation. House himself favoured a rapid

settlement in outline of the major points at issue with Germany, using the machinery and methods of the Supreme War Council to coordinate the Allied and American positions. This outline would be transformed into a more detailed and final agreement by a peace congress. House wanted the preliminary phase to begin almost at once but Wilson was anxious to attend the negotiations in person. This raised two immediate problems: one of timing, the other of protocol. Wilson did not wish to leave for Europe until he had addressed Congress on 2 December, thus mid-December seemed the earliest possible starting date. Further Wilson, as president, was not only head of government but also head of state. Clemenceau had no wish to give his own president, the prickly Raymond Poincaré, any excuse to join the deliberations, neither did he intend, on French soil, to cede the presidency of the conference to Wilson.[3]

Psychologically and practically these questions lacked the immediacy and edge of military operations. The armistice had relaxed the tension of four years of struggle, everyone was exhausted and needed a breathing space, many fell victim to an influenza epidemic, and problems pushed to one side during the war now demanded attention. Wilson's absence made delay inevitable but the Allied leaders discerned compensatory advantages. Clemenceau wanted to savour his triumphant return to Alsace and Lorraine and also to allow the Germans time to organise a constituent assembly which would create a new, hopefully less centralist and more federal, Germany. Wilson hoped that the shape of Germany and the successor states in central and eastern Europe would be clearer. Lloyd George had called an election in the hour of victory but his campaign did not seem to be capturing the imagination of an exhausted and apparently apathetic electorate. He wished to devote his attention to the hustings until polling day on 14 December. Even then he could not be sure of a mandate until 28 December because the soldiers' votes would delay the count. The Christmas and New Year festivities on top of these factors meant the conference was unlikely to begin before January 1919.[4]

There was still much confusion about the shape of the conference. The only detailed proposals for its organisation and protocol were the French drafts informally circulated in Paris on 15 and 21 November and communicated officially to the Allies on 29 November. Many of the proposals came to nothing but the documents do reveal the French vision of peacemaking. The victorious great powers (defined as themselves, Great Britain, Italy and the United States) would dominate throughout. They would first dictate a preliminary peace to Germany and her allies, consulting the small or new states only when their interests or affairs were under discussion. On questions such as Germany's frontiers, the fate of her colonies, the military and naval terms, indemnities, reparations and the trial of war criminals, the Allied decisions would 'be imposed severally on the enemy without any discussion with him'. Later all the participants, Allied, neutral and enemy, would discuss the reordering of the international community and the establishment of the Society of Nations (the French version of the League). Significantly the League was last on the French agenda. They also cast doubt on the Fourteen Points as a basis for negotiation since they were 'not sufficiently defined in their character to be taken as a basis for a concrete settlement of the war'.[5]

Such sentiments and priorities were unlikely to appeal to Wilson and the French document was quietly disregarded though some of its suggestions, particularly those defining the categories of states to be invited to the conference, did evolve into Allied policy. Other piecemeal decisions emerged in November and cleared some, though by no means all, of the confusion. Wilson, reluctantly and with some disappointment, conceded that Clemenceau should preside but insisted that he himself would attend the conference. English might well join French as an official language of the conference. A preliminary inter-Allied conference was now assumed, but whether its decisions would be imposed on the Germans or would form the basis of negotiations with them remained unresolved before (and after) the conference met. The prospect of an eventual congress was becoming increasingly remote.[6]

On 29 November Clemenceau and Foch travelled to London, where they received an enthusiastic welcome. After the weekend, during which Foch gave the British leaders advanced notice of his Rhineland demands, the Italian prime and foreign ministers, Orlando and Sonnino, joined Clemenceau, his foreign minister Stephen Pichon, Lloyd George and Balfour for an inter-Allied conference. House was too ill to attend, leaving the United States unrepresented, and the conference rather stranded. Some provisional decisions were taken, subject to American approval. There was to be a preliminary inter-Allied conference held in Paris or Versailles. This would be controlled by the great powers to whose ranks Japan was now, at least in theory, admitted. Smaller Allied powers, the

British dominions and new nations created since the war would be heard only when their interests were affected. The European leaders proposed the trial of the Kaiser and his principal accomplices before an international court and suggested the establishment of an inter-Allied commission to consider how much the enemy states should pay 'for reparation and indemnity'. When House was informed of this he objected to the word 'indemnity', thus presaging many future struggles. He reserved the trial of the Kaiser for Wilson's considera-tion when he arrived.[7]

Wilson was by now at sea, travelling to Europe aboard the cruiser *George Washington*, not perhaps the happiest choice of vessel given the first president's views on European entanglements. In an age before public broadcasting, air travel or television, Wilson was an un-known quantity, a larger-than-life figure, undiminished by overexp-osure. His precise plans remained obscure even to his companions on the voyage, but despite critics like Lord Curzon who deprecated the nebulous nature of his ideas, few doubted their high moral tone. 'Tell me what is right and I will fight for it', he told his shipmates. There were those who argued that he should maintain an Olympian aloofness in Washington, avoiding a descent into the hurly-burly of the conference, but Wilson, driven partly by intellectual curiosity and partly by a sense of moral responsibility, felt he must come to Paris.[8]

Large crowds greeted him on his arrival, first in France, where flowers were strewn before him in Paris, and later in London and Rome. Of the major Allied leaders, only Balfour and André Tardieu, Clemenceau's close adviser, had met the president, so they were anxious to assess this unknown quantity. Clemenceau was disap-pointed by Wilson's apparent lack of sympathy for France, whilst Lloyd George was distressed by his failure to pay tribute to the British empire's contribution to victory. The real question, however, was whether he could hold his own with such experienced politicians when the conference began, particularly given the setback his Democratic party had just suffered in the mid-term elections, and what some considered to be an unwise choice of American delegates.[9]

THE COUNCIL OF TEN

The Paris Peace Conference was opened formally by President Poincaré on Saturday 18 January 1919. The veteran French diplomat Jules Cambon prophesied, as he left the ceremony, that the result of the negotiations would be 'une improvisation'.[10] The leaders of the great powers, who had been meeting since the previous Sunday seeking to establish the rules and shape of the conference, certainly began in a manner that suggested he would be correct. The meeting on 12 January had comprised the prime and foreign ministers of Britain, France and Italy together with the American president and secretary of state. On 13 January they were joined by M. Matsui and Viscount Chinda of Japan (who were later replaced by Prince Saionji and Baron Makino) thus creating the Council of Ten, the Supreme Council, effective decision-making body of the conference until late March.

The great powers now came face to face with the problems of organisation and principle which they had postponed since the armistice. They had to decide what was the function of the present gathering: preliminary Allied meeting; German/Central Powers peace conference; forerunner to a full congress. Their answers produced more confusion. They established a series of bodies which were partly hierarchical and partly parallel, partly appropriate to an inter-Allied meeting, partly to a peace conference and partly to a congress. Their main concern was to retain control over whatever occurred but they were aware that the smaller powers would resent their exclusion particularly in view of Wilson's pronouncements on diplomacy. Thus these states had to be found a role but not a decisive one. The answer was the Plenary Conference, which all the recognised Allied states would attend but where discussion would be very limited. The real power would lie with the Bureau of the Conference, in effect a cabinet of the great powers. Clemenceau, elected as President of the Conference at the first Plenary Session, made it clear that its role was to endorse great power decisions. 'Clemenceau rather high handed with the smaller Powers. "Y a-t-il d'objections? Non? . . .Adopté." Like a machine gun', commented Harold Nicolson, a junior British diplomat who kept a diary throughout the conference. Faced with the resentment of these states Clemenceau was characteristically blunt: 'I make no mystery of it – there is a Conference of the Great Powers going on in the next room.' His colleagues were more tactful but equally determined, and the small powers found their influence in matters beyond their own direct interests was insignificant. They were invited to comment on international labour legislation and the question of war crimes and responsibility for the outbreak of the war and later were allotted some seats on more sensitive commissions such as reparations and the League though even these places were in the patronage of the great powers.[11]

The establishment of the Plenary Conference (which met only eight times) identified the meetings in Paris as a peace conference, but there was also a simultaneous and interlocking conference of the major Allied powers. There had been suggestions that some problems might be more appropriately handled by a wider body of states, hence the French plan of a treaty with Germany and then consideration of a new international order by a congress. Yet the conference created commissions to consider issues that overlapped such a division. Reparations and War Crimes were peace problems, the League, International Labour Legislation or the future ordering of Ports, Waterways and Railways might be seen as problems of a wider kind for the congress to consider. Other general commissions established by the Conference included Economics, Finance and Aviation. Their work was, in the main, subsumed into that of later bodies or neglected.[12]

The Council of Ten had also to decide which states should be invited to the conference, how many delegates each should receive – a question fraught with international sensitivity – and which languages should be designated as official to the conference. This was not resolved formally in favour of French and English until very late in the proceedings, but both were used during the official business of the conference, and after vigorous protestations, some documents were also produced in Italian. The Ten at first decided to exclude the press from the Plenary Conference but then admitted them to all its meetings except those in May at which the draft treaty terms were communicated to the Allies.[13]

Only two of the five general commissions, created by the Plenary Conference on 25 January, produced results worthy of consideration. The International Labour Organisation grew from the deliberations of the commission chaired by the American labour leader Samuel Gompers (though it has been claimed that the credit more accurately belongs to George Barnes, a Labour member of the War Cabinet and British delegate to the conference).[14] More significantly, the League of Nations was born in the commission chaired by Wilson himself, reflecting the central role he ascribed to his project. Working around a draft prepared by two lawyers, the

American David Hunter Miller and Cecil Hurst from the British Foreign Office, Wilson's commission presented its preliminary plan for the League to a Plenary Session of the Conference on 14 February. The revised version was approved on 28 April but the basic shape had been established by the earlier meeting.[15]

The League commission was remarkable, not only for the calibre of its membership, but also for the speed of its deliberations. Little else was decided by mid-February. There had been an abortive attempt to create a framework of negotiation with the warring factions in Russia by calling a conference at Prinkipo, an island in the Sea of Marmara, but this problem defied solution. An outline of the mandate system for the allocation of former enemy colonies and an agreement not to return any colonies to Germany were the only other positive steps. The root of the problem lay in the size and nature of the Council of Ten which was too unwieldy to tackle the difficult questions it faced. It lacked an agreed list of priorities and the Japanese delegates were largely superfluous for European matters. It lacked the confidentiality and intimacy necessary to allow complex and sensitive issues to be considered in a fruitful manner. At its last meeting on 24 March there were over 50 people present. Significantly they were still discussing a matter raised at its first meeting in January.[16] Whereas the original Supreme War Council had evolved the practice of informal meetings amongst the principals to establish the main points of policy before the formal session, the Council of Ten rejected such a plan.

The Council was to waste much of February hearing the claims of the smaller powers. It did so to appease their ruffled feelings, but learned little that could not have been conveyed more efficiently in writing, though adept performers like Venizelos of Greece could charm where Bratianu of Rumania hectored or bored. Lloyd George and Wilson were, at first, persuaded to delay the appointment of expert committees to advise them on the claims until after the hearings. Their dreary experiences on 29 January, when they heard the Czech and Polish bids, and on 30 January and 1 February, when the Serbs and Rumanians presented their rival demands in the Banat, changed their minds. 'When Dmowski related the claims of Poland, he began at eleven o'clock in the morning and in the fourteenth century, and could only reach 1919 and the pressing problems of the moment only as late as four o'clock in the afternoon', recalled the American expert Isaiah Bowman, 'Beneš fol-

lowed immediately afterwards with the counter claims of
Czechoslovakia, and, if I remember correctly, he began a century
earlier and finished an hour later.' Between 1 and 27 February the
Council established commissions on Rumanian, Greek, Czech, Belgian and Polish affairs to consider the problems and to recommend
solutions. It also appointed, belatedly, on 27 February, the Central
Territorial Commission, to coordinate the work of the existing
commissions particularly where their responsibilities overlapped,
and to deal with questions, such as the Austro-German frontier, that
lay outside their remit.[17]

The Ten had not only to consider the problems of constructing an
Allied agreement on peace terms but were also, as the Supreme
Council and, on occasion, the Supreme War Council, responsible for
a wide range of questions. These spanned the renewal of the armistice, the feeding and supplying of great areas of Europe, and the
dilemma of how to deal with Russia and other revolutionary states.
They were, in effect, a form of emergency European government and
such pressing duties did not ease their main task. They established
further commissions during February to advise them on different
aspects of their responsibilities; a Supreme Economic Council, a
Joint Economic and Military Committee and a Military, Naval and
Air Committee to produce draft military treaty clauses.[18]

Here the confusion as to the exact procedure to be adopted in
making peace with Germany complicated the task of the expert
commissions. Although the French plans had been clear that there
would be no negotiations with Germany, this was not official Allied
policy from the outset (though it was increasingly assumed from
early March). The commissions were unsure whether they should
create final terms or Allied bargaining positions which would probably be modified as a result of discussions with the Germans or at
least considered in their broader and cumulative effect by the Ten or
an equivalent body. Yet in the event there was no negotiation, nor
was there any overall consideration of the total effect of the recommendations of the various territorial commissions which, with
the exception of those of the Polish commission, normally became
the final treaty terms. The hazards of this procedure may be judged
from Nicolson's comment:

We were never for one instant given to suppose that our recommendations were absolutely final. And thus we tended to

accept compromises, and even to support decisions, which we ardently hoped would not, in the last resort, be approved.[19]

Punch cartoonists could fire Lloyd George by cannon from Downing Street and land him in the Champs Elysée five minutes later, but the reality was different, even with a pioneer daily air service between the capitals. More seriously another cartoon portrayed him as a circus rider standing on two horses, 'Paris Conference' and 'Labour Unrest', whose paths were diverging. Indeed all the Allied leaders were aware of pressing domestic issues that required their presence to resolve. On 14 February Wilson departed for Washington for a month. Lloyd George was away from Paris until 5 March, whilst on 19 February Clemenceau survived an assassination attempt (though he carried the bullet inside his chest for the rest of his life). In their absence their substitutes, House, Balfour and Pichon, did their best to speed proceedings. On 22 February the Ten accepted Balfour's resolution that all the expert commissions should report by 8 March and that the main terms relating to the major treaties should be considered without delay. House, who had always favoured a rapid settlement of the preliminary terms – disarmament, reparations, frontiers, colonies – later refuted the charge that this represented a cunning European attempt to railroad the conference in Wilson's absence and this seems a fair assessment. Nonetheless when Wilson returned he ruled out any attempt to produce a preliminary treaty which did not include the League Covenant. This, in effect, telescoped the particulars of the German treaty and the generalities of the world settlement and meant that the leaders would be under increased pressure to conclude their business.[20]

By the time Wilson and Lloyd George rejoined the remarkably resilient Clemenceau at the negotiating table, many of the expert commissions had produced their reports and there were draft recommendations for the military clauses on which agreement was near. They were, however, acutely aware of the need to reach decisions especially in the sensitive areas that had so far not been resolved. These included Germany's frontiers, both in the west and east; reparations; Italian claims to Fiume; Polish claims to Danzig and Anglo-French differences in the Middle East. Hanging like a threatening cloud over the proceedings were the twin menaces of Soviet Russia and bolshevism – a concept not closely defined by the western leaders but which they loosely equated with chaos, famine, disorder and the revolutionary breakdown of authority. This threat was felt to be especially dangerous in eastern and central Europe, where there was much uncertainty as to what would replace the now-defunct traditional hegemony of Germany, Austria-Hungary and Russia. The need to reach firm proposals for the future of these areas was perceived in terms of a race between order and anarchy. The Council of Ten had not lacked diligence; it had met 72 times, initially twice, more latterly once a day, and established 58 subcommittees; but it had not succeeded. A new mechanism was required.

THE COUNCIL OF FOUR

On 7 March Lloyd George met privately with House and Clemenceau for a wide-ranging discussion of outstanding problems. This meeting was the start of a more informal style of business which characterised the conference until the signature of the German treaty. When Wilson returned he replaced House and when Orlando joined them on 24 March, just before the final meeting of the Council of Ten, the Council of Four had evolved. At first it was an exclusive and private body, with only Professor Paul Mantoux in attendance to act as interpreter, but the recruitment of Sir Maurice Hankey, the British cabinet secretary, as its secretary, intermittently from 6 April, permanently from 19 April, transformed its efficiency and effectiveness. It still suffered from a higgeldy-piggeldy agenda, and dealt with issues as they found their way to its presence, but here at last was a body capable of taking decisions.[21]

It met over 200 times, usually in President Wilson's house. Orlando was a member, but he tended to be isolated partly because he understood but could not speak English, their normal language of business, and partly because he was never convinced of Italy's credentials to be in such exalted company. When the Council failed to recognise Italy's demands to Fiume on the Adriatic he withdrew from its meetings from 21 April until 7 May. This, and his subsequent return, without real concessions and hence 'fiuming', only emphasised that the effective power lay in the hands of Wilson, Clemenceau and Lloyd George.[22]

The Council provided a much more informal, though still pressured atmosphere in which to do business. Good humour could defuse awkward situations: Clemenceau records a confrontation between himself and Lloyd George 'so violent that . . .Wilson had to interpose between us with outstretched arms, saying pleasantly, "Well, well! I have never come across two such unreasonable men!" which allowed us to end the angry scene in laughter.'[23] It sought the assistance of informal groups and individuals to suggest solutions to the delicate problems it faced. Sometimes, as with James Headlam-Morley, Charles Haskins and Tardieu over the Saar and Danzig, these succeeded. In other cases, as with Philip Kerr, Sidney Mezes and Tardieu in the Rhineland, or Norman Davis, Louis Loucheur and Edwin Montagu over reparations, they were less successful. The Council's great virtue was that it decided, even if its methods, or its decisions, were not universally applauded: 'These three ignorant men . . . with a child to guide them', Balfour complained after they had adjudicated the fate of Asia Minor with the help of Nicolson.[24]

Balfour's pique was partly caused by his relegation to the second division of the conference. The Council of Ten had now split, unarithmetically, into the Councils of Four and Five, the latter body being the conference of foreign ministers on which Japan retained her seat. The Five met only thirty-two times in all, and although there were five joint meetings of the two bodies between 16 April and 17 June to review progress and to allocate tasks, they were very much the 'second eleven'. The territorial committees reported, in the main, to the Five and most of their decisions became final, though the Four handled Germany's frontiers and retained theoretical responsibility for the rest. The Five also assumed responsibility for some economic matters and dealt with the revision of the Treaties of 1839 (Bethmann-Hollweg's famous scrap of paper) in which the Belgians and Dutch had a special interest.[25]

The real power, however, lay with the Three, and we have a splendid, if jaundiced, view of their proceedings and personalities in the writings of J. M. Keynes, who had served as a British Treasury official at the conference until he quit in disgust in June 1919. Clemenceau, the 77-year-old French cynic who loved France but distrusted his compatriots, sitting opposite the fireplace wearing his grey suede gloves because he suffered from eczema, saying little, but dominating proceedings when he did intervene. Lloyd George, mercurial, a skilful negotiator, but somehow untrustworthy and unreliable, an unscrupulous man who relied upon the quickness of his mind to overcome his deficiencies in knowledge, and the power of his tongue to disguise weaknesses of argument. Wilson incurred Keynes' special wrath by disappointing his high expectations. He was savaged: 'He had no plan, no scheme, no constructive ideas whatever for clothing with the flesh of life the commandments which he had thundered from the White House.' He was an incompetent negotiator who lacked the armoury to cope with his European colleagues, and he deluded himself that the provisions that emerged from the Four were compatible with the Fourteen Points. 'This blind and deaf Don Quixote' was bamboozled and could not be de-bamboozled even when Lloyd George, belatedly, saw the light.[26]

These men laboured until the end of April to resolve the sensitive issues which had threatened to swamp the conference in mid-March. One can obtain a flavour of the pressures and problems they had to face by considering a typical day. On Tuesday 22 April they met first at 11 a.m. to discuss Alsace-Lorraine; the withdrawal of Orlando; a commission on Syria and Palestine; arrangements for meeting the German delegates; the draft articles on the demilitarisation of the Rhineland; guarantees for the execution of the treaty; the future of Danzig; a draft of an American treaty of guarantee to France and finally the situation in Archangel. At 11.30 a.m. there was a lengthy conversation with the Japanese about their claims to Kiaochow and Shantung. In the afternoon they met at 4 p.m. to consider Italian claims in the Adriatic, and again at 4.30 p.m. to hear the Chinese case on Kiaochow and Shantung.[27] It was within this context of wide-ranging and difficult problems that tended to spill into one another that the Council operated, and any historical account must attempt to balance a clear view of the decisions which they reached with some idea of the confusion and stress in which they reached them. Gradually the treaty began to take shape.

They were given some focal points for their discussions by a paper which Lloyd George prepared. His Fontainebleau Memorandum of 25 March was the result of a weekend conference held at Fontaine-bleau on 22 and 23 March, between himself, Sir Henry Wilson (Chief of the Imperial General Staff), Jan Christian Smuts (the South African defence minister and member of the British Imperial War Cabinet), Hankey, Keynes and Philip Kerr (Lloyd George's private secretary and drafter of the memorandum). Lloyd George feared that the Allies might drive Germany to 'throw in her lot with Bolshevism and place her resources, her brains, her vast organising power at the disposal of the revolutionary fanatics, whose dream it is to conquer the world for Bolshevism'. His memorandum represented, he said later, 'the kind of Treaty of Peace to which alone we were prepared to append our signature.' Its general thesis was that 'our terms may be severe, they may be stern and even ruthless, but at the same time they can be so just that the country on which they are imposed will feel in its heart that it has no right to complain.'

British policy had four main bases. Germany should pay reparations, but the payments should cease, if possible, with the passing of the generation responsible for the war. Germany must be allowed equal access to world markets and resources: 'We cannot both cripple her and expect her to pay'. Lloyd George wished to apply Wilson's doctrine of national self-determination as far as was possible in establishing new European boundaries, but he was 'strongly averse to transferring more Germans from German rule to the rule of some other nation than can possibly be helped'. He favoured an all-round limitation of armaments under the aegis of the League of Nations, although he accepted that the initial disarmament of the Central Powers must be unilateral. Finally the treaty should be one that the Germans themselves would enforce: 'A large army of occupation for an indefinite period is out of the question.' Thus, 'If we are wise, we shall offer to Germany a peace, which, while just, will be preferable for all sensible men to Bolshevism.'[28]

Lloyd George's thoughts were not universally acclaimed by his colleagues, not least because his own actions sometimes seemed at variance with them. Clemenceau's view was that Lloyd George, with the main threats to Britain removed, could afford to be magnanimous, whereas France faced a powerful neighbour without the benefit of a natural boundary like the Channel. The French attempts, strongly favoured by Foch and Poincaré, to gain a Rhine frontier, or at least to detach the Rhineland from Germany, had foundered in the face of implacable opposition from Wilson and Lloyd George, but Clemenceau did achieve a package of linked concessions. In addition to Anglo-American treaties guaranteeing France against a future German attack, Clemenceau secured an Allied occupation of the left bank of the Rhine and strategic bridgeheads on the right bank for at least 15 years, and also the permanent demilitarisation of the left bank and a 50 kilometre strip paralleling the river on its right shore. These decisions were spread between the offer of the guarantees, on 14 March, and the reluctant acquiescence of Lloyd George to the extended occupation of the Rhineland, on 22 April.[29]

Clemenceau's other main territorial concern of direct interest to France produced the dilemma of the Saar. France wished to exploit the coalmines of the area, in order to compensate herself for those mines deliberately destroyed by the retreating Germans in 1918. Whilst there was general sympathy for this claim, there was resistance to the French argument that, in order to exploit the mineral resources of the region, they must also take over its government. Lloyd George was prepared to waive German self-determination, but Wilson was not, and a new crisis loomed when Clemenceau left the Council of Four in disgust on 28 March, frustrated at his inability to achieve progress on this problem, the Rhineland, and reparations. An expert committee, James Headlam-Morley, Charles Haskins and André Tardieu, suggested a compromise whereby Germany would cede the ownership of the mines to France, and the sovereignty of the area to the League of Nations, for 15 years. After this the inhabitants could choose to return to Germany, become French, or retain their special status under the League. By 10 April the Four accepted this solution.[30]

Wilson had promised Poland free and secure access to the sea, but the obvious port of Danzig was indisputably German in population, whilst there were many Germans in the lands between the sea and territory that was incontrovertibly Polish. Lloyd George was alarmed at the prospect of allocating too many Germans to Polish rule, and he spoke, movingly, of the dangers of creating Alsace-Lorraines in reverse on Germany's eastern border. At first he was isolated, but Wilson came to recognise the problem, and the Four renegotiated the Polish-German frontier, making provision for plebiscites in the districts of Allenstein and Marienwerder, and reducing the area of the Polish corridor to the sea. Danzig itself was to become a free city under the League, though linked economically to Poland. The Four adopted this policy on 9 April and, despite vigorous protests by the Poles, stuck by its essentials. This solution, which has much in common with the Saar compromise, was suggested by the same experts. There was some consolation in the notion that, if the problems overlapped, so at least did some of the possible answers.[31]

The most difficult and contentious problem that the Ten had been unable to unscramble was that of reparations. Here abstruse economic theory, an urgent need to repair the dreadful consequences of the war, and the grubbier considerations of electoral politics, combined to create a dilemma that was both emotionally highly charged, and yet of vital practical importance. There was no doubt that, in addition to the enormous damage that was a casual consequence of industrialised warfare, some destruction had been quite deliberately caused by the Germans as they retreated in 1918. They had accepted, in the pre-armistice agreement, that they should make a contribution towards repairing the devastation, but to what extent was left unclear. Essentially the problem revolved around four issues but, because of the interplay between them, their implications were enormous. What was Germany's liability? How much could she afford to pay? How, and for how long, should she pay?

Did Wilson's acceptance of the Allied gloss on 'restoration' in his speeches entitle them to claim their entire war costs from Germany, or were they permitted to seek redress only for damage done to civilians and their property? Was Germany's ability to pay to be measured against her straitened circumstances of 1919, or against some more optimistic forecast of her future prosperity? Should Germany escape at less than the maximum economic penalty? Furthermore, there was an intense political risk if the British and French electorates, whose expectations had been irresponsibly raised before the conference, perceived their leaders to be asking for too little. Finally, how, and over what period should the German payments be made? The most common assumption was that 30 years was, in both a practical and a moral sense, an appropriate period, but there was much confusion as to what a 30-year limitation actually meant.

The resolution of these complex and interlocking difficulties began before the Four resumed responsibility for them from their expert advisers. There would be no payment of war costs as such, but Lloyd George and Clemenceau were afforded some protection against public disappointment by a formula asserting Germany's liability for such debts in theory because she was responsible for the war, but disclaiming them on the grounds of her practical inability to pay. Wilson had also defied logic, and his experts' advice, by accepting the dubious and shabby argument that civilian damage could be interpreted as covering pensions and allowances paid to Allied soldiers and their dependants. The crucial issues of defining Germany's total liability, and of producing a viable scheme for the discharge of this debt, were returned unanswered to the Four, who themselves produced proposals that postponed the real decisions, leaving Germany responsible for an unspecified, and largely unlimited debt.

They did so because this seemed to them the only way to avert a collapse of Allied unity at this crucial stage of the negotiations. Both Clemenceau and Lloyd George resisted any total sum being named in the treaty, fearing public disappointment, neither would they accept any time limit on payments. The way out of this impasse was to create a Reparations Commission which would, in May 1921, produce a statement of account to Germany based upon a list of damages (including military pensions and allowances) for which compensation could be claimed. Thus the Four bought themselves two years of grace to settle the reparations dilemma, but at the cost of continuing uncertainty as to Germany's economic and financial future, and enormous German resentment at the 'War Guilt' clause (Article 231).[32]

In his diary House noted: 'Saw Mezes, Haskins, and other of our experts many times during the day trying to work out some solution of the Dantzig [sic], Sarre [sic], and reparations controversies.'[33] These problems combined to produce the crisis of the conference, which lasted from mid-March until mid-April. During this period Clemenceau had stormed out of a meeting with Wilson, who had threatened to summon the *George Washington* to take him home. Lloyd George had to quell a possible parliamentary revolt over his handling of reparations. Gradually the Four untangled the separate threads and began to resolve the issues, and the conference moved ahead. The solutions proposed by the experts and approved by the Four were passed rapidly to the legal advisers to be couched in diplomatic language and, by 13 April, the Four felt sufficiently confident that their task was nearing completion to invite the German delegates to Versailles. There ensued an extraordinary duel between Clemenceau and Foch, who refused at first to pass the message to the Germans on the grounds that French security had not yet been assured. Clemenceau prevailed and, on 18 April, the Allied invitation reached Berlin. Eleven days later the German plenipotentiaries arrived at Versailles.[34]

Yet the drama was not complete. Italy had substantial territorial claims along her frontier with Austria, and in the Adriatic. Wilson was prepared to adjust his principles to accommodate Italian ambitions in the Tyrol, but he would make no concessions elsewhere, particularly over the fate of Fiume, a port claimed by both Italy and the emerging state of Yugoslavia. When Orlando realised this, he withdrew from the Council on 21 April, and by 23 April there was a complete deadlock, which Wilson sought to solve in American presidential style by an appeal to the Italian people over the heads of their state leaders. He did not succeed, but Orlando's boycott alienated his colleagues and prejudiced Italy's position, not only in Europe, but also in the Near East. In her absence the Three sought to limit Italian influence in Anatolia by authorising the landing of a Greek force at Izmir. The results of this action were to have enormous consequences for the whole Near Eastern settlement. Turkish resentment at the Greek invasion inspired the nationalist revolt which, under the brilliant leadership of Mustapha Kemal, undid the Treaty of Sèvres and forced the Allies to negotiate a new treaty at Lausanne. All of this lay in the future, and Orlando's chief current concern was Fiume and the Adriatic. His return, empty-handed, to the Four on 7 May, was an Italian humiliation.[35]

In these circumstances, the Japanese claims to former German colonial possessions in China left the Four with a particularly embarrassing choice between principle and the realities of power. Their decision, in favour of Japan, must have been galling to the Italians. Worse, the Chinese refused to sign the treaty. The Four were reminded, by the imminent arrival of the German delegation, that the treaty would recognise the creation of several new states, which would need to be apprised of their international responsibilities, in both practical matters such as posts, telephones and telegraphs, and more principled questions such as the proper treatment of minorities within their borders. Furthermore, there was a queue of smaller enemy states waiting, neither patiently nor peacefully, for their fates to be settled, and indeed these matters became more prominent in May.[36]

The attention, however, still centred on the draft treaty with Germany. All the varied and disparate decisions reached separately, and under great pressure, by the Ten, the Five, and the Four, were now assembled for the first time into a single document. For some the effect was shattering. Foch was still dissatisfied about French security, and embarrassed Clemenceau by saying so in public, on 6 May, at the Allied Plenary Session to receive the treaty. Many, in a gloomy British delegation, found the cumulative effect too harsh upon Germany. It appeared as if the treaty as a whole was greater than the sum of its parts, a mathematical absurdity that Keynes would have found apt.[37]

The text was handed to the German delegates at the Hotel Trianon on 7 May, in a formal ceremony attended by all the Allied powers. The icy atmosphere was not improved when Count Brockdorff-Rantzau, the head of the German delegation, made his speech seated. Whether this was nervousness, or a calculated gesture, not even he appeared sure. Balfour had not noticed: 'I make it a rule never to stare at people when they are in obvious distress.' 'A. J. B. makes the whole of Paris seem vulgar', commented Nicolson.[38] The Germans now had 15 days to make their written observations on the draft, there would be no meetings, and the main shape of the treaty was not open to negotiation. In what were understandable, but possibly counter-productive tactics, they initially subjected the individual clauses to a barrage of notes which were repulsed by Allied expert committees, and led to a very few minor changes of wording. Later Brockdorff-Rantzau requested an extension of a week, and the Germans began preparing an overall reply and covering letter, which they presented on 29 May.[39]

Meanwhile Lloyd George, fearing that the Germans would not sign the treaty as it stood, sought approval to renegotiate parts of it from a cabinet meeting, specially convened in Paris, on 31 May. On 1 and 2 June, the cabinet met in joint session with the British delegation, and authorised the prime minister to seek plebiscites in Upper Silesia, and other areas disputed by the Poles and Germans; the early admission of Germany to the League; concessions on reparations, and the withdrawal of the Rhineland occupation. He could, if necessary, withdraw the navy from the German blockade, and refuse to allow British troops to participate in a renewal of hostilities.[40] Thus armed, he returned to his colleagues in the Council of Four. He was neither welcomed nor, except in the important matter of the Silesian plebiscite, was he very successful. He obtained minor concessions as to the costs, but not the length, of the Rhineland occupation, and an anodyne form of words which offered Germany some prospect of joining the League after a period of probation. Although he made much of British objections to the reparations draft, he resisted Wilson's final attempt to name a fixed sum in the treaty.

Clemenceau was irritated at what he saw as another British

attempt to make concessions at other people's expense. Moreover he was fairly certain that the Germans would sign. Fearing that the French might have installed microphones to eavesdrop on their deliberations, the Germans employed a pianist to confuse the listeners, but with the telephone and telegraph wires tapped, the French knew that the German mood was one of bitter, but resigned, indignation.[41] Wilson accused Lloyd George of 'funk', and his exasperation was increased when the prime minister combined with Clemenceau to thwart any radical change to the reparations clauses. He was so cross that Lloyd George had a difficult task to convince him that his principles demanded his support for the Upper Silesian plebiscite. In its essentials, therefore, the draft treaty was little affected by Lloyd George's intervention, though it might be argued that British revisionism dated from this episode.[42]

Neither did the Germans have much effect on the treaty. When they were handed the final version on 16 June the original text had been amended in red ink in a few places. The Allies' covering letter maintained their condemnation of Germany both for provoking the war and for the manner in which she had fought it. It allowed her five days to sign though this was extended until 23 June. The German delegation returned home and advised against signing but the military provisions of the armistice had crippled Germany's ability to fight. Brockdorff-Rantzau resigned, the government fell and Bauer, the new premier, in accepting the treaty, tried to enter caveats against the war-guilt and war-crimes clauses. The Four rejected this plea on 22 June and presented the Germans with a final ultimatum – sign within 24 hours or hostilities would recommence. Germany capitulated.[43]

On Saturday 28 June 1919, the fifth anniversary of the Sarajevo assassinations, the Treaty of Versailles was signed in the Hall of Mirrors in Louis XIV's great palace. Some Frenchmen were disappointed that it was Müller and Bell, Social Democratic representatives of the new order, and not the Kaiser and his generals, who had to witness this carefully staged revenge for the humiliation of 1871. Some of the British observers felt the ceremony lacked dignity and the treaty lacked hope. Orlando, whose government had fallen on 19 June, was, perhaps aptly, not there. For Clemenceau it was 'une belle journée'. The triumph of the Three as they stood on the steps of the palace after the ceremony was captured by the newsreel cameras, though not all appreciated their presence: 'The Press is destroying all romance, all solemnity, all majesty. They are as unscrupulous as they are vulgar', complained Frances Stevenson. Harold Nicolson drank bad, if free, champagne, and retired 'To bed, sick of life'.[44]

THE FINAL PHASE

The signature of the German treaty was the most spectacular, but by no means the final, moment in the lengthy process of peacemaking. The Three held one last business meeting after the ceremony before Wilson and Lloyd George left Paris that evening. Now a new Supreme Council, the Heads of Delegation, assumed the main decision-making role in Paris, supervising the closing stages of the negotiations for the Austrian treaty, the main shape of which had been determined by the Four in May and June. The Austrians received their draft treaty on 20 July, presented their reply on 6 August and were given the final text on 2 September with a five-day deadline for acceptance. The Treaty of St Germain was signed on 10 September. Thereafter the pace noticeably slackened. The Bulgarians were handed a draft treaty on 19 September, produced their counter-proposals on 24 October and received the final text and a ten-day ultimatum on 3 November. The Treaty of Neuilly was signed on 27 November. The Hungarian delegation was summoned to Paris on 1 December, arrived on 7 January 1920 and finally signed the Treaty of Trianon on 4 June. The final act was the signing of the Treaty of Sèvres with the Ottoman empire on 10 August 1920, though this was later renegotiated and a fresh treaty signed with Turkey at Lausanne on 24 July 1923.

Meanwhile events in America during the autumn of 1919 cast doubts upon the future of the decisions so painfully reached in Paris. Faced with powerful opposition to the settlement he had negotiated, and particularly to what were portrayed as the entangling obligations of the League of Nations and dangerous concessions to the Japanese in the Pacific, Wilson had embarked upon a whistle-stop crusade seeking the support of his fellow citizens in the coming debate over ratification of the treaty in the Senate. Following so closely upon his exertions in Paris, the strain proved too much and he suffered a stroke, which paralysed both the president and the presidency. Neither the efforts of House, nor those of Lord Grey, whom the British had sent on a special mission to Washington, could reconcile Wilson and his opponents and on 19 November the Senate rejected the treaty. It did so again, and finally, on 19 March 1920. The United States signed separate peace treaties with Germany, Austria and Hungary in August 1921. Wilson had played an always vital, and sometimes decisive, role in the drafting of the settlement. Its character would have been very different without his presence, and much of the execution of the treaty also required the United States to take an active and responsible part. There was no aspect of the treaty which could fail to be affected by this defection, but the future of the League, the shape of the Middle East and the continuing history of reparations would be markedly different as a result.[45]

The later stages of the Paris conference were complicated by increasing doubts as to its authority and status. Clemenceau was on hand to attend its meetings but his fellow premiers could no longer neglect their other responsibilities. Yet Lloyd George in particular was loath to allow too much authority to a body of which he was not a member and he sought to devalue it by substituting a diplomat for Balfour as British representative. Nonetheless important questions remained, quite apart from peace terms for the smaller enemy states. There was a long, unexpected delay between the signature of the German treaty and its entry into force on 10 January 1920 and this raised difficult armistice and treaty execution problems. The Supreme Council had also to decide what penalty to exact for the June scuttling of the German fleet in Scapa Flow. When negotiations on this point broke down in December, Lloyd George was dismayed to find his government apparently on the brink of renewed hostilities as a result of an ultimatum delivered by the Paris conference to the Germans. He was now determined to conclude its role and the conference ended on 21 January 1920 but this did not resolve his problems.

A new organisation, the Conference of Ambassadors, meeting in Paris, assumed part of its functions as peacemaker and executor of the treaties but without a clear distinction between its role and that of a revived, peripatetic Supreme Council of senior Allied politicians. This body, meeting intermittently in a variety of Allied capitals and desirable watering places, inaugurated the era of 'diplomacy by conference'. Matters reached an extreme pitch of confusion when, in March 1920, these two bodies, one in Paris and the other meeting in London, each claiming to be the Peace Conference, took simultaneous but opposite decisions on the same question.[46] Thus it is not perhaps surprising that the final stages of peacemaking took so long. It was not possible to sustain the intensity or the high-powered level of personnel of the Council of Four and the continuing press-ures of domestic and international politics distracted attention from the smaller enemy states. The organisational confusion that had dogged the conference from its outset was thus sustained to the very end. In such circumstances it is remarkable that any treaties emerged, but the men of 1919 succeeded, however imperfectly, in producing a global settlement despite the enormously complex problems they faced. The following chapters will isolate the main headings of that settlement and examine the negotiations in greater detail.

3 The League of Nations

There are few better illustrations of the complexities and paradoxes of the peacemaking process in 1919 than the ideas and negotiations that combined to produce the Covenant of the League of Nations. Seeking to build upon past experience but also attempting to create a new framework for diplomatic activity, the League represented a revolutionary basis for future international stability. It sought to limit the untrammelled exercise of national sovereignty that had allegedly characterised the 'international anarchy' of 1914, yet it stopped far short of supranational power. It thus embodied the paradox of an attempt to combine collective security with the continued existence of national sovereignty. In theory based on the idea of equality among nations but in practice controlled by the great powers, it aimed at producing a peaceful world by threatening a determined aggressor with, as a last resort, war. Designed to guarantee the territorial integrity and political independence of its members but also to permit peaceful changes to frontiers and treaties that had become inappropriate, the League is an apt symbol of the idealism, vision, difficulties and contradictions of the 'new diplomacy'.

THE ORIGINS OF THE LEAGUE

In his Fourteen Points address of 8 January 1918, President Wilson's final demand was for 'a general association of nations . . . formed under specific convenants for the purpose of affording mutual guarantees of political independence and territorial integrity to great and small states alike.' The idea of a general alliance to preserve peace was not new; Henry IV's friend and adviser, Sully, had suggested something of the kind in the seventeenth century, whilst the ideal of a united Christendom predated his 'Grand Design' by several hundred years. It was during the nineteenth century, however, that serious consideration was given to the practicability of such an idea. The Holy Alliance of 1815 sought to stabilise the frontiers and internal regimes of post-Vienna Europe though neither Castlereagh, nor his successor, Canning, was prepared to join any blanket guarantee of the *status quo*. We shall find echoes of this attitude in the British concern to build some mechanism for peaceful change into the Covenant in 1919.[1]

On the other hand, successive British foreign secretaries upheld the Concert of Europe, an informal and less ambitious instrument of great power diplomacy that replaced the congress system in the 1820s. The concert was essentially a club of the major powers in which they habitually, but not invariably, consulted one another when important matters affecting the general European situation arose. With the exception of the turbulent years between 1854 and 1871 the concert helped to keep the European peace from 1815 to 1914, but it was an optional device that no one was obliged to use, as Grey discovered in 1914 when he strove, unsuccessfully, to call the conference which, he remained convinced, would have prevented the war. Hence his strong commitment to the idea of a league which could force international consultation and delay the resort to arms in such a crisis. For many British advocates of a league, the concert model (given a more formal and powerful structure) was what they desired.[2]

The increasing trade and improving communications of the nineteenth century prompted practical examples of international cooperation. Postal, railway, port and shipping arrangements, the combating of disease and the slave trade, the regulation of international rivers and waterways, were tackled successfully despite the intense national rivalries of the period. This helped to promote the use of international law to resolve certain types of problem and some powers were prepared to sign international arbitration treaties for the settlement of such disputes as impinged neither on their 'honour nor vital interests'. The first Hague Conference of 1899 made little progress on the disarmament question it had been called to tackle, but it did establish a Permanent Court of Arbitration, though this remained an obscure body.[3]

There were thus two strands of nineteenth-century thought and practice that fed into the League: the idea of disputes which could be tackled by law and an international court, and the habit of great power consultation. There were further developments in the early twentieth century. In 1908, Léon Bourgeois, a French lawyer and politician who was a member of the Hague court, published a book entitled *La Société des nations* from which came the eventual French name for the League, but little else. The outbreak of war in 1914 added intensity to the search for an alternative diplomacy.[4]

WARTIME DEVELOPMENTS

In both Great Britain and the United States there were small groups of enthusiasts advocating new methods in international relations. Their influence, despite the support of ex-Presidents Taft and Roosevelt in America and Lord Bryce, Robert Cecil and Edward Grey in Britain, was not great. This was particularly so in the early days of the war, when such activities had a faintly unpatriotic air about them but the stalemate and cost of the war began to change the public perception of groups like the League to Enforce Peace, the League of Nations Society and the League of Nations Union. Each helped to promote an image in the public mind, even if the final Covenant had little in common with their suggestions for its organisation.[5]

A number of other wartime developments helped to promote the league idea. The need to make a favourable impression in the United States reinforced Grey's enthusiasm for reform, whilst his cordial contacts with Wilson's unofficial adviser, Colonel House, convinced him that here was an opportunity for Anglo-American cooperation which might assist in bringing America and the Allies closer together. When Wilson spoke to the League to Enforce Peace on 27 May 1916 endorsing their ideas, the League of Nations acquired its most effective champion. His call for a

> universal association of the nations to maintain the inviolate security of the highways of the seas for the common good and unhindered use of all nations of the world, and to prevent any war begun either contrary to treaty convenants or without warning and full submission of the causes to the opinion of the world – a virtual guarantee of territorial integrity and political independence

might contain ideas not entirely welcome to Britain but this was offset by the attractive possibility of American assistance in the war.[6]

The Bolshevik seizure of power in November 1917, and their publication of some of the secret wartime deals between the Allies, increased the importance of the League as a disclaimer of such venal policies. Furthermore, Wilson found that the Bolsheviks had annexed much of his programme, leaving the League as one of the few distinctive elements in his battle for reformist capitalism against Lenin's revolutionary socialism. In the grim winter of 1917–18, the need to carry organised labour along with the war effort grew in importance. Hence, when Lloyd George made the first substantial and detailed statement of British war aims, he spoke, on 5 January 1918, to the Trades Union Congress and he included a reference to his belief that 'a great attempt must be made to establish by some international organisation an alternative to war as a means of settling international disputes'. Three days later Wilson made his historic address to Congress. Thus, as George Egerton states: 'By 1918 the league of nations idea stood at the center of the ideological response of British and American liberalism to the tragedy of modern war and the fear of revolution.'[7]

Yet it was an idea with little agreed substance since none of the major powers had advanced any firm proposals for the organisation and functions of a league. In early 1918 a series of semi-official studies and reports in Great Britain, France and the United States revealed the divergent approaches and philosophies of the three major Allies. The process began in Britain where, on 3 January 1918 and prompted by Robert Cecil, Lloyd George appointed the Phillimore Committee to investigate 'particularly from a judicial and historical point of view' the background and feasibility of earlier proposals. The chairman, Sir Walter Phillimore, was a High Court judge who had already published, in 1917, a study of the historical precedents and advanced his own plan of a league. The other members were three historians, Julian Corbett, A. F. Pollard and J. H. Rose, and three Foreign Office officials, Eyre Crowe, William Tyrrell and Cecil Hurst. They met nine times before submitting an Interim Report to the foreign secretary, Arthur Balfour, on 20 March 1918, in the hope that he might be able to use it to initiate inter-Allied discussions before the end of the war.

The essence of the Phillimore proposals was an alliance to preserve peace amongst its members. Initially at least, membership would be restricted to the present Allies, with the possible addition of some neutrals. The League would have a permanent base but its functions would be limited to the solution of urgent international disputes and little else. They recommended arbitration as the best method of resolving problems but did not provide for a permanent international court or similar mechanism. If arbitration seemed an unsuitable or unacceptable method, then Phillimore envisaged that a conference would meet, probably consisting of the normal diplomats representing the members at whatever capital was chosen as its base. This conference would assemble, only in a crisis, to recommend a solution 'calculated to ensure a just and lasting settlement'.[8]

As the first of the semi-official league studies, Phillimore's report naturally raised many of the key issues that were to be debated in Paris. Its initial premise, that the League would be an organisation of states, was never seriously disputed. Indeed the report throughout showed great sympathy to the idea of national state sovereignty and, in most cases, rejected proposals that seemed to trespass on the authority of the member governments. On one question, however, Phillimore did propose a new and radical idea which did limit their freedom of action. If a member broke the alliance, and went to war without exhausting the established procedures, then Phillimore suggested that the offending state 'will become *ipso facto* at war with all the other Allied states, and the latter agree to take and support each other in taking jointly and severally all such measures – military, naval, financial, and economic – as will best avail for restraining the breach of the covenant.' Here was the kernel of the idea of collective security, and the fate of this proposal would determine the eventual shape of the League.[9]

Such an automatic sanction was exactly what Grey had felt was lacking in 1914, but it was highly controversial. Phillimore also raised another delicate matter: in this new alliance of equals, would some be more equal than others? Should the votes of the great powers be given extra weight in such issues, or stages of a decision, where majority voting was acceptable? Whilst commonsense, and a recognition that the greater share of any burden of enforcement would fall upon them, suggested that they should, Phillimore warned of the likely resentment of the smaller powers and declined to make any firm proposal.[10] Phillimore's suggestions, with the exception of automatic sanctions, amounted to a minor reform of existing diplomatic practice. His League was a close relative to the concert, and probably represented the mainstream of British official thinking on the matter, though not necessarily that of the prime minister and his advisers, Hankey and Kerr. Whether these ideas would prove compatible with those of their allies and, in particular, with those of President Wilson, remained to be seen.[11]

The French produced an equivalent document on 8 June 1918, following an investigation by a committee headed by Léon Bourgeois. His proposals were equally characteristic and revealing. There should be an International Council of heads of government held each year, and a smaller permanent committee working throughout the period between the full Councils. Disputes would be divided into those that could be settled by law (justiciable disputes) – these should be referred to an International Tribunal – and those that could not (non-justiciable disputes) which the Council would consider. Although these ideas were more elaborate than Phillimore's, they represented proposals that were common in Anglo-American league circles and were unlikely to cause serious differences of principle between France and her friends. In addition to legal and economic weapons, however, Bourgeois proposed to give the League its own military forces, to be provided by contingents from member armies, and the nucleus of an independent, international general staff. This force would be available to enforce League decisions and to afford protection to members against outside powers. Since, like Phillimore, Bourgeois envisaged only the current allies as founder members of the League, his proposals amounted to a perpetuation of the wartime alliance against Germany. Such a suggestion attracted little support in Britain or America, but remained a recurring theme in French plans.[12]

It is perhaps surprising that Wilson's ideas on the shape of the League remained very vague at this stage. He was, however, adamant in refusing to be drawn into inter-Allied discussion on the matter, despite approaches from the French, and especially the British, governments. He was reluctant to commit himself too early to any particular model, though he declared himself unimpressed with either the Phillimore or Bourgeois plans. Even so, when House produced his first draft of a proposal on 16 July 1918, it leaned heavily on Phillimore's suggestions for the settlement of disputes. House added his own practical touches to the funding and administration of the League and he stressed the role of arbitration. The distinctive feature of House's approach lay in his commitment to a moral code in international relations. Seeking to render unnecessary the 'abominable custom of espionage', he believed that, 'the same standards of honor and ethics shall prevail internationally and in the affairs of nations as in other matters'. Wilson did not share this idiosyncratic approach to diplomacy, but he did use House's proposals as the basis of his own first draft in the summer of 1918.[13]

Wilson's first version of the Covenant included compulsory and binding arbitration for all disputes which could not be settled by diplomacy. He envisaged a Body of Delegates, consisting of the ambassadors of member states to the state chosen as the League's headquarters, as well as the foreign minister of the host state. This prototype of what became the Assembly would establish a Secretariat and act as a court of appeal in arbitration cases where the arbitrators' decision was contested. The members could guarantee to 'each other political independence and territorial integrity' but Wilson did allow for peaceful change in certain circumstances. The draft reflected his commitment to disarmament and his distrust of private armaments manufacturers. He was firmer in his sanctions than House, writing of the obligation 'to use any force that may be necessary' to discipline recalcitrant powers. He offered little guidance on membership and he left the practical details to be established by the Body of Delegates.[14]

This then was the state of play just before the German request for an armistice. Wilson disliked the British approach as being insufficiently different from the mechanisms that had failed in 1914. He was suspicious of the more radical French plans which he feared sought to cast the United States as her permanent guarantor against a resurgent Germany. The British also found the French proposals too extreme and were nervous of the implications of Wilson's ideas on territorial and political guarantees, which they felt might stultify peaceful adjustments to any post-war *status quo*. The French rejected the Anglo-Saxon alternatives as inadequate safeguards of their position as a victorious power. Although there was general agreement that there would be no superstate or federation, and their differences on the bureaucratic structures did not seem irreconcilable, there were clear distinctions in the scope and ethos of their respective proposals.

FROM THE ARMISTICE TO THE CONFERENCE

The next few months saw the British and American positions move closer together. For this much of the credit belongs to Cecil who was supported by a strong, but not unopposed, body of opinion in the

British War Cabinet which held that Britain should seek to coop-erate with the United States rather than France at the forthcoming peace conference. If such a strategy was followed then, as Lloyd George pointed out to his colleagues on 30 December 1918, the League 'was the only thing which he [Wilson] really cared much about' and British cooperation here 'would ease other matters, such as the question of the "Freedom of the Seas", the disposal of the German colonies, economic issues, etc.' International expediency thus reinforced domestic electoral considerations, for the Coalition whips, before and during the 1918 election, had stressed the appeal of the league idea to the voters.[15]

For whatever motives, Lloyd George was astute enough to appoint, as the major British spokesmen on the issue, Jan Christian Smuts and Robert Cecil, who though not without their own interests, were genuine in their enthusiasm for Wilson's project. It was indeed Smuts who, in his *The League of Nations: A Practical Suggestion* of 16 December 1918, produced perhaps the most influential of the pre-Paris drafts. Cecil also made his own, unofficial, suggestions before the conference met and remained a committed Wilsonian, sometimes exceeding his authority and embarrassing his own government in an enthusiastic quest for an Anglo-American agreement on a draft Covenant.

Smuts' proposals contained the germs of several ideas that later developed in the final Covenant, though not necessarily quite in the manner he had envisaged. His original mandates scheme was in-tended for use in the Middle East and eastern Europe rather than in the ex-German colonies, but it proved to be invaluable in resolving apparently intractable problems between the president and the Dominion prime ministers over the future of areas like South-West Africa or New Guinea. He argued for small and middle rank powers to join the major states on an Executive Committee, or Council, which would meet on a more frequent basis than the Assembly of all League members. He proposed to abolish conscription and to nationalise armament works. 'Europe', he declared, 'is being liquidated and the League of Nations must be the heir to this great estate.' His moving and eloquent plea that the League should be the cornerstone of the peace negotiations evoked a sympathetic response from Wilson.[16]

Cecil's ideas were not entirely at one with those of Smuts. Basing his draft on an earlier paper prepared in the Foreign Office by Alfred Zimmern, the 'Cecil Plan' was much closer to the mainstream of sympathetic British government thinking on the question. He preferred to see only great powers on the Council and he hinted at some kind of international control over former German colonies in Africa, a cause not close to the heart of his South African colleague. Cecil suggested Geneva as the seat of the League, which he thought might be controlled by a meeting of the General Conference of all members once every four years, and an annual meeting of the great powers. Where both Smuts and Cecil did agree was in their adoption, in broad outline, of the Phillimore proposals for the settlement of disputes. Both also adopted Phillimore's sanction of *ipso facto* war against members who did not observe the League's procedures and embarked on an unauthorised war. Indeed, Cecil's plan extended the threat of force to non-members as well, though it is not obvious why the Foreign Office had made this proposal, given its overall lack of enthusiasm for sanctions.[17]

Robert Lansing, the American secretary of state, reacted strongly against any proposal of this kind, warning that it would violate the constitution of the United States, but his ideas had little effect. Wilson was given similar advice by David Hunter Miller, a lawyer who had been a member of the Inquiry and who now had an especial interest in the League. Nonetheless Wilson's second attempt at an outline proposal, his first Paris draft, did include the sanction of *ipso facto* war. This document was completed in Paris on 10 January 1919, and shows strong influences of the Smuts paper. Wilson adopted Smuts' model for the Council and abandoned his earlier proposal for obligatory arbitration in favour of the Smuts/ Phillimore plans for reference either to arbitration or to the Council. He agreed with the abolition of conscription but on the question of mandates, Wilson followed Cecil in making them apply to ex-German colonies. In addition he elaborated schemes for the fair treatment of workers, and of racial or national minorities.[18]

PARISIAN PROPOSALS

Cecil's paper was part of a process of Anglo-American cooperation and discussion which had begun when he arrived in Paris on 6 January 1919. On 8 January he met House and Lansing, and despite wide differences of approach, they did agree that it would be wise to 'settle between them their policy on the League of Nations before they met their Allies'. There was clear evidence of goodwill in both delegations but, alone, this would not bridge the obvious gaps between them, nor could it disguise the opposition, within both camps, from members less enthusiastic about the whole concept of a League. Henry Wilson thought the League 'futile nonsense', Leo Amery said it was 'moonshine' and Lord Milner called it 'flapdoodle'. Nonetheless, the continuing dialogue and exchange of ideas between the British and Americans played a vital role in the emergence of the Covenant and, some hoped, offered encouraging signs for future Anglo-American cooperation on the rest of the treaty.[19]

Perhaps because he was trying too hard to create common ground, Wilson's first Paris draft was not well received by his American colleagues and, in particular, Hunter Miller attacked it as adopting 'unconsciously no doubt, the British Empire point of view which looks for protection by the United States against the future without a thought of changing or improving the past'. In addition to his fears about the constitutionality of the *ipso facto* war proposal, he was disturbed at the lack of any mention of much of the president's programme: the freedom of the seas, economic equality and effective minority protection. Hunter Miller also wished for a specific clause to safeguard the Monroe Doctrine.[20]

Wilson's reaction was to try again and he produced a second Paris draft on 20 January. Most notably it retreated from the wording of his earlier paper on the question of sanctions. Whereas he had originally written: 'Should any Contracting Power break or disregard its covenants . . . it shall thereby *ipso facto* become at war with all the members of the League' the new wording was: 'Should any Contracting Power break or disregard its covenant . . . it shall thereby *ipso facto* be deemed to have committed an act of war against all the members of the League'. Thus, the idea that national governments could be committed to war by the actions of others was replaced by the more realistic but less dramatic proposition that they could, if they wished, take action on behalf of an injured party. Collective security came a predictable second to national sovereignty. Less significantly he added a clause relating to the freedom of the seas and others against religious discrimination and secret treaties.[21]

Cecil too was refining his ideas in Paris. On 14 January he revised his earlier proposals and produced a 'Draft Sketch of a League of Nations', and with further minor alterations, this formed the basis of the official British draft of 20 January. Cecil revived the idea of a Permanent Court of International Justice, part of whose remit should be to advise the Council or Assembly of the League on disputes that they might refer to it. He revealed his enthusiasm that the League should be led by a man of standing and authority whom he entitled the 'Chancellor'. He opened a new controversy by claiming separate representation in the League for the British Dominions and India. He accepted the principle of a territorial guarantee, though with some provision for peaceful change. The remainder of his suggestions were much as before: a League controlled by the great powers; the settling of disputes as recommended by Phillimore; the retention of the sanction of *ipso facto* war, though with the draconian provision that such actions as the League took to enforce its decisions 'shall be carried on without regard to any limitations hitherto imposed on belligerent States by any convention or rule of international law'.[22]

It was from this exchange of suggestions and ideas that the draft Covenant emerged. Cecil met Wilson on 19 January and discussed with him the proposals advanced in their forthcoming papers. They agreed that a common draft would be desirable and hence discussions between Cecil and Hunter Miller began on 21 January. They met again on 25 and 27 January with the intention of combining as much as was possible of their programmes into a joint draft and isolating, for further consideration, such differences that they did not feel competent to resolve. Working around Wilson's paper of 20 January, they succeeded in producing a joint draft on 27 January: the Cecil–Miller draft. Cecil had been remarkably successful in achieving the modifications that he sought. Miller agreed, at least provisionally, to the separate representation of the Dominions and India, and also to the ideas of a Chancellor and a permanent international court. The League would be controlled by the great powers and might also involve itself in a wider range of non-political activities than Wilson's draft had envisaged. In return Cecil accepted Wilson's amended wording on sanctions in place of his own proposal of *ipso facto* war.[23] There were still several outstanding issues and Cecil was not particularly pleased with the draft, but a broad measure of agreement had been established in these informal sessions, and it was now important, and urgent, to build on this foundation. On 22 January the Council of Ten accepted a resolution, drafted by Cecil, calling for the establishment of the League as an integral part of the peace treaty, and on 25 January the Plenary Conference created the League of Nations Commission to draft the Covenant. There was thus a pressing need for the Anglo-Americans to finalise their proposals.[24]

Cecil faced two problems: he had to gain not only Wilson's agreement to the Cecil–Miller draft, but also that of his own government. This did not prove easy for he had acted on his own initiative since arriving in Paris. This was not entirely of his own volition, since it was partly a reflection of Lloyd George's lack of interest in the League, but he did now require approval of the steps he had taken and permission to continue. This he sought on 29 January, sending the prime minister a copy of the Cecil–Miller draft. Two important meetings took place on 31 January, the first between Smuts, Cecil and Lloyd George, and the second between the two British delegates and Wilson, House and Miller. Lloyd George was not pleased with the direction the League negotiations were taking: his preference, as expressed in a memorandum prepared by his private secretary, Philip Kerr, was for a much more functional League, based on the experience and practice of the Supreme War Council. He felt that the present conference should establish the principle of the League, but that the practical details should be the task of a second, larger gathering. He was particularly unhappy with any idea of territorial guarantees involving automatic sanctions, believing that such a provision would so far infringe the sovereignty of members that states simply would not join. Knowing he was soon to meet the president to finalise their joint draft, Cecil found Lloyd George's attitude unacceptable (he ascribed it to ignorance of the issues) and, characteristically, ignored it.[25]

Cecil and Smuts did not tell Wilson of Lloyd George's misgivings when they met that evening. Wilson accepted the separate representation of the Dominions, the predominance of the major powers and also the idea of an international court. It was decided that Miller and the British legal expert, Cecil Hurst from the Foreign Office, should now meet to produce an Anglo-American draft, referring any outstanding problems to Cecil and House.[26] Working through the afternoon, night and early morning of 1 and 2 February, Hurst and Miller produced the Hurst–Miller draft: the document that would form the basis of discussions in the League Commission. This was not immediately clear, since Wilson, believing that too much of his original draft had disappeared, now set about producing an independent paper, his third Paris draft. Neither did the prime minister's advisers like the Hurst–Miller version though Cecil was more concerned by Wilson's opposition. Fearing that the agreement between the League's main proponents was about to evaporate, he had a tense meeting with the president on 3 February, but he was relieved when Wilson, with some reluctance, agreed that when the League Commission began its deliberations that day, it would use the Hurst–Miller draft as the basis of its discussions.[27]

The Hurst–Miller draft consisted of a preamble and 22 articles. Articles 1 to 5 defined the shape of the League. There was to be a Body of Delegates (the later Assembly) representing all the members, which was to meet periodically, and an Executive Council (the Council) which would meet more frequently. This would always be composed of the representatives of the great powers, but could include the representatives of powers whose interests were affected by the matter under review. The League would have a permanent base, its capital, as yet unnamed, a Chancellor and a permanent bureaucracy. Article 6 established conditions for admitting new members. Article 7 was an unreserved promise to 'respect and preserve as against external aggression the territorial integrity and existing political independence' of member states. Article 8 endorsed the principle that members would reduce their armed forces to 'the lowest point consistent with domestic safety and the enforcement by common action of international obligations' and envisaged the Council making proposals for disarmament.

Article 9 made any threat of war a matter of concern to members and endorsed the 'friendly right' of any member to refer such a threat to the League. Article 10 was a promise not to resort to war without submitting the problem to the League, and then only after a delay of three months following a League award or recommendation. Members further agreed that, in no circumstances, would they use force against another member who complied with a League recommendation or award. Article 11 obliged members to submit suitable disputes that they could not settle by diplomacy, to arbitration, with an undertaking to execute any decision reached.

Article 12 established the principle of a Permanent Court of International Justice, whilst Article 13 covered the compulsory referral of disputes that were not suitable for arbitration to the Council, or to the Body of Delegates. If the Council reached a unanimous recommendation, then members agreed not to resort to war against any member carrying out the recommendation. Article 14 declared that any member found to have broken its obligations under Article 10 'shall *ipso facto* be deemed to have committed an act of war against all other members of the League'. The Council would recommend the level of forces or contributions that each member should make in such a case, and members agreed to offer each other mutual support in off-setting possible losses and to allow free passage to League forces protecting its covenants.

Article 15 defined the role of the League in dealing with disputes involving one or more non-League members. Article 16 entrusted the League with the supervision of the international arms trade whilst Article 17 defined the Mandate system for the colonial territories of the defeated powers. Article 18 declared the League's interest in fair hours and humane working conditions within member states and Article 19 established non-discrimination on religious grounds within the League. Article 20 concerned fair trading conditions between members. Article 21 provided for the publication of all treaties concluded between members and Article 22 proclaimed the paramountcy of obligations assumed under League membership over any other obligations.[28]

DRAFTING THE COVENANT

The role of the great powers, both in the commission to establish the League and on the proposed Council, was a matter of extreme sensitivity to the smaller powers. If Wilson's proposals for a 'new diplomacy' had real meaning then the touchstone must surely be the manner in which its central feature, the League, was created and the influence which they might hope to have on its subsequent workings. The Council of Ten proposed a commission of fifteen, ten delegates from the great powers, five from the smaller powers of Belgium, Brazil, China, Portugal and Serbia. At its second meeting, and despite the efforts of Wilson and Cecil, the small powers forced a vote and added a further four representatives from Czechoslovakia, Greece, Poland and Rumania. In the event, this, and the subsequent expansion of the Council to include four small power representatives, proved to be rare exceptions to the dominance established by the Anglo-Americans in the commission, and probably eased the passage of a document to which the smaller powers had contributed relatively little, but for which they now shared responsibility.[29]

Despite its size, the commission worked with a speed and determination that was unique at this stage of the Paris negotiations. It met ten times in eleven days (on average for three hours a session) and produced the draft Covenant for the Plenary Session of

14 February. Wilson chaired all but the final meeting and worked closely with his deputy chairman, Cecil, together with Smuts and House. The French delegates, Bourgeois and Larnaude, and the Italians, Orlando and Scialoja, played only a secondary role and had relatively little impact on the final Covenant. The Japanese representatives, Makino and Chinda, also had little influence on this stage of the proceedings. From the moment that the commission agreed, at its first meeting on 3 February, to work from the Hurst–Miller draft despite alternative French and Italian proposals, there was little doubt of Anglo-American ascendancy.[30]

Wilson was at his best during these proceedings, which were marked by a business-like informality. In the key debate on the status of the Monroe Doctrine, his eloquence won the day, but was so powerful that even the secretaries stopped work to listen. With a rare display of humour he opposed recording a full transcript of the sessions on the grounds that 'he wished to keep his mind wide open, so that he could say the opposite of what he had said before if he saw fit'. Instead only a brief official record of the discussion and decisions was kept, though Hunter Miller's informal notes show that the meetings, around the large red-covered table in Room 351 of the Hotel Crillon, were often frank and direct.[31]

The commission decided at its first meeting that it would discuss, amend, and then adopt, each article in turn. In general the pattern was that the Anglo-American draft was accepted with more or less minor amendment but there were a number of issues that were keenly debated. In the course of discussions some new clauses were added and the original draft altered and amended. (The final text of the Covenant is printed as an appendix to this chapter.) On 4 February the representatives of the small powers made it plain that the Anglo-American suggestion of an exclusively great power Council was unacceptable. The Belgian foreign minister, Hymans, described by one American observer as a 'pestiferous mosquito', raised the spectre of a new Holy Alliance, and led the small powers to press for either equality of representation on the Council or, at the very least, four members to the five of the major powers. When they were supported by the French and Italians, Cecil, with deep misgivings, bowed to this pressure for an elected minority of smaller powers. He fought a rearguard action for several days to restrict the smaller powers to two representatives but it was agreed, on 13 February, that there should be four.[32]

If Hymans perceived the Holy Alliance as the epitome of great power domination, for the British it had represented an attempt to preserve indefinitely the *status quo*. Hence when, on 6 February, the commission considered Article 7 of the Hurst–Miller draft, the guarantee of political independence and territorial integrity that was to become the basis of Article 10 of the final Covenant, Cecil was anxious to amend it. He preferred a passive undertaking to respect other members' independence to the active obligation 'to preserve as against external aggression [their] territorial integrity and existing political independence'. Wilson insisted on the central importance of the draft clause; without it, he said, the League would be 'hardly more than an influential debating society'. 'Yes', remarked Cecil, 'but do any of us mean it?' He and Smuts were completely isolated and had to accept the Article although its effect was considerably reduced by an amendment, proposed by Wilson, that the Council should advise how the obligation should be fulfilled in each particular circumstance. Since the Council had to be unanimous, the strength of the theoretical guarantee was certainly weakened, perhaps even destroyed.[33]

Later, on 11 February, the British introduced a draft article which permitted the League to 'make provision for the periodic revision of treaties which have become obsolete'. Since this wording could be taken to infringe the sovereignty of members, the final version (Article 19) spoke of the right of the Assembly to 'advise the reconsideration by . . . members . . . of treaties which have become inapplicable, and of international conditions, the continuance of which may endanger the peace of the world'. It was not clear whether this could be compatible with Article 10, nor indeed how effective it might be, but it did offer some comfort to Cecil.[34] The French refused to contemplate the possible abolition of compulsory military service, a proposal of particular importance to the British and especially to Lloyd George. Instead, on Wilson's suggestion, it became the responsibility of the Council to determine what levels of military equipment and armaments would be appropriate for each power, given the scale of forces laid down in the League's programme of disarmament and the needs of national safety. Such levels could only be exceeded with the permission of the Body of Delegates (later amended to the Council.)[35]

Cecil resisted Belgian pressure for compulsory arbitration when, on 6 and 7 February, the commission considered the various proposals for the peaceful settlement of disputes. There were few changes made but Hymans wished to amend Article 13 of the Hurst–Miller draft so that it became obligatory for members to comply with a unanimous report by the Council. He proposed that the original draft, which expected members not to go to war with states which executed the recommendations, should now apply to majority reports. Neither Wilson nor Cecil was prepared to accept these proposals and they lapsed, although it was later agreed that the Council should consider what steps were necessary to implement unanimous recommendations. Cecil also prevented Hymans expanding the scope of sanctions under Article 16 of the final Covenant to include violations of the territorial and political guarantee of Article 10.[36]

The most serious difference of principle that arose in the February discussions concerned the predictable French attempt to create an international army to provide the League with its own independent strike force. Bourgeois was adamant that, in Wilson's words, though not his meaning, without 'a force so superior to that of all nations or to that of all alliances' the League would become 'nothing but a dangerous facade'. Both Wilson and Cecil opposed this idea with great firmness. Wilson, who had earlier favoured the possibility of an international police force, now stressed his philosophical objections and the constitutional problems that such a proposal would pose for the United States. Cecil was prepared to countenance a permanent advisory commission on military and naval matters for the League but not an independent military force. Even though Cecil warned the French that there could be no independent League force and that the alternative to the League was an Anglo-American alliance, it was only after a tense final session in which their proposals were defeated, that the French reluctantly settled for the advisory commission.[37]

The commission now polished its draft for presentation to the Plenary Conference. It was at this stage that Cecil abandoned his plan to make the head of the League, the Chancellor, a man of political weight and standing. Cecil had hoped that, if Wilson himself would not stand, the Greek premier Eleutherios Venizelos would accept this role. When he declined and no other figure of suitable stature acceptable to all the major powers could be found, the post became one more appropriately filled by a bureaucrat. The title was thus amended to Secretary-General and Cecil now hoped that Sir Maurice Hankey, the secretary to the British cabinet, would become the first incumbent. Hankey dabbled with this idea but declined, after gaining the impression, from Curzon and others, that the League was unlikely to enjoy enthusiastic support. It was thus a British diplomat, Sir Eric Drummond, who became the first Secretary-General, serving from April 1919 until June 1933, with the Frenchman, Jean Monnet, as his deputy.[38]

On 14 February Wilson, his hand resting on the Bible, presented the draft Covenant to the Plenary Conference with the words 'a living thing is born'. This might be considered premature since the Conference was not yet required to decide whether to accept the proposal, but both Wilson and Cecil had reason to be pleased with the progress they had made in barely a month in Paris. 'This is our first real step forward', Wilson told his wife, 'for I now realise, more than ever before, that once established, the League can arbitrate and correct mistakes which are inevitable in the treaty we are trying to make at this time'. On the other hand the draft did not occasion universal acclaim. The French and Japanese had objections and wide sections of both the British establishment and radical opposition made it clear that they wished for substantial amendments (in differing directions) before the Covenant reached its final form. The government's military advisers criticised the disarmament clauses, whilst two Dominion premiers, the formidable Australian William Hughes and the Canadian Robert Borden, together with Lloyd George himself, all expressed similar misgivings about the League's potential encroachment on vital areas of national sovereignty.[39]

Immediately after the presentation Wilson left Paris for the United States, where he knew he faced opponents of the calibre of the implacable Henry Cabot Lodge, backed by a round robin supported by sufficient senators to block the progress of the Covenant through the Senate. On the other hand there were hopes that concessions and amendments could persuade some of the signatories to change their minds. Wilson was advised, by his own supporters and by Republican ex-President Taft, that he must safeguard the national sovereignty of the United States by excluding domestic issues from the League's competence, obtaining recognition of the special status of the Monroe Doctrine, making provision for states to quit the League and clarifying certain matters, particularly the wording of Article 15. Taft cabled, on 18 March, that the 'Monroe Doctrine reservation alone would probably carry the treaty, but others would make it certain'. Unfortunately

Wilson's methods in his attempts to conciliate his political opponents proved to be counter-productive, and there was no sign of a more favourable climate after his visit.[40]

When Wilson returned to Paris in mid-March he was alarmed that House, in his absence, had apparently sought to advance the more pressing practicalities of peace, which did not include the League. Wilson made it clear that there would be no treaty without the Covenant, but this meant that both he and Cecil knew that the draft must be revised, despite any embarrassment that this might occasion him. In fact there were close parallels between many of the amendments sought by critics of the draft Covenant on both sides of the Atlantic, and it was not especially difficult to find suitable formulations to cover many of the difficulties. By the end of March the commission had reconvened and agreed to exclude domestic issues from the competence of the League, a state might withdraw from membership by giving two years notice, and it was made clear that no member could be required to go to war in defence of the Covenant, against the provisions of its own constitution. Wilson also announced his intention of introducing a clause clarifying the relationship of the Covenant and the Monroe Doctrine. In addition, the Body of Delegates now became the Assembly, and provision was made (with Russia and Germany in mind) to allow the Council to be enlarged in the future.[41]

Despite this relatively painless process it was inevitable that, as the conference as a whole approached the crisis of late March and early April, the Covenant would become part of a larger game. Each delegation was anxious to retain a bargaining angle in the complex problems – reparations; the Rhineland; the Saar; Danzig; the Polish frontiers; the Middle East and so on – which were all meshed together. Hence progress on any front was dependent on concessions and bargains on another. The French, for example, admitted that their stance on an international general staff for the League was linked to the progress of negotiations on Germany's western borders, whilst Lloyd George gambled that Wilson would compromise on the American plans to build a formidable navy in return for British acquiescence to a special status for the Monroe Doctrine. Cecil's focus was tightly fixed on the Covenant, and he resented deeply any attempt to use the League as a political pawn but, for most of the negotiators, the League was not the most pressing or important issue of the crisis. When the general crisis broke, the Covenant once more made progress. House and Cecil reached a face-saving compromise over American naval construction and, when the commission met on 10 and 11 April to finalise their proposals, Cecil backed Wilson in his attempt to prevent the League interfering in the American hemisphere without United States approval. There was no doubt, as the French assiduously pointed out, that this was illogical. 'If, therefore, there was nothing in the Monroe Doctrine inconsistent with the Covenant it would not be affected . . . if it was not inconsistent with the terms of the Covenant, it was unnecessary to refer to it. What was unnecessary might be dangerous.' Whereas Wilson was anxious to exclude European interference in the Americas, the French feared that the United States might not fulfil its League obligations in Europe. Even after strenuous denials by Wilson and Cecil, the French pushed the matter to a vote, which they lost.[42]

One further debate soured the last meeting of the commission. The Japanese had, early in February, stated their wish to introduce a clause on racial equality into the Covenant. It proved impossible to discover a form of words which would satisfy them and yet not alarm the Australians, New Zealanders, British Columbians and Californians who feared unlimited Japanese immigration. Now they insisted upon an open confrontation, and Cecil was faced with the embarrassing task of opposing a principle of obvious justice. Wilson, having failed to induce the Japanese to withdraw their proposal, had finally to resort to procedural devices to save the face of both himself and Cecil. Since the only result of earlier attempts to produce a compromise had been the dropping of the guarantee of religious toleration, this was hardly an edifying episode.[43]

Several points were clarified: Geneva was chosen as the seat of the League and Drummond as its first Secretary-General; Belgium, Brazil, Greece and Spain became the first temporary members of the Council; the British Dominions and India were not, technically, independent states and therefore the wording of the Covenant was altered to make it plain that they were full members. Later these 'six votes for the British Empire' would become an emotive, if meaningless, issue in the battle over ratification in the United States. On 28 April, the Plenary Conference adopted, unanimously, the Covenant of the League, which was then incorporated as the first section of all the treaties comprising the Versailles Settlement.[44]

The Covenant reflected the compromises that had helped to construct it. The British and Americans had the most cause for satisfaction since the League most closely represented their vision, although it was not clear how far Cecil and Wilson enjoyed the support of their respective establishments. Despite Wilson's insistence on the collective guarantee, the League was never a collective security system and, in most areas, the Covenant was more concerned to safeguard the integrity of its members' rights to control their own destiny, though its opponents did not accept this. The Italians failed to include guarantees on access to trade and raw materials, the Japanese did not achieve a racial equality clause and, most significantly of all, the French failed to transform the League into a perpetual guarantee of the Versailles Settlement, thus for them it was a toothless organisation.

At its heart the League was a permanent international conference, more an aid to the 'old diplomacy' than an embodiment of the 'new'. Yet it did seek, under Article 11, to spread the revolutionary gospel that peace, in the twentieth century, was indivisible, and that any threat to peace, anywhere on the globe, was of vital importance to all members, no matter how remote they were from the dispute. It reflected a belief in the rationality of mankind, and of states, and the hope that international disputes might be controlled, and war averted, by detailed and impartial investigation, and the application of goodwill. At the very worst, war would be delayed for at least three months, and this stay of execution might create new opportunities for international and national public opinion to influence the outcome. Wilson and Cecil had great faith in the benevolence of public opinion. Cecil pointed out that:

> For the most part there is no attempt to rely on anything like a superstate: no attempt to rely upon force to carry out a decision of the Council or the Assembly of the League. What we rely upon is public opinion . . . and if we are wrong about it, then the whole thing is wrong.

Clemenceau was less sanguine: '*Vox populi, vox diaboli*' (the voice of the people is the voice of the devil), he growled. His representative on the commission, Ferdinand Larnaude, was equally scathing, asking his colleague, Bourgeois, in an audible undertone, 'Am I at a Peace Conference or in a madhouse?'[45]

Its role expanded during the Paris negotiations to include a close relationship with the International Labour Organisation, a watching brief over attempts to control drug trafficking and the slave trade, and the authority to coordinate internationally the control and prevention of disease. It became interwoven with other areas of the settlement, having responsibility for mandates, the government of the Saar and Danzig, and an overall concern for the welfare of minority protection. It was to oversee international disarmament. In 1921 the Permanent Court of International Justice was founded at The Hague and became the legal backbone of the League. Given the ambiguities which existed between its different provisions, the guarantee of political and territorial integrity under Article 10 (which was not, apparently, covered by the sanctions of Article 16), and the status of peaceful change under Article 19, it was clear that, if nothing else, the League offered improved career prospects to international lawyers.

The fate of the League was in doubt even before the Paris negotiations were concluded. The attitude of the American Senate remained hostile, despite Taft's optimism, and the prospects for the Covenant in that quarter were, at best, dubious. Wilson's insistence that the Treaty of Versailles and the Covenant were an indivisible whole rebounded when, on 19 November 1919, the Senate refused to ratify the Treaty. The British Dominions were not pleased with the final draft and the Canadians were quick to point out that they were not keen to become suppliers of security to European states which did not enjoy Canada's strategic and geographical advantages. After 1923, their restrictive interpretation of the execution of Article 10 would, in practice, be adopted by the League. The French distrusted it as impotent and warned that they would continue to seek security in more traditional ways. Wilson and Lloyd George had already recognised this in their offers of Anglo-American guarantees to France during the Rhineland debates in March. The British establishment distrusted the threat which it perceived that the League posed to the diplomacy which it understood and to its jealously guarded control of national affairs. In addition, the defection of the United States meant that no British government could consider operating a naval blockade on behalf of the League without first consulting Washington, for fear of becoming embroiled in an unnecessary dispute with the Americans.[46]

There can be no doubt that Wilson played the major role in ensuring the birth of the League, and that, without the need to defer to the controller of the vast power of the United States, it would have remained an idealistic concept without practical reality. Wilson was the inspiration and progenitor of the Covenant but much of its text was British in origin and, without the commitment and negotiating tenacity of Robert Cecil, it would not have emerged, as Wilson himself generously acknowledged. It would also be unfair to omit men like David Hunter Miller and Cecil Hurst, who sought to provide a legal framework for the dreams of the politicians, and those like James Headlam-Morley, who strove to ensure that the League would not merely form part of the text of the treaties, but would become a living part of the settlement. Others hoped that the inevitable mistakes made in Paris would be fielded and corrected by the League. Certain of its provisions were incompatible, some were downright illogical, and some represented no more than pious hopes. Yet, despite the embarrassment of the racial equality issue, and the expediency of the exclusion of the Monroe Doctrine, there was a nobility of purpose to the League that transcended the pettiness of its drafting, even if its eventual fate remained, at best, uncertain.[47]

THE COVENANT OF THE LEAGUE OF NATIONS

THE HIGH CONTRACTING PARTIES

In order to promote international co-operation and to achieve international peace and security:

by the acceptance of obligations not to resort to war;

by the prescription of open, just and honourable relations between nations;

by the firm establishment of the understandings of international law as the actual rule of conduct among Governments;

and by the maintenance of justice and a scrupulous respect for all treaty obligations in the dealings of organised peoples with one another.

Agree to this Covenant of the League of Nations.

Article 1

1. The original Members of the League of Nations shall be those of the Signatories which are named in the Annex to this Covenant and also such of those other States named in the Annex as shall accede without reservation to this Covenant. . . .

2. Any fully self-governing State, Dominion or Colony not named in the Annex may become a Member of the League if its admission is

agreed to by two-thirds of the Assembly, provided that it shall give effective guarantees of its sincere intention to observe its international obligations, and shall accept such regulations as may be prescribed by the League in regard to its military, naval and air forces and armaments.

3. Any Member of the League may, after two years' notice of its intention so to do, withdraw from the League, provided that all its international obligations and all its obligations under this Covenant shall have been fulfilled at the time of its withdrawal.

Article 2

The action of the League under this Covenant shall be effected through the instrumentality of an Assembly and of a Council, with a permanent Secretariat.

Article 3

1. The Assembly shall consist of Representatives of the Members of the League.

2. The Assembly shall meet at stated intervals and from time to time as occasion may require at the Seat of the League or at such other place as may be decided upon.

3. The Assembly may deal at its meetings with any matter within the sphere of action of the League or affecting the peace of the world.

4. At meetings of the Assembly, each Member of the League shall have one vote, and may have not more than three Representatives.

Article 4

1. The Council shall consist of Representatives of the Principal Allied and Associated Powers, together with Representatives of four other Members of the League. These four Members of the League shall be selected by the Assembly from time to time in its discretion. Until the appointment of the Representatives of the four Members of the League first elected by the Assembly, Representatives of Belgium, Brazil, Spain and Greece shall be members of the Council.

2. With the approval of the majority of the Assembly, the Council may name additional Members of the League whose Representatives shall always be Members of the Council; the Council with like

approval may increase the number of Members of the League to be selected by the Assembly for representation on the Council.

3. The Council shall meet from time to time as occasion may require, and at least once a year, at the Seat of the League, or at such other place as may be decided upon.

4. The Council may deal at its meetings with any matter within the sphere of action of the League or affecting the peace of the world.

5. Any Member of the League not represented on the Council shall be invited to send a Representative to sit as a member at any meeting of the Council during the consideration of matters specially affecting the interests of that Member of the League.

6. At meetings of the Council, each Member of the League represented on the Council shall have one vote, and may have not more than one Representative.

Article 5

1. Except where otherwise expressly provided in this Covenant or by the terms of the present Treaty, decisions at any meeting of the Assembly or of the Council shall require the agreement of all the Members of the League represented at the meeting.

2. All matters of procedure at meetings of the Assembly or of the Council, including the appointment of Committees to investigate particular matters, shall be regulated by the Assembly or by the Council and may be decided by a majority of the Members of the League represented at the meeting.

3. The first meeting of the Assembly and the first meeting of the Council shall be summoned by the President of the United States of America.

Article 6

1. The permanent Secretariat shall be established at the Seat of the League. The Secretariat shall comprise a Secretary-General and such secretaries and staff as may be required. . . .

Article 7

1. The Seat of the League is established at Geneva.

2. The Council may at any time decide that the Seat of the League shall be established elsewhere.

3. All positions under or in connection with the League, including the Secretariat, shall be open equally to men and women. . . .

Article 8

1. The Members of the League recognise that the maintenance of peace requires the reduction of national armaments to the lowest point consistent with national safety and the enforcement by common action of international obligations.

2. The Council, taking account of the geographical situation and circumstances of each State, shall formulate plans for such reduction for the consideration and action of the several Governments.

3. Such plans shall be subject to reconsideration and revision at least every ten years.

4. After these plans have been adopted by the several Governments, the limits of armaments therein fixed shall not be exceeded without the concurrence of the Council.

5. The Members of the League agree that the manufacture by private enterprise of munitions and implements of war is open to grave objections. The Council shall advise how the evil effects attendant upon such manufacture can be prevented, due regard being had to the necessities of those Members of the League which are not able to manufacture the munitions and implements of war necessary for their safety.

6. The Members of the League undertake to interchange full and frank information as to the scale of their armaments, their military, naval and air programmes and the condition of such of their industries as are adaptable to warlike purposes.

Article 9

A permanent Commission shall be constituted to advise the Council on the execution of the provisions of Articles 1 and 8 and on military, naval and air questions generally.

Article 10

The Members of the League undertake to respect and preserve as against external aggression the territorial integrity and existing political independence of all Members of the League. In case of any such aggression or in case of any threat or danger of such aggression, the Council shall advise upon the means by which this obligation shall be fulfilled.

Article 11

1. Any war or threat of war, whether immediately affecting any of the Members of the League or not, is hereby declared a matter of concern to the whole League, and the League shall take any action that may be deemed wise and effectual to safeguard the peace of nations. In case any such emergency should arise, the Secretary-General shall, on the request of any Member of the League, forthwith summon a meeting of the Council.

2. It is also declared to be the friendly right of each Member of the League to bring to the attention of the Assembly or of the Council any circumstance whatever affecting international relations which threatens to disturb international peace or the good understanding between nations upon which peace depends.

Article 12

1. The Members of the League agree that if there should arise between them any dispute likely to lead to a rupture they will submit the matter either to arbitration or to inquiry by the Council, and they agree in no case to resort to war until three months after the award by the arbitrators or the report by the Council.

2. In any case under this article the award of the arbitrators shall be made within a reasonable time, and the report of the Council shall be made within six months after the submission of the dispute.

Article 13

1. The Members of the League agree that whenever any dispute shall arise between them which they recognise to be suitable for submission to arbitration, and which cannot be satisfactorily settled by diplomacy, they will submit the whole subject-matter to arbitration.

2. Disputes as to the interpretation of a treaty, as to any question of international law, as to the existence of any fact which, if established, would constitute a breach of any international obligation, or as to the extent and nature of the reparation to be made for any such

breach, are declared to be among those which are generally suitable for submission to arbitration.

3 [adopted after 1919]. For the consideration of any such dispute, the court to which the case is referred shall be the Permanent Court of International Justice, established in accordance with Article 14, or any tribunal agreed on by the parties to the dispute or stipulated in any Convention existing between them.

4. The Members of the League agree that they will carry out in full good faith any award that may be rendered, and that they will not resort to war against a Member of the League which complies therewith. In the event of any failure to carry out such an award, the Council shall propose what steps should be taken to give effect thereto.

Article 14

The Council shall formulate and submit to the Members of the League for adoption plans for the establishment of a Permanent Court of International Justice. The Court shall be competent to hear and determine any dispute of an international character which the parties thereto submit to it. The Court may also give an advisory opinion upon any dispute or question referred to it by the Council or by the Assembly.

Article 15

1. If there should arise between Members of the League any dispute likely to lead to a rupture, which is not submitted to arbitration in accordance with Article 13, the Members of the League agree that they will submit the matter to the Council. Any party to the dispute may effect such submission by giving notice of the existence of the dispute to the Secretary-General, who will make all necessary arrangements for a full investigation and consideration thereof.

2. For this purpose, the parties to the dispute will communicate to the Secretary-General as promptly as possible, statements of their case with all the relevant facts and papers, and the Council may forthwith direct the publication thereof.

3. The Council shall endeavour to effect a settlement of the dispute, and if such efforts are successful, a statement shall be made

public giving such facts and explanations regarding the dispute and the terms of settlement thereof as the Council may deem appropriate.

4. If the dispute is not thus settled, the Council either unanimously or by a majority vote shall make and publish a report containing a statement of the facts of the dispute and the recommendations which are deemed just and proper in regard thereto.

5. Any member of the League represented on the Council may make a public statement of the facts of the dispute and of its conclusions regarding the same.

6. If a report by the Council is unanimously agreed to by the members thereof other than the Representatives of one or more of the parties to the dispute, the Members of the League agree that they will not go to war with any party to the dispute which complies with the recommendations of the report.

7. If the Council fails to reach a report which is unanimously agreed to by the members thereof, other than the Representatives of one or more of the parties to the dispute, the Members of the League reserve to themselves the right to take such action as they shall consider necessary for the maintenance of right and justice.

8. If the dispute between the parties is claimed by one of them, and is found by the Council, to arise out of a matter which by international law is solely within the domestic jurisdiction of that party, the Council shall so report, and shall make no recommendation as to its settlement.

9. The Council may in any case under this article refer the dispute to the Assembly. The dispute shall be so referred at the request of either party to the dispute provided that such request be made within fourteen days after the submission of the dispute to the Council.

10. In any case referred to the Assembly, all the provisions of this article and of Article 12 relating to the action and powers of the Council shall apply to the action and powers of the Assembly, provided that a report made by the Assembly, if concurred in by the Representatives of those Members of the League represented on the Council and of a majority of the other Members of the League, exclusive in each case of the Representatives of the parties to the dispute, shall have the same force as a report by the Council concurred in by all the members thereof other than the Representatives of one or more of the parties to the dispute.

Article 16

1. Should any Member of the League resort to war in disregard of its covenants under Articles 12, 13 or 15, it shall, *ipso facto*, be deemed to have committed an act of war against all other Members of the League, which hereby undertake immediately to subject it to the severance of all trade or financial relations, the prohibition of all intercourse between their nations and the nationals of the Covenant-breaking State, and the prevention of all financial, commercial or personal intercourse between the nationals of the Covenant-breaking State and the nationals of any other State, whether a Member of the League or not.

2. It shall be the duty of the Council in such case to recommend to the several Governments concerned what effective military, naval or air force the Members of the League shall severally contribute to the armed forces to be used to protect the covenants of the League.

3. The Members of the League agree, further, that they will mutually support one another in the financial and economic measures which are taken under this article, in order to minimise the loss and inconvenience resulting from the above measures, and that they will mutually support one another in resisting any special measures aimed at one of their number by the Covenant-breaking State, and that they will take the necessary steps to afford passage through their territory to the forces of any of the Members of the League which are co-operating to protect the covenants of the League.

4. Any Member of the League which has violated any covenant of the League may be declared to be no longer a Member of the League by a vote of the Council concurred in by the Representatives of all the other Members of the League represented thereon.

Article 17

1. In the event of a dispute between a Member of the League and a State which is not a member of the League or between States not members of the League, the State or States not members of the League shall be invited to accept the obligations of membership in the League for the purposes of such dispute, upon such conditions as the Council may deem just. If such invitation is accepted, the provisions of Articles 12 to 16 inclusive shall be applied with such

modifications as may be deemed necessary by the Council.

2. Upon such invitation being given, the Council shall immediately institute an enquiry into the circumstances of the dispute and recommend such action as may seem best and most effectual in the circumstances.

3. If a State so invited shall refuse to accept the obligations of membership in the League for the purposes of such dispute, and shall resort to war against a Member of the League, the provisions of Article 16 shall be applicable as against the State taking such action.

4. If both parties to the dispute when so invited refuse to accept the obligations of membership in the League for the purposes of such dispute, the Council may take such measures and make such recommendations as will prevent hostilities and will result in the settlement of the dispute.

Article 18

Every treaty or international engagement entered into hereafter by any Member of the League shall be forthwith registered with the Secretariat and shall, as soon as possible, be published by it. No such treaty or international engagement shall be binding until so registered.

Article 19

The Assembly may from time to time advise the reconsideration by Members of the League of treaties which have become inapplicable and the consideration of international conditions whose continuance might endanger the peace of the world.

Article 20

1. The Members of the League severally agree that this Covenant is accepted as abrogating all obligations or understandings *inter se* which are inconsistent with the terms thereof, and solemnly undertake that they will not hereafter enter into any engagements inconsistent with the terms thereof.

2. In case any Member of the League shall, before becoming a Member of the League, have undertaken any obligations inconsistent with the terms of this Covenant, it shall be the duty of such

Member to take immediate steps to procure its release from such obligations.

Article 21

Nothing in this Covenant shall be deemed to affect the validity of international engagements, such as treaties of arbitrations or regional understandings like the Monroe doctrine, for securing the maintenance of peace.

Article 22

1. To those colonies and territories which as a consequence of the late war have ceased to be under the sovereignty of the States which formerly governed them and which are inhabited by peoples not yet able to stand by themselves under the strenuous conditions of the modern world, there should be applied the principle that the well-being and development of such peoples form a sacred trust of civilisation and that securities for the performance of this trust should be embodied in this Covenant.

2. The best method of giving practical effect to this principle is that the tutelage of such peoples should be entrusted to advanced nations who, by reason of their resources, their experience or their geographical position, can best undertake this responsibility, and who are willing to accept it, and that this tutelage should be exercised by them as Mandatories on behalf of the League.

3. The character of the mandate must differ according to the stage of development of the people, the geographical situation of the territory, its economic conditions and other similar circumstances.

4. Certain communities formerly belonging to the Turkish Empire have reached a stage of development where their existence as independent nations can be provisionally recognised subject to the rendering of administrative advice and assistance by a Mandatory until such time as they are able to stand alone. The wishes of these communities must be a principal consideration in the selection of the Mandatory.

5. Other peoples, especially those of Central Africa, are at such a stage that the Mandatory must be responsible for the administration of the territory under conditions which will guarantee freedom of conscience and religion, subject only to the maintenance of public

order and morals, the prohibition of abuses such as the slave trade, the arms traffic and the liquor traffic, and the prevention of the establishment of fortifications or military and naval bases and of military training of the natives for other than police purposes and the defence of territory, and will also secure equal opportunities for the trade and commerce of other Members of the League.

6. There are territories, such as South West Africa and certain of the South Pacific Islands, which, owing to the sparseness of their population, or their small size, or their remoteness from the centre of civilisation, or their geographical contiguity to the territory of the Mandatory, and other circumstances, can be best administered under the laws of the Mandatory as integral portions of its territory, subject to the safeguards above mentioned in the interests of the indigenous population.

7. In every case of mandate, the Mandatory shall render to the Council an annual report in reference to the territory committed to its charge.

8. The degree of authority, control or administration to be exercised by the Mandatory shall, if not previously agreed upon by the Members of the League, be explicitly defined in each case by the Council.

9. A permanent Commission shall be constituted to receive and examine the annual reports of the Mandatories and to advise the Council on all matters relating to the observance of the mandates.

Article 23

Subject to and in accordance with the provisions of international Conventions existing or hereafter to be agreed upon, the Members of the League:

   (a) will endeavour to secure and maintain fair and humane conditions of labour for men, women and children, both in their own countries and in all countries to which their commercial and industrial relations extend, and for that purpose will establish and maintain the necessary international organisations;

   (b) undertake to secure just treatment of the native inhabitants of territories under their control;

   (c) will entrust the League with the general supervision over the

execution of agreements with regard to the traffic in women
and children, and the traffic in opium and other dangerous
drugs;

(d) will entrust the League with the general supervision of the
trade in arms and ammunition with the countries in which
the control of this traffic is necessary in the common interest;

(e) will make provision to secure and maintain freedom of communications and of transit and equitable treatment for the
commerce of all Members of the League. In this connection,
the special necessities of the regions devastated during the
war of 1914–18 shall be borne in mind;

(f) will endeavour to take steps in matters of international concern for the prevention and control of disease.

Article 24

1. There shall be placed under the direction of the League all
international bureaux already established by general treaties if the
parties to such treaties consent. All such international bureaux and
all commissions for the regulation of matters of international interest
hereafter constituted shall be placed under the direction of the
League.

2. In all matters of international interest which are regulated by
general Conventions but which are not placed under the control of
international bureaux or commissions, the Secretariat of the League
shall, subject to the consent of the Council and if desired by the
parties, collect and distribute all relevant information and shall
render any other assistance which may be necessary or desirable.

3. The Council may include as part of the expenses of the
Secretariat the expenses of any bureau or commission which is
placed under the direction of the League.

Article 25

The Members of the League agree to encourage and promote the
establishment and co-operation of duly authorised voluntary national
Red Cross organisations having as purposes the improvement of
health, the prevention of disease and the mitigation of suffering
throughout the world.

Article 26

1. Amendments to this Covenant will take effect when ratified by the Members of the League whose Representatives compose the Council and by a majority of the Members of the League whose Representatives compose the Assembly.

2. No such amendments shall bind any Member of the League which signifies its dissent therefrom, but in that case it shall cease to be a Member of the League.

(Appendix I from *The League of Nations* by Ruth Henig is reprinted above by kind permission of Ruth Henig.)

4 Reparations

THE cost of the Great War in human life and suffering, material damage and misery had been enormous, even leaving aside the expenditure of treasure and the disruption of trade. No one knows the true casualty figures for the fighting but perhaps 8 million dead on both sides is approximately accurate. Many more died after the armistice in further fighting or as a result of the influenza epidemic of 1918–19 which wrought havoc in war-wasted Europe. As a direct result of the fighting France lost 1.35 million men, the British Empire nearly 1 million, Germany 1.6 million and Russia 2.3 million. Italy suffered 650,000 dead and the United States, which had entered the war in April 1917, lost 100,000 men. In addition, perhaps two or three times as many men were wounded, some severely and some crippled for life, whilst wartime conditions occasioned a fall in the birthrate. A hasty survey of the battlefields by the American General McKinstrey, estimated material damage at between £3000m and £5000m whilst the British Treasury calculated the cost of the total Allied war effort at £24,000m. In France 8 million acres (an area the size of Holland) had been devastated and much of her industrial wealth destroyed. A later estimate suggests French losses at £2200m. In so far as it could be expressed in terms of money, someone had to pay this bill and there was little doubt, in the atmosphere of 1918, that Germany would be expected to shoulder much of the burden.[1]

From its very inception the debate over the extent and discharge of this responsibility was seen by both participants and commentators alike as crucial in setting the content and tone of the peace settlement. Moral and material considerations were always mixed both in the discussions in Paris and in later negotiations and critical assessments. Not only was the problem one of the most dramatic elements of the conference in the short term, threatening at one point to drive Wilson to quit Europe and at another to bring down Lloyd George's government, it was also one of the most enduring of the long-term difficulties of Treaty execution. Finally it was a topic always in the forefront of the assaults on the practicality, morality and effectiveness of the Treaty which began in 1919 with J. M.

Keynes' *The Economic Consequences of the Peace* and which grew in volume if not in intensity, throughout the 1920s and 1930s.

⟨The reparations discussions in Paris focused on four key issues: the extent of Germany's liability; the question of her capacity to pay; and the problem of how, and over what period, the necessary payments could be made.⟩Of these the first was the most contentious but, at various stages of the negotiations, other themes became entangled in the reparations debate, most notably the questions of Allied economic policy towards Germany and towards each other after the war and the particularly charged problem of the debts which the Allies had contracted between themselves but especially from the United States during the war. Furthermore the reparations issue was an integral part of the interlocking complex of negotiations to conclude a peace settlement with Germany and hence there was bound to be a process of osmosis between it and other contentious areas of discussion.

The generally received view of the reparations settlement portrays France as anxious to establish as high a German debt as possible, often intransigent and unwilling to face economic reality. At the opposite extreme the United States sought a much more realistic settlement with less punitive overtones, whilst on this issue, perhaps with a slightly shamefaced air, Great Britain moved away from America and closer to France. Finally the sort of figures discussed in Paris are condemned as 'fantastic' and beyond the bounds of economic possibility. As we shall see, each of these propositions requires some modification before a more accurate picture emerges.[2]

REPARATIONS OR INDEMNITY?

The contemporary Allied assumptions on Germany's liability are well expressed in the earliest major history of the conference.

> For her own unjust ends Germany had provoked a war, which brought on the world unparalleled loss and suffering. In defeat it was right that, like any other wrongdoer brought to justice, she should make all amends within her power.

But amends for what? Some of the Allied representatives believed that Germany should pay, quite literally, for the entire cost of the Allied war effort. 'L'Allemagne paiera' (Germany will pay), Louis-

Lucien Klotz, the French finance minister, is alleged to have said, apparently drawing from the caustic Clemenceau the comment that, if Klotz believed that, then he was the only Jew who did not understand finance. Whilst, as a recent authority has argued, this may do less than justice to Klotz, there is no doubt that Allied opinion was encouraged to believe that its negotiators would be searching German pockets and squeezing their economy to the utmost, and that, furthermore, they would succeed. More cautious and pessimistic politicians tried to suggest that there might be a striking difference between what Germany should pay and what she could pay. An even smaller minority argued that the Allies had no right to demand payment of their war costs but there seems to have been no serious suggestion denying Germany's liability to repair the civilian damage she had caused in the countries she had invaded or attacked. Indeed there were those who argued that a simple bill for all such damage would far exceed her capacity to pay and that therefore hopes of an indemnity to cover Allied war costs were illusory.[3] There were thus in simple terms two main schools of thought: those who believed in an indemnity policy, under which Germany should pay all, or part of, the Allied war costs; and those who argued for a reparations policy, under which Germany would restore only civilian damages. At the centre of the debate over Germany's liability was the interpretation of the pre-armistice agreement and whether this precluded the Allies from seeking an indemnity.

Wilson believed that, since Germany had invaded Belgium illegally in 1914, Belgium was entitled to her war costs but this was a unique case. Referring to other invaded Allied territory, the president said only that it should be 'evacuated' and 'restored'. He pursued and clarified this theme in his 'Four Ends' speech of 11 February 1918 when he declared that 'There shall be . . . no contributions, no punitive indemnities'. Clemenceau and Lloyd George well understood the implications of Wilson's invitation to consider an armistice leading to a treaty based on his policy speeches. On 25 October Lloyd George warned the War Cabinet to voice any objections to these: 'Otherwise the Germans would have a perfect right to assume that the Fourteen Points were the worst conditions that could be imposed on them.' Their request, on 29 October, for a clarification of what Wilson meant by 'restoration' was a tacit admission that a war costs indemnity was not negotiable. On 3

November House approved a definition which Wilson incorporated into the pre-armistice agreement with the Germans on 5 November. The final draft read: 'By it [restoration] they understand that compensation will be made by Germany for all damage done to the civilian population of the Allies and their property by the aggression of Germany by land, by sea, and from the air.' This draft included an important change from the original approved by House. That had referred to Germany's 'invasion of Allied territory'. The amended version submitted by Britain on 4 November substituted 'aggression'. The practical justification was to safeguard British claims to compensation since she had not been invaded, but there were moral overtones to the new wording reflecting the unspoken assumptions of German guilt in 1914.[4]

Whatever the long-term consequences of such a moral judgement, there seemed to be no justification within the pre-armistice agreement for any indemnity claim. Yet when the Peace Conference opened, every delegation, except that of the United States, put forward a claim for reimbursement of their entire war costs. They could find some basis for such claims in the preamble to Paragraph 19 of the Armistice of 11 November 1918 which stated: 'With reservation that any future claims and demands of the Allies and the United States remain unaffected, the following financial conditions are required: Reparation for damage done . . .' This 'lamentably obscure' wording had been suggested by Klotz before the agreed definition of 'restoration', and in their reply in June 1919 to the German observations on the draft treaty, the Allies admitted, at least tacitly, that this caveat could not overturn the pre-armistice agreement.[5] In the short term, however, the British and French claims in particular require explanation.

THE BRITISH DEMAND FOR AN INDEMNITY

Robert Bunselmeyer has shown how in Britain a combination of public opinion, pressure from some newspaper proprietors, relations with the Dominions and a general election campaign in which two-thirds of the electorate were newly enfranchised, all had a part to play. Although some politicians, most notably Andrew Bonar Law, the Conservative leader, tried to moderate public expectations, many candidates were swept along by anti-German feeling. Winston Churchill and David Lloyd George may have spent the evening of

Armistice Day discussing ways of relieving acute shortages in Germany but they were not typical. The anti-German mood of the country owed much to fears for the safety of British prisoners-of-war in Germany. It was also testimony to the highly effective wartime propaganda campaign waged by the Department of Information with its atrocity stories and exploitation of incidents such as the executions of Nurse Cavell and Captain Fryatt. The vindictive sinking of the Irish mail packet *Leinster* with the loss of 451 lives on 10 October 1918, whilst Germany was negotiating with Wilson, drove even the normally urbane Arthur Balfour into a fury. There was thus no immediate urge to forgive and forget and moderate voices like those of C. P. Scott, editor of the *Manchester Guardian*, or George Bernard Shaw were drowned in a growing chorus for revenge and retribution. On 28 October a group of Tory MPs, calling themselves the National Party, placed an advertisement in *The Times* stating 'Germany can pay. Germany must pay'. This theme became increasingly common in the press in November and December, particularly in those papers controlled by Lord Northcliffe.[6]

A powerful spur to newspaper demands for an indemnity came from the Australian prime minister, William Hughes, an irascible and difficult man. 'Hughes was partly deaf, easily irritated, and seldom afflicted by doubt. Many of his British Empire colleagues regarded him as "l'enfant terrible", to be avoided when possible and accommodated when necessary.'[7] He arrived at an Imperial War Conference on 6 November convinced that he had been excluded deliberately from the armistice discussions and anxious that Wilson's programme might prevent an effective scheme of imperial preference and deny the Allies proper restitution. Soothed by Lloyd George and Bonar Law at that meeting, he returned to the charge the next day when he became the first political figure of significance in Britain to make a public call for an indemnity. Both this demand, and his formal complaint, made on 9 November, of a lack of consultation about the armistice, were embarrassing for Lloyd George. Hughes pointed out that, whereas reparations would help France and Belgium and offer at least some recompense to Britain, the empire stood to recover none of its considerable contribution to the Allied cause. Hughes was creating a potential rift both in the empire and amongst Conservative supporters of the Coalition. With the idea of an indemnity gaining press and public support in the midst of the election campaign, Lloyd George had a difficult problem.

He sought to solve, or at least to evade it by establishing, on 26 November, an Imperial War Cabinet Committee on Indemnity, forcing the reluctant Hughes to become its chairman. The committee had reached the main part of its conclusions by 2 December, including a recommendation that Germany could pay £24,000m in annual instalments of £1200m which would include 5 per cent interest. It offered no empirical evidence for this claim, which was wildly in excess of Treasury estimates of German capacity which ranged from £900m to £3000m. Starting from the premise that the cost of the war would ruin either the Allies or Germany, the committee had decided, in a member's words: 'On the whole I think we had better ruin them.'[8]

This sentiment accorded well with the mood of the general election in Britain. It had been called by the Coalition partners on 12 November and Lloyd George and Bonar Law asked the electorate to support candidates whom they had endorsed with what Asquith scathingly called a 'coupon'. The current parliament had far exceeded its constitutional span but more important to the government was the chance to gain a firm mandate from a grateful public in the euphoria of victory. In particular Lloyd George, whose political base was unsure, needed to establish his premiership at a time when his political credit was at its zenith with his Conservative allies. The government had planned to concentrate its campaign upon domestic issues such as Irish Home Rule, tariff policy and the disestablishment of the Church of England in Wales. Foreign policy was not given a high profile, though Lloyd George's speech to Liberal party workers on 12 November stressed the moderation of his diplomacy. This was hardly heady stuff and was unlikely to catch the imagination of the electors. Constituency reports suggested that voters were largely apathetic, though they were keen to make Germany pay, in every sense of the word. There was enthusiasm for the trial of the Kaiser and other German leaders, for the expulsion of German aliens from Britain, and for an indemnity. Feeling that he could not afford to be out of touch with this new electorate, Lloyd George responded to the anti-German mood.

In a major speech at Newcastle on 29 November he called for the trial of the Kaiser and for Germany to pay for the cost of war to the limit of her capacity to do so. Thereafter the anti-German theme became dominant and although Lloyd George did not call for the hanging of the Kaiser, and neither did he promise to squeeze the

German lemon until the pips squeaked,[9] he did not repudiate his colleagues when they did so. On 11 December he encouraged the voters of Bristol to believe that the optimistic predictions of the Hughes' committee might be more accurate than the Treasury's, and he pledged his government to demand the whole cost of the war from Germany. Lloyd George's main task was to win the election and this he proceeded to do by a landslide. He had thus turned potential embarrassment to electoral advantage and ridden a wave of popular and press opinion for a punitive economic settlement with Germany. For the moment this was sufficient; he would deal later with the problem of his conflicting promises to the Germans and the British electorate and he would ignore the fact that his strong parliamentary position depended entirely on Conservative support. He therefore had little option, in the light of his election campaign, but to include a British demand for war costs. Whether this was a reluctant gesture or something which he had always planned is a matter for speculation.[10]

FRENCH POLICY REVIEWED

The French, who also claimed their war costs, have been cast traditionally as the villains of the reparations drama. Their policy has been interpreted as malevolent and vindictive, and as a quite deliberate attempt to bankrupt Germany, even to the extent that, although France needed German assistance to restore her devastated regions, she preferred to ruin Germany rather than adjust her claims to a level at which Germany could make at least some contribution. Reparations policy is thus seen as an extension of security policy since a drained and destitute Germany could not threaten France.[11] More recent research, whilst not entirely discounting such explanations, has suggested that French policy was more subtly motivated and flexible than the cartoon caricature of a large Frenchman demanding money with menaces from a destitute German child. Marc Trachtenberg in particular argues that reparations was only one strand and, initially, not the most important one, in a more general French economic and financial strategy. Indeed reparation demands may have been seen by the French as a lever more against the Americans than the Germans, and their subsequent higher profile has to be seen in the context of a set-back for other aspects of French policy.[12]

During the war Britain and France had considered an arrangement to maintain economic penalties against Germany in peace-
time. The resolutions of the Paris Economic Conference of 14 to 17
June 1916 envisaged a tightening and greater coordination of wartime measures against Germany, but also a post-war arrangement
whereby priority of access to key raw materials would be assured
those countries despoiled by Germany. The policy included restrictions on trade with Germany and was disliked by British free-
traders. It was the subject of political controversy in 1917 and 1918.
Wilson's objections to any idea of continuing an economic war
against Germany after peace had strengthened the hand of those
opposed to the resolutions, whilst in Britain, Germany's collapse in
the autumn of 1918 removed much of the policy's motivation. Now
the scenario of a compromise peace with an undefeated Germany
was no longer relevant and the idea of imposing an indemnity as
part of a victorious settlement gained ground.

In France the Paris resolutions, or the thinking behind them,
continued to be an important part of government strategy. The
leading spokesman for the policy was the Minister of Commerce,
Etienne Clémentel, who strove in 1917 and 1918 to convince Britain
and America of the need for inter-Allied economic cooperation. He
was successful to the extent that a number of inter-Allied committees were created to coordinate the purchasing, supply and
transportation of war materials. Of these the Allied Maritime
Transport Council, which allocated shipping space, was the most
developed but Clémentel hoped that the system could be elaborated
and maintained after the war so as to create an inter-Allied control
of world supplies of raw materials.[13] Some of the British officials on
the various inter-Allied commissions also favoured the idea but they
were realistic about the probable American response. For the
French, who lacked a powerful mercantile marine and whose industrial areas had been hard-hit, the attractions of such a policy were
obvious and they adopted Clémentel's idea of an Allied economic
union despite clear signs that Wilson was not impressed by the
arguments in its favour. On the eve of the armistice then, French
policy was less concerned with reparations than with establishing an
inter-Allied economic structure to enable her to rebuild her industrial and financial base. Furthermore, the restriction of supplies to
Germany might enable her to contribute to French reconstruction
whilst limiting her potential for aggression.[14]

It was a policy doomed to failure. Wilson made clear on 27 September that there could be no 'special selfish economic combinations within the League' and, more privately, he advised his representatives abroad that America would not accept any inter-Allied control of her resources after the war. He was an unrepentant free-trade liberal and seems to have had no economic dimension to his plans for a brave new world. Even less ambitious schemes for American government loans to finance French reconstruction failed. With the armistice the Americans began to dismantle the agencies of inter-Allied cooperation and to resist with gathering firmness any attempts to link reconstruction, reparations and inter-Allied debts into a package representing the financial and economic legacy of the war.[15]

Clémentel's ideas had one brief final flicker of life when he became chairman of the Economic Drafting Committee established in early February by the peace conference. He tried to make any French concessions dependent upon inter-Allied economic cooperation and implied that, failing such an arrangement, France would insist upon a punitive peace. The Americans at first seemed receptive, at least to the idea of assistance for the devastated regions, but their enthusiasm evaporated and Clémentel also faded into the background.[16] Nonetheless, argues Trachtenberg, his replacement as Clemenceau's main economic adviser by Louis Loucheur and the new French emphasis on reparations should not necessarily be seen as more than a change of tactics. The ultimate aim was still to involve the United States in an all-round settlement, but the means would now be to demand impossibly high compensation from Germany. When the Allies came to recognise the justice of the French claim but Germany's inability to meet it, they would themselves undertake a share of the task. Thus the French too claimed an indemnity when the Conference opened.[17]

THE COMMISSION ON THE REPARATION OF DAMAGE

Lloyd George tried (as he had at the London conference in December) to introduce 'indemnity' into the title of a commission on 'reparation and indemnity' which he proposed on 22 January. In the face of Wilson's vigorous objection he made a tactical retreat, and the Commission on the Reparation of Damage was established on 25 January, with terms of reference drafted by Lloyd George. Each of the five major powers had three members whilst Belgium, Serbia,

Greece, Poland and Rumania had two each. The Czechs and Portuguese were added in February but it was the American, British and French delegates who dominated this cumbersome body.

Wilson appointed Vance McCormick, chairman of the War Trade Board, Bernard Baruch, chairman of the War Industries Board, and Norman Davis, the United States Treasury representative in London. The French delegates were Louis-Lucien Klotz, the Finance Minister, Louis Loucheur, Minister of Industrial Reconstruction and Albert Lebrun. Lloyd George's choices, for reasons that have been disputed, were William Hughes of Australia, Lord Cunliffe, an ex-governor of the Bank of England, and Lord Sumner, a judge. The latter two were irreverently dubbed the 'Heavenly Twins' by their British colleagues.[18] The commission met for the first time on 3 February, under the chairmanship of Klotz, and established three subcommittees on evaluation, capacity to pay and guarantees.

The achievement of this commission lay more in the problems it identified than in the solutions it proposed. Nonetheless, when reparations was handed back to the Council of Four in late March, possible answers to some of the difficulties were emerging. In particular, there was a hint of a possible compromise in the heated controversy as to whether the claims for war costs were admissible. Lloyd George and Clemenceau argued that they were but the young American John Foster Dulles was adamant, on 13 February, that the pre-armistice agreement ruled out such claims. Given the high expectations of public opinion in Britain and France this fundamental disagreement was potentially disastrous.

THE ORIGINS OF THE 'WAR GUILT' CLAUSE

It was Dulles who on 21 February suggested a way out of this impasse when he outlined a clause affirming Germany's theoretical responsibility for the entire cost of the war but limiting any actual claim to a sum within her capacity to pay. When the matter was later discussed in the Council of Four, Wilson maintained his objection to war costs but Lloyd George argued along Dulles' line: there would be no actual demand for such a payment but there should be a theoretical statement of Germany's liability. After further debate the Council agreed to consider a draft based on Norman Davis' suggestion: 'We can write that Germany is morally responsible for the war and all its consequences and that legally she is responsible for damage to property and persons according to the formula adopted.'[19]

From this sprang Article 231, the 'War Guilt' clause which stated:

The Allied and Associated Governments affirm and Germany accepts the responsibility of Germany and her allies for causing all the damage to which the Allied and Associated Governments and their nationals have been subjected as a consequence of the war imposed upon them by the aggression of Germany and her allies.

Article 232 followed and qualified this by recognising

that the resources of Germany are not adequate . . . to make complete reparation for all such loss and damage. The Allied and Associated Governments, however, require, and Germany undertakes that she will make compensation for all damage done to the civilian population . . . and to their property.[20]

The intention then, was to differentiate between what they claimed was their moral entitlement and their actual demands. This was unsure ground but the pressing political needs of the European leaders had been, temporarily, met. The other aspects of the reparations debate now claim our attention.

THE CENTRAL POINTS OF DEBATE

In essence there were only a few key issues but these were so inextricably linked that it proved impossible in Paris to reconcile principles, commitments and expectations. The three subcommittees of the main commission had to wrestle with the questions of exactly how much damage had been done; how to find a fair way of valuing that damage; what categories of damage could legitimately be charged to Germany; whether Germany's liability should be assessed simply by adding up the sums established once these earlier problems had been resolved; or whether the whole issue should be approached rather by asking what Germany could afford and then settling for a figure which would be less than their full entitlement but which might at least be paid.

If the latter approach – the 'fixed sum' – was adopted, this raised new and difficult questions about how to assess Germany's capacity to pay. Not so much in 1919 but, given reasonable recovery, what would be attainable in, say, 1930? Supposing an answer to these problems was forthcoming, how was Germany to pay? The assumption was that she would make annual instalments but in what form – money or goods? Should the capital sum bear interest? Should there be a limit after which payments should cease – 30 years was often mentioned? Finally, how and on what basis should any receipts be shared amongst the Allies?

Each was a difficult technical, legal or political problem in its own right, but the complexities were compounded by the interplay between them. If, for example, the Allies agreed upon a distribution of receipts amongst themselves and agreed also upon a fixed sum to discharge all Germany's debts then, in essence, it did not much matter what categories of damage had been considered. The Allied distribution agreement would eliminate that part of their function, and it was always assumed that the fixed sum meant a reduction of the full Allied claim. On the other hand, if the German debt was calculated by adding the totals claimed under each reparation heading then the definition of legitimate categories became vital. Interpreted literally this would determine both Germany's debt and how the receipts would be distributed. On each of these issues the essential feature of the Versailles Settlement was that no firm conclusion was reached. Throughout the negotiations all the options were either in continuous contention or lurking just outside the conference room. Even the treaty postponed the decisions, leaving them to various agencies and later conferences. Expressed crudely, the Germans were asked to buy a pig in a poke.

The Allies came close to agreeing how to divide the spoils. Lloyd George opened the bidding on 25 March, suggesting 50 per cent for France, 30 per cent for the British empire and 20 per cent for the rest. The French countered by claiming a priority for themselves and Belgium on the grounds that material damage should be repaired first. Later they agreed to discuss a proportional distribution without such a priority. On 26 March, Loucheur began by proposing a French/British division of 72:18 but later floated options ranging from 55:25 to 56:28. When Sumner accepted the latter, which the Americans also favoured, it seemed agreement was near, but then Loucheur reverted to 55:25 and no conclusion was reached during the conference. Later, in December 1919, Britain accepted

55:25 whilst the final agreement was struck at 52:22 in June 1920 at Spa.[21] In Paris therefore, this variable remained unresolved and certainly affected Allied attitudes towards the other interconnected problems.

When it came to Germany's capacity to pay, or the actual amount of damage suffered by the Allies, there was a common dilemma: a lack of detailed knowledge and a fear of setting either too low. A full survey of the battlefields would take two years, any earlier figures would be guesses, and in the subcommittee on evaluation of damages, the French and Belgians refused to deal in guesses. They rejected McKinstrey's rapid survey and estimate of £3000m to £5000m as inadequate. This left the subcommittee able to deal only with what were the legitimate categories for compensation, and how to compute their value. Their findings formed the basis of the list of headings under which reparations might be claimed, adopted by the Four on 8 April. Controversially that list included not only damage caused to civilians and their property during the war, but also the pensions and allowances paid to Allied servicemen and their dependants. It is impossible to find a logical argument which permits such an interpretation of the pre-armistice and armistice agreements without simultaneously conceding the case for an indemnity. Wilson admitted as much when, on 1 April, he declared: 'Logic! Logic! I don't give a damn for logic. I am going to include pensions', thus overturning his earlier strong objections to this British initiative.[22]

He had allowed the South African delegate, Jan Christian Smuts, to persuade him that since soldiers were merely civilians in uniform, injuries to them constituted civilian damage. Quite why he succumbed to this palpable nonsense is uncertain, but Lloyd George had left him in no doubt of the strength of British feeling, threatening, apparently, to quit the conference unless this concession was made. The British probably made the case to justify a larger share of any receipts than a strict interpretation of civilian damage would allow. Under such a definition, Great Britain would receive relatively little despite contributing more heavily, in financial terms, than France, whilst Australia, which had expended more men and money than Belgium, would receive nothing. Wilson, knowing Lloyd George was under political pressure both within his own delegation and in parliament, may have believed that there was an element of rough justice in the inclusion of pensions in so far as it affected the distribution of receipts amongst the Allies. He may still have hoped that he could persuade his colleagues on the Council of Four to accept a fixed sum solution, yet he must have realised this was improbable.[23]

The difficulties in agreeing a fixed sum revolved around finding a figure which Allied public opinion would accept as sufficient and, initially, the Americans and, ultimately, the Germans, would see as practical. No one really knew what Germany could afford to pay, neither were they sure how much she owed, but the figures bandied about in discussions suggested deep divisions amongst the Allies. In simple terms they had to establish what Germany could afford to pay in annual instalments, and then to multiply that amount by a number of years, usually assumed to be 30, to produce a capital sum. Thomas Lamont, of the United States, suggested a capital sum of between £3000m and £5000m – significantly the same amounts as McKinstrey's estimates of damage on the Western Front. As a gesture to Allied public opinion, however, Lamont increased this to £6000m. Yet on 21 February, Lord Cunliffe at first maintained his 1918 estimate of £24,000m, whilst the lowest total he would consider was £9500m. Loucheur, for France, was closer to Lamont with £8000m, but although the committee agreed that Germany should make a preliminary payment of £1000m, it made no further headway. The problem of Germany's capacity to pay was returned, unresolved, to the Council of Four.[24]

REPARATIONS IN THE COUNCIL OF FOUR

Lloyd George thus found himself in a difficult position. His Treasury experts believed that £3000m was the most Germany could pay, but both Cunliffe and Sumner refused to compromise. Having appointed the 'Heavenly Twins' as his representatives, he was now trapped by their adamance. This became particularly clear when the Council of Four appointed a new three-man committee, on 10 March, to untangle the figures. Lloyd George replaced Cunliffe with Edwin Montagu, his Liberal Secretary of State for India. Together with Loucheur and Davis, Wilson's main financial adviser, he agreed to £6000m. Since half this sum was payable in paper marks, the true figure was £3000m. Furthermore, in a private meeting on 15 March, Lloyd George apparently endorsed this figure, but given the extreme sensitivity of the issue, it was not surprising when on 22 March he made his approval conditional upon the agreement of Cunliffe and Sumner. Their refusal meant a resumption of deadlock.[25]

Lloyd George's appeal for moderation in his Fontainebleau Memorandum of 25 March must therefore have been particularly galling to the American and French reparations negotiators. His words were pious: 'we must offer terms which a responsible Government in Germany can expect to carry out' and 'I would say that the duration for the payment of reparations ought to disappear, if possible, with the generation which made the war', but his actions pointed elsewhere. Lamont believed that it was British not French intransigence, which had prevented the March committee reaching agreement, and his exasperation must have been compounded by the new estimates of German capacity advanced that day. Sumner proposed £11,000m, the French between £6200m and £9400m and the Americans £5000m to £7000m.[26] Indeed Lloyd George's next initiative was not to moderate Germany's liability but to begin, on 28 March, a successful campaign which practically ensured that the treaty would not name her total obligation.

That day the Council of Four considered two schemes put forward by Klotz and the British expert, John Maynard Keynes. Klotz proposed that the treaty should name only a deposit sum together with a list of damages which the Allies deemed legitimately chargeable to reparations. The only negotiations with Germany would be about the items on the list. An Allied commission would then compute Germany's total bill after the treaty was signed. Keynes preferred to say to Germany: 'Here is what you owe; but we have not yet determined how much you can pay'. Wilson thought the two plans were incompatible and condemned Klotz's as 'equivalent to asking the Germans to extend us unlimited credit'. Lloyd George, however, declared:

> I see real advantages in not stating now any figure to represent the total sum owed to us by the Germans. Be assured that, whatever this figure, many people in England as well as in France, will immediately exclaim 'This is too small'.

He wanted Klotz's commission to decide what Germany owed and then Keynes' system would establish what Germany could pay. It is not clear which figure Lloyd George saw as having priority. Although

Wilson reserved his position, he was isolated and this meeting effectively ruled out the naming of any final bill, however computed, in the German treaty.[27]

If there was to be any limitation on Germany's debt therefore, it required the Allies to set a term for reparations payments. Wilson now tried to persuade his colleagues to agree to a 30-year period, beyond which payments would cease. With the Fontainebleau Memorandum barely a week old, he must have hoped for Lloyd George's support when the question was raised in the Four on 5 April. If so he was to be disappointed. They were considering the draft clauses prepared by the experts. The first two became Articles 231 and 232 of the Treaty, the third envisaged an inter-Allied commission establishing, by May 1921, a list of damages to be claimed from Germany. It would review all the Allied demands and grant Germany an audience before reaching its decision. It was also to fix a schedule of payments 'up to or within the total sum thus due, which in their judgement Germany should be able to liquidate within a period of thirty years, and this . . . shall then be communicated to Germany as representing the extent of their payments'.[28]

The Four wanted this explained, and Davis, pointing out that this was a British text, obliged:

this is how I now understand it: Two years from now, the Commission must declare the total sum due to us. If it finds that this sum exceeds Germany's capacity to pay within 30 years, it will determine what Germany should pay, according to this capacity. But this latter sum must be integrally paid, even if it discovered thereafter that this period must be lengthened.

In other words the principle of a fixed sum but with the announcement of the figure itself postponed for two years. Lloyd George and Klotz both objected vigorously to such a limitation on Germany's debt, but House, deputising for Wilson who was sick, entirely missed the point at issue when he declared: 'Everyone was agreed that if the Germans could not pay in 30 years, then they must pay the amount in 40 years. He did not understand, therefore, what the discussion was all about.'[29] Effectively the second battle to limit the German debt had failed.

'In other words', said the American expert Vance McCormick, 'everything will be paid, whatever the period necessary.' Davis was completely exasperated; according to him the whole debate had now moved away from the basic principles of the past three months: 'We had always spoken of taking into account, on the one hand, the capacity to pay, always held by us to be less than the debt [and agreed] . . . that Germany would have to pay what she could in 30 years or 35 years, not more.'[30] It is possible that the experts were working on these assumptions (beyond 35 years the interest payments would apparently outstrip repayments and make the debt perpetual) but the principals were never so clear in their understanding of the principles involved. Instead they wavered between various incompatible options, always coming up short against the political inconveniences of each as it was revealed.

THE REPARATIONS SETTLEMENT

Thus the eventual shape of the reparations settlement emerged from a series of decisions whose main motives were to put off unpalatable choices, to preserve a facade of Allied unity, and to obscure their lack of principle. On 5 April the Four agreed that Germany should make a preliminary payment of £1000m in gold to an inter-Allied Reparation Commission by May 1921. This money would be used to pay army-of-occupation costs and for the supply of essential raw materials to Germany. Only any remaining balance would be credited to reparations. The French did not like this but lost the point. On 7 April the texts of Articles 231 and 232 were accepted together with 233 which established a Reparation Commission. On 8 April the Council approved the final list of legitimate damages for which reparation could be demanded. The day same Lloyd George received a sharply worded telegram from 233 MPs, reminding him that they expected a bill to be presented to Germany which, at least in the first instance, represented nothing less than the full imperial financial claim. On 16 April he routed his critics in the Commons but the threat to his freedom of manoeuvre had seemed clear.[31]

The Reparation Commission was to consist of one member each from France, Great Britain, Italy and the United States with the fifth seat alternating between Belgium when Germany was under discussion, Japan for maritime matters, and Yugoslavia, for matters concerning the former Austro-Hungarian empire. By 1 May 1921 it was to determine Germany's debt by adding the sums due under the approved categories, and also to decide how and when Germany was to pay, and at what rates of interest. Payments were to be completed within 30 years but the Commission could allow post-ponements in certain circumstances. Indeed it had wide-ranging powers – taken literally the treaty meant that, without the Com-mission's permission, the German government could spend nothing on its normal business until it had met its reparations commitments. For matters affecting the sovereignty of the Allied powers, the Commission had to be unanimous – abstentions counted as con-trary votes. Thus on major issues such as the cancellation of all, or part, of the debt, or lengthy postponements of instalments, the individual governments retained a veto.[32]

Wilson insisted on such an American veto on the timing of the issue of German government bonds to cover all, or part, of her reparations debt. There were obvious attractions for her creditors in such bonds. If they were sold on the international market or used as collateral for loans, then the Allies could touch their money sooner and widen the responsibility for enforcing payment beyond a per-petual Allied/German confrontation. Lloyd George believed that the Commission could, within 48 hours of the signature of peace, calculate a substantial proportion of the reparations bill and then instruct Germany to issue bonds for that amount. Not surprisingly Wilson was amazed: 'he was mystified by this discussion. Months had been spent in trying to reach a figure, then it had been decided to drop the attempt. Now it was proposed to ask the Commission to name it right away.'[33]

Thus, once again, the eventual decision on 12 April to approve Sumner's proposals for a bond issue was ambiguous. The German government was to issue bearer bonds to the value of £5000m in three parts. The first, an immediate issue of £1000m, represented the sum it had already been decided to ask Germany to pay before 1921. It would bear no interest. The second issue of £2000m would take place after the treaty had been signed. The bonds would carry interest of 2.5 per cent from 1921 until 1926 and thereafter 5 per cent. The third tranche of £2000m was to be held by the Commission until it judged the German economy could afford its release.[34] But did the bonds represent the complete German debt?

Bond issues needed a unanimous Commission vote – Wilson could insist on this because most bonds sold would find their way to the American market. Now some of the American experts claimed that the bonds to be issued did cover all Germany's liabilities. In effect a total of £3000m with an American veto over a possible further £2000m but this view was firmly rejected by Britain and France. It does seem inherently unlikely that Clemenceau and Lloyd George, having battled to prevent a total sum being named in the treaty, would now relent.[35]

A further example of hasty and unclear judgement arose when the French suggested specific penalties for any German default in reparations payments. Lloyd George and Wilson were suspicious of French intentions and were anxious to preserve their future freedom of action. Wilson's alternative draft, approved by the Four on 23 April, insisted that any German default must be deliberate and continued:

> The measures which the Allied and Associated Governments shall have the right to take, and which Germany hereby agrees not to consider as acts of war, may include economic or financial prohibitions and reprisals, and in general such other measures as the respective Government may determine to be necessary in the premise.

His attempt to improve the French original left much to be desired. The wording apparently permitted individual governments to take unilateral action – which Britain was quick to do when she renounced certain treaty rights in October 1920. The French not only exploited this loophole, but also interpreted 'such other measures' as allowing their occupation of German territory in the Ruhr in January 1923. The Americans believed that their wording, whilst vague, had by its tone and content confined sanctions to economic and financial measures.[36] Given the imprecision of the reparations clauses, there is something apt about this confusion.

Part of Germany's obligations were to be paid in kind and the treaty gave the Allies various options to buy or receive coal, dyestuffs and shipping, and to have restored items stolen or requisitioned during the war. These included large numbers of farm animals for France and Belgium – over 40,000 horses, 220,000 cattle and 121,000 sheep. More bizarre demands included the restoration of the original Koran of the Caliph Ottoman and the skull of Sultan Mkwawa.[37] Germany's obligation to supply coal reparations is treated more fully in the next chapter, on the German settlement.

REACTIONS TO THE DRAFT PROPOSALS

German reaction to the reparations section of the draft treaty was predictably bitter: 'Those who will sign this Treaty will sign the death sentence of many millions of German men, women and children.' Nonetheless the delegation was aware that it must make some counter-proposal, and it did offer to pay £5000m in reparations. This sum, however, would not bear interest and the maximum payment in each of the first ten years was £50m. She was also prepared to make special arrangements to deliver coal to Belgium and France, but implied that this entailed continuing German sovereignty in the Saar and Upper Silesia. Perhaps hoping that Wilson might yet improve the terms and conditions, the Germans ignored tentative explorations by the French of possible special arrangements between the two countries in the fields of reconstruction and economic cooperation.[38]

Meanwhile part of the British alarm, having seen the treaty as a whole for the first time, was directed towards the reparations clauses. Faced with the possibility that the Germans, and even some of his own delegation – Smuts and Barnes – might not sign the draft treaty, Lloyd George called a special meeting of the British cabinet and Dominion prime ministers in Paris on 1 June. He found them strongly in favour of revision of the terms and, as far as reparations were concerned, pressing for the treaty to name a total sum for German payments, or for the Germans themselves to have an opportunity to offer, within three months of the treaty's signature, a complete reparations package.[39]

Yet, although Lloyd George told Clemenceau and Wilson on 2 June that his colleagues 'most stressed criticism was the indefinite and unlimited nature of the debt imposed on Germany' and that 'all are in agreement in believing we are asking Germany to pay more than she will ever be able', he did not press the Council so hard on this aspect of British revisionism as on others. Indeed, when the Council considered his objections over the following days, Lloyd George and Clemenceau once again combined to defeat Wilson's final attempt to name a total sum in the treaty. On 9 June he proposed that Germany's maximum liability under Article 232 should be £6000m. Lloyd George replied that:

The conclusion he had come to was that if figures were given now

they would frighten rather than reassure the Germans. Any figure
that would not frighten them would be below the figure with
which he and M. Clemenceau could face their peoples in the
present state of public opinion. . . . The statement of a figure at
the present time would also raise inconvenient questions between
the Allies.

Thus, despite his earlier protestations, Lloyd George preferred to
leave the treaty unchanged but to permit the Germans to make a
counter-offer within three or four months.[40]

Wilson was furious at Lloyd George's expediency – Clemenceau
at least had the virtue of consistency – and privately berated the
British for being 'unanimous in their funk . . . they are afraid the
Germans won't sign, and their fear is based upon things that they
insisted upon at the time of the writing of the treaty; that makes me
very sick'. Scorning Lloyd George's proposals as mere verbosity,
Wilson declared that he stood by the treaty, but was prepared, if
Britain and France wished, to make concessions to induce Germany
to sign. However, 'If we must make concessions then he was in
favour of perfectly definite concessions'. In the event the terms were
little changed, but Germany could make a full counter-offer within
four months of the signature of the treaty.[41]

REPARATIONS IN PERSPECTIVE

What verdict then should be returned on the reparations clauses and
the main actors in the drama? Keynes, himself a minor player, had
little doubt. Leaving Paris in despair in June 1919 he had, within six
months, published a stinging attack on what he saw as the economic
madness of the treaty. His magnificent polemic, *The Economic Consequences of the Peace*, has dominated later debate and tended to carry
all before it, particularly in his attempt to demonstrate the impossi-
bility of Germany transferring such large sums of money to her
creditors without, paradoxically, ruining them. Without seeking to
'prove' conclusively that Germany could have paid reparations of
the magnitude discussed in Paris, Marc Trachtenberg does at least
show that the figures were not entirely meaningless in economic terms.
A German debt of £6000m, he argues, meant annual payments of
£300m or roughly 7 per cent of German GNP in the late 1920s.
Between 1911 and 1913 Great Britain had exported approximately 8.7

per cent of her GNP. Thus, whilst not discounting the complexities of the issues, and recognising the political and psychological elements involved, Trachtenberg's analysis does cast doubt on some of the more extravagant condemnations of this aspect of the treaty. Sumner's calculations, however, still seek a champion of sufficient weight to defend them.[42]

No one, including the Germans, denied that Germany should pay something towards repairing the enormous damage caused by four years of industrialised warfare. The problem was to find a figure which enabled everyone to feel they had, in some sense, 'done well'. Britain and France needed a sufficiently large German cheque to placate a public whose expectations had been deliberately over-inflated. The Germans needed a bill which was less than their own private calculations of their ability to pay. Such a happy compromise was probably unobtainable in Paris, but it is interesting that the American experts present blamed this failure more on Britain than on France.[43]

Lloyd George later claimed credit for creating a breathing space in which tempers could cool and wiser counsels prevail. He was to pillory Loucheur for not facing economic reality and for deceiving the French public over the magnitude of likely receipts.[44] There is something disarmingly disingenuous in both these propositions: Lloyd George showed little inclination to offer Loucheur an example in honest assessment, whilst his 'virtue' in seeking more time is rather like an arsonist claiming credit for calling the fire brigade. It may be that his lawyer's instinct, as he so often declared, inclined him to seek a possible settlement rather than an impossible bill, yet both during the conference and after, the case for his moderation on this issue rests more on words than on figures or deeds. He tended to discount German objections to reparations. At the time of the Fontainebleau Memorandum he told the Council of Four that the real German difficulties lay in the territorial sphere but that they would accept even 'a very heavy indemnity'.[45] When his colleagues sought revision of the draft treaty, Robert Cecil remarked that he was 'curiously reluctant to make any changes' to the reparations clauses.[46] In part this was clearly due to public and parliamentary pressure, but this is not a sufficient explanation. Later, in 1920 and 1921 as Keynes' book began to have an effect and the public mood changed, Lloyd George still pressed for a high reparations settlement at the conferences of Spa, Boulogne, London and Paris.

Perhaps this is an issue on which it would be unwise to underestimate the calvinism in the prime minister's soul. 'It was not vengeance but justice', he told his cabinet colleagues '. . . whether we ought not to consider lashing her [Germany] as she had lashed France.'[47]

Equally, any assessment of Wilson's position on reparations would have to recognise his strong conviction that, before there could be forgiveness, there must first be retribution. He was also aware of, and sensitive to, the political problems of his colleagues on the Council of Four, and was thus prepared to make concessions which, as he forcefully admitted, lay beyond logical justification. Nonetheless, without wishing to be 'soft on Germany', American policy was consistent in its efforts to limit reparations to a sum as near as possible to their estimate of her maximum capacity to pay – about £3000m or £4000m – though it was accepted that it might be necessary to camouflage this figure with 'phoney money', German currency payments or undated bonds that had no value but made the total look impressive.

The weakest part of the American position was their refusal to admit any link between reparations and the inter-Allied debts contracted to pay for the war. In approximate figures these totalled £3,703,500,000 of which £2,965,250,000 was owed to the United States.[48] The Europeans saw these sums as part of a common effort to defeat Germany, and believed that the United States should ease the burden of repayment to pave the way for a more moderate reparations settlement. Wilson never quite descended to the crude commercialism of President Coolidge – 'Well they hired the money didn't they?' – but he and his advisers declined forcefully to admit any notion of an overall financial and economic package encompassing the various legacies of the war. This problem continued to bedevil America's relations with her friends, and attempts to resolve the reparations muddle, but the presidents concerned faced political difficulties just as severe as those Lloyd George and Clemenceau encountered in 1919. In particular any attempt to forgive British debts would have put any administration under heavy strain.

The most interesting new research has concerned French policy and has revealed early traces of the more imaginative responses to the 'German problem' in all its aspects that emerged in the post-1945 period.[49] In the short term, however, French attempts to induce the United States to shoulder broad responsibility for post-war reconstruction failed, and it would, in any case, be unwise to abandon completely an explanation of Clemenceau's policy which did not encompass the security angle. Given the curiously centrifugal nature of French ministerial decision-making it might be dangerous to base an analysis of French policy too firmly on the archives of any one ministry and finance was clearly only part of the reparations problem. It is also plain that, even if Klotz did not say 'l'Allemagne paiera', French public opinion expected German contributions, and Clemenceau, like Lloyd George, had to be wary of these expectations.

The Allies, as the Germans uncomfortably reminded them on 29 May 1919, had set themselves higher standards than the time-honoured formula of 'winner takes all' when establishing their terms of peace.[50] Seen in this light there is something inherently shabby in the reparations negotiations in Paris. The British and French leaders knew they had debarred themselves from seeking an indemnity, yet they still encouraged their public to expect one. Hence, fearful of public anger, they took refuge in the dubious legality of the pensions and allowances claim (which approximately doubled the eventual 'legitimate' claims against Germany)[51] and in the insensitive and unfortunate phrasing of Article 231. There is no doubt that the 'War Guilt' clause accurately represented contemporary Allied opinion, and the later researches of Professor Fischer and his disciples have suggested that this judgement was not entirely unfounded.[52] Nevertheless, there seems to have been no thought of expressing such a condemnation of Germany in the treaty, until the reparations negotiations posed a political problem for the Allied powers. The Preamble to the treaty speaks, in much more neutral tones, of the war originating in the Austro-Hungarian and German declarations of war in July and August 1914,[53] and the Allies, apparently, had no intention of basing the moral validity of the whole treaty on an assertion of German culpability. German reaction was extremely hostile but, simultaneously, it recognised a possible lever to use to overturn the treaty. If the judgement of Article 231 could be refuted, then would not the moral foundations of the entire treaty be undermined, and force a revision of its practical consequences?

During the Allied conference with the Germans in London in March 1921, Lloyd George was, foolishly, to go a long way to justify such a view: 'For the Allies', he told the German delegates, 'German responsibility for the war is fundamental. It is the basis upon which

the structure of the treaty has been erected, and if that acknowledge-
ment is repudiated or abandoned, the treaty is destroyed'.[54] Predictably, Germany spared no efforts in the 1920s to repudiate the 'War
Guilt' clause. Five volumes of carefully edited documents were
published in 1919, and a periodical and a special subsection of the
Foreign Ministry were established. The whole *Kreigsschuldfrage* (war
guilt question) industry culminated in the forty volumes of *Die Grosse
Politik der Europaischen Kabinette* published between 1922 and 1927.
These efforts were relatively successful, at least on a historical level,
leading to sympathetic accounts of Germany's policy in, for example
S. B. Fay's *The Origins of the World War* published in 1929, and
contributing towards the generally held view in the 1930s that the
war had been more the result of miscalculation than malice.[55]

The effect of the long-drawn-out battle to collect reparations
played havoc with Anglo-French relations and provided embittered
Germans with a stick to beat the Allies and to stir the political pot at
home. The Allies had taken their stance on the high moral ground
throughout the peace negotiations. They had a legitimate and
pressing claim against Germany, particularly for the deliberate
damage she had inflicted in the closing stages of the war, but also,
under the terms of the pre-armistice agreement, for the earlier
devastation of Allied property and resources. Their attempts to
inflate their claims squandered a strong moral position. When the
treaty as a whole began to lose the sympathy of informed opinion
throughout the world, then the nature of the reparations settlement
played a major, perhaps a decisive, role.

5 The German Settlement

THE signature of the armistice ensured that the map and, in part, the institutions of Germany would be recast by the peace conference but the extent and method of this reshaping remained obscure. Much would depend on the overall assessment that each of the Allied states made of the future intentions and political stability of the new German regime, which sought, as best it could, to distance itself from the ambitions and methods of the Kaiser and his government. Was this death-bed conversion genuine or expedient, and who would control the new, apparently democratic, Germany? Furthermore, what roles did the Allies see for Germany in the new international system? The shape of the new Germany would depend on the outcome of the debate between their widely differing viewpoints.[1]

In the west, Alsace and Lorraine were evacuated by Germany and occupied by Allied troops under the terms of the armistice, thus allowing Clemenceau and Poincaré, united for once, to make an emotional and triumphant return to Metz and Strasbourg on 8 and 9 December 1918. Although formally a matter for the conference to decide, there was no doubt as to the fate of the lost provinces, despite German rearguard pleas for a plebiscite. France had further claims on Germany: she sought compensation in the Saarland for the deliberate destruction of her coalmines in the north-east, and she hoped for a readjustment of the frontier in the Rhineland. The extent and motivation of these ambitions remained obscure. Belgium wanted Eupen and Malmedy, and had ambitions to control Luxemburg. She also wished to improve her defensive position by taking territory on the left bank of the Scheldt from Holland and this had implications for Germany, since it was assumed that the Dutch would, in turn, seek compensation from her. The Danes wished to reopen part of the settlement of the Schleswig-Holstein question brutally engineered by Bismarck in the 1860s.

The situation on Germany's eastern borders was more complex still, since her new frontiers here would be with states that were only now in the process of being formed and established. Indeed, in certain areas, the German army provided the only authority and the

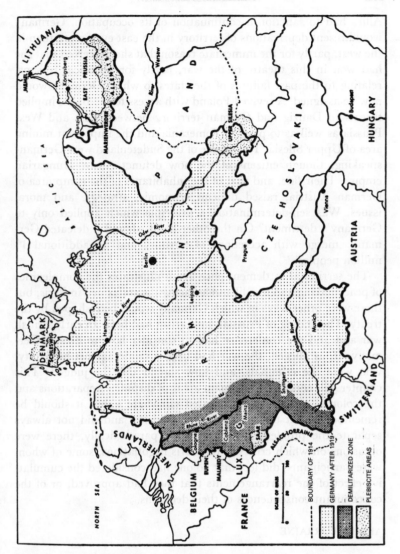

Map 1 Germany after 1919. The final boundary settlement 1919–23
(Reprinted with permission from H. I. Nelson, *Land and Power*,
Routledge & Kegan Paul, 1963, p. 363)

Allies had to sanction a continuation of its occupation. Germany would resent deprivations of territory in the east even more than in the west, partly for the immediate reason that she perceived that she had won in this theatre of the war, partly for historical reasons, relating to the past failures of the states to which Germans would now be assigned. A revived Poland with access to the Baltic implied threats to Danzig and German territory between East and West Prussia as well as to parts of Pomerania and the important mining area of Upper Silesia. The people of the Sudetenland were German-speaking, though citizens of the now defunct Austro-Hungarian empire. Their fate, and that of the inhabitants of the rump area of German Austria, raised difficult economic, strategic and moral issues. Was self-determination a principle which applied only to Germany's detriment? On the other hand, should a defeated Germany emerge with accretions of territory and an additional 11 million people?

The territorial settlement once again illustrates the complexities of peacemaking and the dilemmas facing the statesmen in Paris, but there were other ways in which Germany would be reshaped by the treaty. The ending of Prussian militarism had been an early British war aim and the conference had to consider how to disarm Germany. If, as alleged, the war had been a crime against humanity, who were the criminals, and how should they be judged? This chapter will consider these main areas of dispute – reparations and the colonial settlement are treated elsewhere – but it should be remembered that the peacemakers could not and did not always separate the problems so neatly. Yet, paradoxically, there were occasions on which critics of the Paris negotiations, some of whom were participants, did feel that no one had considered the cumulative effect of the rearrangements that they had approved, or of the concomitant consequences of their decisions.

ALSACE-LORRAINE

France did not enter the war in 1914 to regain Alsace-Lorraine, but it was inevitable that, once at war, she would demand the return of the two provinces as part of her war aims. Her allies knew this as early as 5 August 1914, although it was not until 22 November that the prime minister, Viviani, claimed their return in the Chamber. From 1915 onwards, semi-official groups and organisations within

France prepared for the eventual reincorporation of Alsace-Lorraine, and these hopes and demands were shared across the political divides of the Third Republic, although the Socialist party did believe that a plebiscite should determine the fate of the disputed provinces. It is interesting to note that official circles discouraged any such idea, partly because they were not entirely confident of its outcome.[2] There was a general sympathy for the French claim, but it was tinged, in the cases of Great Britain and the United States, with a certain suspicion that French ambitions might be greater than the simple restoration of the pre-1870 frontiers. In their January 1918 speeches, both Lloyd George and Wilson chose their words with care, speaking of reconsidering, or righting, 'the great wrong of 1871'. Neither wished to encourage wider French demands, and Lloyd George was anxious not to commit Britain to continue the war until Germany agreed to return the provinces.[3]

When the Germans demanded an armistice in October 1918, Clemenceau was, at first and surprisingly, prepared to follow Lloyd George's advice that Alsace-Lorraine should be evacuated by German troops without being occupied by the Allies. It was Foch who insisted that he change his mind, and the terms of the armistice allowed the Allies to garrison the region. Its special status was emphasised by the fact that the costs would be borne by the Allies, whereas Germany was responsible for the remainder of the Rhineland occupation expenses. In theory, it was only on 30 April 1919 that the Four agreed to restore the frontier of 1815–70 (rejecting Clemenceau's earlier suggestion that the 1814 frontier be adopted), but the French forces in the provinces had anticipated the outcome, and were re-establishing French rule long before that. The treaty, in fact, emphasised that their return to France dated from 11 November 1918.[4]

The return of the two provinces had interesting implications for the Third Republic. Its anti-clericalism had altered the face of France since 1871, whilst, with a certain irony, it was the Catholic clergy who had provided an important focus for French nationalism in Alsace-Lorraine throughout the German occupation. To what extent would France be prepared to compromise her ideological principles in order to allow a harmonious reintegration? This problem continued to tax politicians well into the 1920s, before common sense prevailed. Furthermore, the increased riches in iron that came with Alsace-Lorraine required extra resources, particularly in coking coal, a deficiency which would not be alleviated directly by any arrangement in the Saar. Wine-lovers, however, could anticipate the restoration of the production of the strong and distinctive wines of Alsace, suspended under German rule.[5]

THE RHINELAND

France welcomed the return of Alsace-Lorraine but this neither satisfied her ambitions nor allayed her fears as to her future security. Facing a German state which would, despite any foreseeable outcome to the present conference, be significantly more populous and industrialised than herself, France sought additional safeguards by suggesting changes to the frontiers and status of the Rhineland. Under the first Peace of Paris in 1814, the French had retained their frontier of 1792, which included Saarlouis and Saarbrucken, but the Hundred Days cost her these territories. The second Peace of Paris reduced France to her 1790 boundaries, and the 1815 Vienna settlement assigned much of the Rhineland to Prussia, with the immediate objective of strengthening the barriers against renewed French aggression. In coming to terms with this role, and with the unexpected riches of the Ruhr, Prussia had transformed herself from a relatively weak, central and eastern European state, into a powerful, industrial and political European colossus. If the decision of 1815 could be reversed or modified, France stood to benefit, and the question had exercised ministers and publicists throughout the war.[6]

Some Frenchmen argued that the natural frontier of Germany was the Rhine, and that the left bank territories or even the entire Rhineland should be incorporated into France. They supported their case by claiming Carolingian precedent and asserting that the celtic origins and Roman Catholicism of the inhabitants, if not their fundamental economic interests, would favour such a policy. More sensible and realistic commentators, such as the historian Aulard, acknowledged the French dilemma: 'Either we annex the left bank of the Rhine and violate principle, or we do not annex it and France remains in perpetual danger of invasion.' He believed that the Rhineland should be detached from Germany and become a neutral buffer state, or states. This belief was shared, with more or less conviction, by various French ministers, but they were aware of the pitfalls of too public a debate.[7]

Thus successive French governments approached their international partners with great caution on the Rhineland issue. Nicholas II of Russia was the most enthusiastic, telling the French ambassador in March 1915, 'Take the left bank of the Rhine; take Mainz; take Coblenz; take even more if you like', but the French were later embarrassed when the Russian government note of 14 February 1917 supporting their position on the Rhineland was published by the Bolsheviks after they had seized power. The British were cautious to the point of disapproval. On 2 July 1917 Paul Cambon communicated the view of the prime minister, Aristide Briand, that 'Germany must henceforth have but one foot across the Rhine' and called into question the future status of the Rhineland. Balfour replied that the French 'desire to see the territory west of the Rhine separated from the German Empire and erected into something in the nature of a buffer state' was a 'rather wild project' which he would not encourage. Later in the Commons, on 19 December 1917, Balfour claimed that the British government was never aware of any serious French statesman supporting such a project and indeed, French enthusiasm was muted after the American entry into the war.[8]

Nonetheless both Wilson and Lloyd George must have anticipated that Clemenceau would advance the idea of detaching the Rhineland from Germany during the conference. Lloyd George had clear warning when Foch seized the opportunity, on 1 December 1918, during the visit that he and Clemenceau made to London, to raise the question informally with British ministers. Lloyd George and Bonar Law responded politely but coolly to Foch's suggestions that the Rhineland be detached from Germany (by implication, becoming a neutral state) and that Britain should join all the left bank states in an alliance against future aggression. Foch was not discouraged, however, and became a persistent advocate of a revision of the status of the Rhineland throughout the conference.

Clemenceau's absence on this occasion and indeed his whole attitude to the Rhineland issue has been variously interpreted. Lloyd George commented that the Tiger relied upon others, notably Foch and Tardieu, to present the case, whilst he confined himself to unofficial approaches to his allies. Lloyd George felt that this avoided Clemenceau suffering an official rebuff, and it has also been suggested that Clemenceau never really had much faith in the policy, except as a bargaining counter. Much has also been made of a possible crisis in civil-military relations within France over the future of the Rhineland and over French policy in the area. On the other hand, Clemenceau does seem to have been committed to the 1814 frontier, and to have given vigorous support to Tardieu, at least until he became convinced of the depth of Anglo-American resistance.[9]

Foch continued his campaign by issuing a note on 10 January 1919, in his capacity as Allied commander-in-chief. He argued that the Allies must seize this unique opportunity to establish the Rhine as the military frontier of Germany. They should install a permanent army of occupation on the left bank and in three strategic bridge-heads, and integrate the area economically with France and Belgium. He was silent as to the future political status of the region. 'Marshal Foch has not explained what his plan really meant', Lloyd George remarked to Clemenceau, hinting at the widely-held British suspicions that the French had deep-rooted annexationist ambitions in this area. This distrust was to cloud Anglo-French relations, not only during the Paris conference, but also during their attempts to enforce the peace in later years. Faced with persistent French pressure to bring Germany to heel by occupying the Ruhr, the British foreign secretary Lord Curzon warned the Imperial Conference meeting in London on 26 June 1921, 'The Ministers present will see at once what her object is – with Lorraine, the Saar Valley and the Ruhr in her occupation, she becomes the mistress of Europe in respect of coal, iron and steel, and with those countries under her military command she would also become the military monarch.'[10]

The French thus encountered fierce and sustained British resistance to their Rhineland proposals. André Tardieu and Paul Mantoux both record Lloyd George as saying, in almost identical words on separate occasions: 'The strongest impression made upon me by my first visit to Paris was the statue of Strasbourg veiled in mourning. Do not let us make it possible for Germany to erect a similar statue.'[11] It was a theme to which the prime minister frequently returned when any of Germany's frontiers was under discussion, but it was obviously of especial relevance to the Rhineland debate. The Americans followed a similar line. House remarked to Balfour on 9 February: 'The French have but one idea and that is military protection. They do not seem to know that to establish a Rhenish Republic against the will of the people would be contrary to the principle of self-determination.'[12] Clemenceau felt that he was faced by adamant opponents: 'When confronted with the Rhineland question Mr. Wilson shook his head in an uncompromising fashion, and Mr. Lloyd George assumed a determined air of antagonism.' This placed him on the horns of a dilemma; he had told House on 22 February that a Rhineland republic was vital to French security, yet he was insistent that the continuation of the Anglo-American alliance with France was the fundamental plank of his peace strategy.[13] It appeared that these two objectives were incompatible.

This Clemenceau was not yet prepared to accept, and he moved the Rhineland discussions from private and informal conversations into the conference itself. On 25 February, Tardieu submitted formally a memorandum on behalf of the French government 'on the Fixation of the Rhine as the Western Frontier of Germany and on the Inter-Allied occupation of the Rhine Bridges'. Tardieu's arguments used and emphasised those of Foch: Germany's enormous military strength; the uncertainty of disarmament; the question mark over the speed and effectiveness of any guarantee offered by the League; and the French need for physical barriers against renewed German aggression. He tried, however, to stress the more general importance of the problem, looking to the security of the new states of eastern Europe, and the stability of the entire settlement. 'There is no question of annexing an inch of German soil, only of depriving Germany of her weapons of offence . . . France expects from an inter-Allied occupation of the Rhine what Great Britain and the United States expect from the maintenance of their naval forces; nothing more or less.'[14]

Like Foch, Tardieu made no effort to dispel the confusion as to French plans for the political future of the area, and this did not help their cause.[15] Despite strong support from Clemenceau, Wilson and Lloyd George remained unmoved, and the problem reached an apparent impasse; with French security needs and Anglo-American principles in opposition. It was one of the key issues in creating the crisis of the conference. Lloyd George commented: 'At one time a serious rupture between France and her Allies was threatened.'[16]

An attempt to end the deadlock by creating a small working-party failed. Tardieu, Sidney Mezes (House's brother-in-law) and Philip Kerr (Lloyd George's private secretary) made no progress in their two-day discussion on 11 and 12 March. The main protagonists were Tardieu and Kerr, the latter supported by Mezes. Tardieu proposed a three-part plan: the German frontier should be the

Rhine; the left bank territories should form an independent state; there should be an inter-Allied occupation of the Rhine bridgeheads. Each of the three aspects of the plan was indispensable. Kerr (and Mezes) resisted both an army of occupation and an independent Rhineland. In their place, Kerr could offer only the moral support of public opinion in Britain and America, provided both peoples were convinced of the justice of the settlement, but he stressed the importance of plans to demilitarise the Rhineland (suggested in the draft disarmament clauses then under consideration), and the continued existence, near at hand, of substantial British forces. 'It was clear', said Tardieu, 'that there was a deep difference of opinion between the British and French governments.'[17]

Lloyd George was aware of the wider implications of an Anglo-French rift, particularly in the Middle East, and he hinted at a possible compromise. On 4 March he suggested to the British cabinet that 'if the United States and ourselves would guarantee France against invasion, France would be satisfied'.[18] His enlistment of Wilson's support, and their joint offer to Clemenceau on the very afternoon of the president's return to Paris on 14 March, put pressure on the French leader. They proposed an 'immediate military guarantee against any unprovoked aggression on the part of Germany against France' but in return Clemenceau must accept that the Anglo-Americans would not agree to either a Rhineland buffer state or a prolonged occupation of the left bank.[19]

Clemenceau received the offer with mixed feelings: clearly the Anglo-American guarantee – provided that it actually materialised – would fulfil one part of his strategy but what of the rest? He consulted Tardieu, Loucheur and Pichon, and resolved to accept the offer but to continue to press, in addition, for the demilitarisation of the Rhineland. This should be verified by a permanent British, French and American inspection commission, and backed by the sanction of a French occupation of the line of the Rhine and five bridgeheads if there were infractions. Any German troop movement into the area should trigger the Anglo-American guarantee. He sought a 30-year inter-Allied occupation of the left bank and the bridgeheads of Mainz, Coblenz and Cologne, the frontier of 1814 rather than 1815, and the right of occupation, without annexation, of the mineral basin of the Saar not included in the 1814 frontier. He presented these demands in a forceful memorandum on 17 March and followed up with an emotional appeal in the Council of Four on

27 March, during the debate on the Fontainebleau Memorandum, in which Lloyd George had reiterated his fears about new Alsace-Lorraines in reverse.[20]

Lloyd George's forecast that a security guarantee would satisfy the French proved incorrect and a further month of hard and sometimes bitter bargaining ensued, contributing in no small measure to the general air of crisis in Paris at the time. There was no difficulty for the Anglo-Americans in accepting the principle of a demilitarised zone in the Rhineland but they did resist the more extreme French attempts to define the scope of demilitarisation and the extent of the zone.[21] One of Lloyd George's major concerns, however, was to avert any long-term occupation of Germany, partly because of the strain on British resources, but more importantly because of the likely resentment this would create in Germany. Wilson had initially supported him, but whilst Lloyd George was in London tackling his parliamentary critics, the president succumbed. Clemenceau offered to accept Wilson's proposals on the outstanding Rhineland issues and Wilson reluctantly agreed to a 15-year inter-Allied occupation of the left bank and the three bridgeheads. Clemenceau was elated: 'I have the fifteen years. I now consider that the peace is made'.[22] Lloyd George was disgruntled but isolated and feeling the strain of all the interwoven problems of reparations, disarmament, the League, Germany's eastern frontiers, the Rhineland and the Saar. On 22 April, with great reluctance, he too agreed.[23]

The final package represented an interesting compromise. The Allies would occupy the left bank and the appropriate bridgeheads for 15 years, but their troops would be withdrawn in three stages. Subject to satisfactory German treaty execution, the first zone would be evacuated after five years and the second after ten. If the Germans executed the entire treaty before 15 years were up, then the occupation would cease at once. On the other hand, if the Germans did not fulfil their reparations obligations, then all, or part of the area could be reoccupied. The left bank, and a 50 kilometre strip paralleling the river on its right bank, were to be permanently demilitarised. Any German infraction would be deemed a 'hostile act', but would not automatically trigger the Anglo-American guarantee. Clemenceau failed to gain an inspection commission, instead the League was to be notified of suspected breaches, and Germany had to respond to any League request for information.[24]

The Anglo-American guarantee was now defined more precisely. Britain and the United States would each offer a separate guarantee, which would continue until the signatories considered that the League offered sufficient protection to France. The British guarantee only became operative, however, upon the ratification of its American counterpart. This reflected the growing underlying anxiety in Paris as to Wilson's ability to honour his pledges upon his return to the United States. Thus Clemenceau secured a further concession permitting a prolongation of the Rhineland occupation beyond 15 years if 'at that date the guarantees against unprovoked aggression are not considered sufficient by the Allied and Associated Governments'.[25]

Clemenceau had thus compromised on the detachment of the Rhineland, much to the disgust of Poincaré and, especially, Foch,[26] but he had forced important concessions from Wilson and Lloyd George, to the extent that he boasted: 'I shall make a prediction: Germany will default and we shall stay where we are, with the alliance'.[27] In any case, the French generals would have many opportunities, during the occupation, to encourage the anti-Prussian (though not pro-French) sentiment in the area. A recent authority has argued: 'It is probable that Clemenceau's reluctant acceptance of the Rhineland compromise is attributable to his awareness of a long-term policy in the French zone designed to loosen the ties between the Rhineland and the German Reich.'[28]

The extent of Clemenceau's commitment to a genuine 'politique rhénane' remains debatable, but the Rhineland discussions represent a microcosm of many of the wider treaty issues. For France, the problem was how best to secure her future, and to ensure German execution of the treaty, without abandoning her pretensions to the status of a great power. For the British the question was entirely different and centred upon their perceptions of French ambition. Headlam-Morley pointed out that the demilitarisation of the Rhineland might protect France, but it exposed south Germany to a French attack. It was thus a policy based 'on the assumption that Germany will remain a strong, vigorous and aggressive military Power, but that France will remain peaceful and unambitious; this is an assumption that it will be difficult to justify'.[29] Hence, whilst Wilson's primary concern may have been for German self-determination, Lloyd George had to consider also the wider implications of the future European power balance.

The Anglo-American offer of guarantees to France represented, for both states, an unprecedented departure from their foreign policy traditions. It is tempting to ask if they were ever intended to operate. House commented at the time, 'I have my doubts as to the Senate accepting such a treaty but that is to be seen. Meanwhile, it satisfies Clemenceau and we can get on with the real business of the Conference.'[30] The British guarantee depended upon the ratification of the American treaty and therefore when Wilson's administration failed to submit it to the Senate, Britain was left with only a moral obligation to the French. It proved to be a pledge that she did not hasten to redeem, and the French had cause for complaint.

THE SAAR

If it had been Lloyd George who led the Anglo-American opposition to French ambitions in the Rhineland, it was Wilson who assumed this role in the negotiations over the future of the Saar. British and American advisers sympathised, to an extent, with the argument that the deliberate German destruction of the coalmines in the Pas-de-Calais and Nord departments entitled France to work the Saar mines in compensation. They feared, however, that France would seek to annex the land within the 1814 frontier and additional territory in the region. The root of the problem, from an Anglo-American viewpoint, was how to ensure that the French could work the mines in an efficient and effective manner, without depriving the inhabitants of their right to self-determination.

On 21 February, as part of the House–Balfour initiative to speed the preliminaries of peace, British and American experts met to establish a common approach to German frontier questions. They agreed, within a loose framework, on a programme which would transfer the ownership and management of the Saar mines to France, but not the sovereignty of the area, though they remained vague as to what should happen in this respect. They decided to await French proposals,[31] although the British expert, James Headlam-Morley, was already wrestling with the problem.[32] André Tardieu advanced the French case in a memorandum of 27 March. Relying partly on historical arguments, soon exposed as spurious, but more on economic grounds, he claimed the 1814 frontier, ownership of all coal deposits in the region, and also the right to administer and work the mines in that part of the Saar which lay beyond the 1814 frontier. He envisaged the economic integration of the whole area into the French customs and monetary system.[33]

The Four debated the issue on 28 March. Lloyd George disposed rapidly of France's historical claims but accepted her right to reparation, and indeed, showed sympathy to her wider vision. He suggested a degree of autonomy for the Saar, with the French exercising a control analogous to the British regime in the Isle of Man or the Channel Islands. Wilson would have nothing to do with this thinly disguised annexation, 'to grant a people an independence they do not request is as much a violation of the self-determination principle as forcibly handing them over from one sovereignty to another'. Furthermore, whereas Lloyd George was prepared to transfer the ownership of the Saar mines to France, Wilson spoke only of their 'use'. Clemenceau, who appears to have had a deeply felt sentimental urge to regain territory that he wished to believe was French in sympathy, made one of his most moving and emotional interventions, but to little avail.[34]

There was thus a wide difference in the positions taken up by the three main protagonists. Wilson, whilst acknowledging the French right to compensation, preferred to leave the mines and territory in German ownership, with an obligation to deliver coal to France. Clemenceau's policy, in the face of American opposition, was to make a tactical withdrawal from the demand for outright annexation, but instead to seek the permanent ownership of the mines and a temporary regime, under the supervision of the League of Nations, for 15 years. Only after a proper period of 'de-germanisation', argued Clemenceau, would the truly French character of the Saar re-emerge. Once again he could hope that the French occupation forces would have opportunities to sway the allegiance of the inhabitants towards France in the plebiscite which would be held after 15 years.[35] Lloyd George was prepared to go much further than Wilson to meet the French demands, though he began to seek some form of compromise.

The Four formed a small expert committee to consider the problem from its various angles. Charles Haskins was the west European specialist from the American Inquiry team, James Headlam-Morley was the German expert in the Foreign Office's unorthodox Political Intelligence Department, whilst Tardieu represented France. They had little difficulty in producing a plan for the economic exploitation of the region, based upon an amended French draft, but, commented Headlam-Morley on 5 April in a covering letter to the Four: 'The only result of our work so far is . . . to show that it is impossible to secure to the French that which they may reasonably demand without introducing a much more extended political control'. He advised them to consider a special regime for the Saar. The Four agreed on 8 April.[36]

The experts proposed that Germany should cede sovereignty of the area to the League and ownership of the mines to France. A League Commission would govern and permit the French to exploit the mineral resources. After 15 years a plebiscite would offer the inhabitants three choices: to return to Germany; to become French; or to perpetuate the League regime. If the region voted to rejoin Germany, then she must repurchase the mines from France. Headlam-Morley described this scheme as 'a very honest attempt to solve an extremely difficult problem'. Even so, it took five days of discussion to persuade the reluctant Wilson to agree.[37]

The problem of the fate of the Saar raised a number of noteworthy points. Despite his aversion to Alsace-Lorraines in reverse, Lloyd George was, surprisingly, prepared to consider virtual French sovereignty in the area. Wilson showed how stubborn he could be when he chose, but despite his dramatic gesture (reminiscent of Disraeli in Berlin) of summoning the *George Washington* to Brest, he bowed to pressure. The expert committee of diplomatic irregulars produced a solution which had a strong family likeness to the Danzig proposals, with which Tardieu and Headlam-Morley were also closely associated. Haskins and Headlam-Morley, perhaps uniquely amongst the territorial committees, actually inspected the frontier they proposed for the Saar.[38]

There are two further points of interest: the relationship of Saar coal production to the other coal deliveries demanded of Germany; and the question of what motivated French policy in this region. French coal production in 1912–13 was about 41 million tons, and it was generally agreed that the war, and especially German sabotage, had reduced her capacity by 20 million tons. Hence Germany was obliged to supply France with 20 million tons of coal for the first five years of the treaty, and 8 million tons for the next five years. Germany had also to deliver an additional 7 million tons annually for ten years to assist France to absorb the extra strain on her resources occasioned by the return of Alsace-Lorraine.[39] Yet it was in compensation for the lost 20 million tons of Nord and Pas-de-

Calais coal that France sought to gain control of the Saar, which had produced 17.5 million tons in 1912–13. It has been argued that, since the other German deliveries were to be purchased by France (at a price reached by a complex formula to ensure that German deliveries did not destroy the important British market in France), these deliveries strictly should not be classed as reparations. Hence 'it seems unreasonable to maintain that an act of injustice has been committed'.[40] Purchased or not, the German obligation to deliver coal was part of the reparations section of the treaty, and there does appear to be an element of double jeopardy.

There are interesting and differing interpretations of the motivation of French policy. One commentator argues that it should be seen as part of 'a vast project seeking to slow and restrain German industrial development, and . . . to facilitate that of France, Belgium, Italy and Poland. At the heart of this plan, there appears to be the ambition to alter profoundly the balance of European industrial power'.[41] Another, however, argues that Clemenceau, and even Tardieu, based their policy on the hope of reviving French sympathy in the area, and comments: 'The Saar claim, with its flimsy economic and still more flimsy ethnographic base, was the closest to a French demand of sheer unreason, unsupported either by convincing arguments from national self-determination or by the logic of a broader strategic design'.[42] Whether from delusion or by design, Clemenceau invested much effort in these negotiations, and felt he had dealt his successors a reasonable hand.

BELGIUM

Belgium's direct territorial claims against Germany at the conference were modest, but her declared ambition to revise the 1839 Treaty provisions had wider implications.[43] There was no doubt as to the illogicality of her 1839 frontiers, or of their economic and strategic inconvenience, but Belgian hints at the possibility that the Dutch might be persuaded to relinquish control of Flemish Zeeland and lower Limburg in return for compensation at Germany's expense, raised difficult questions of legality and morality. James Headlam-Morley was sympathetic to the Belgian case, but pointed out the fundamental and fatal objection:

The idea of separating territory from one State and giving it territory belonging to another State merely on the ground of compensation belongs to the order of ideas which ruled at the Congress of Vienna and which have been generally repudiated: it is by its rejection of this conception that the Paris Conference is to show its superiority to Vienna.[44]

When the Four considered the problem they ruled out any transfer of German territory, and later the Council of Five rejected any readjustment of the Dutch-Belgian border.[45]

Belgium enjoyed greater success in her demands for the transfer of Moresnet and Malmédy from Germany, and she was also awarded Eupen, for which she had decided to ask only after much consideration and doubt because of its Germanic nature. Eupen also caused the most difficulty to the Allied territorial commission on Belgium established by the Council of Ten on 12 February but, on 12 March, the British and American representatives accepted Tardieu's arguments for its transfer, subject to the right of protest of its inhabitants – an interesting example of a negative plebiscite.[46] In total she gained under 400 square miles of territory and 64,000 people, less indeed than neutral Denmark.[47]

In these circumstances Belgium might well have expected British support for her desire to control Luxemburg, whose future status was in doubt because of its behaviour in 1914 and the pro-German sympathies of its wartime ruler, Grand Duchess Marie Adelaide. Her abdication in favour of her sister Charlotte, in January 1919, saved what Clemenceau dubbed 'the German dynasty'. The wish of the inhabitants to be free of German economic domination left the Grand Duchy poised between France and Belgium, perhaps inclining towards the latter. France had, in 1917, apparently renounced any claim to Luxemburg, but British and Belgian scepticism was reinforced by the proselytising activities of the French occupation forces after the armistice.[48]

British officials were indeed alarmed that a disappointed Belgium might become too firmly attached to France, and pressed for Luxemburg to be assigned to Belgium; as Balfour told Lloyd George, 'it would be most unjust, and in the long run most inexpedient, that France should get Alsace-Lorraine and the Saar coal – and Belgium *nothing*'.[49] It might have been possible, in March 1919, to bargain British support for French claims to the Saar for French support for Belgian claims to Luxemburg, but Lloyd George missed the opportunity.[50] Instead Clemenceau's insistence that there must be a plebiscite in the Grand Duchy prevailed, Luxemburg was released from the German customs and railway unions, and a double vote on 28 September 1919 approved both the continuation of the dynasty and an economic union with France.[51]

As with Luxemburg, so with many of Belgium's other aspirations; the signature of the treaty on 28 June left much unresolved. Her negotiations with Holland dragged on, largely fruitlessly, for several months, whilst her hopes of maintaining a British guarantee without the humiliating obligation (as she saw it) to perpetual neutrality, also came to naught, but not until 1920, when she abandoned her attempted balancing act and reached a military agreement with France.[52]

SCHLESWIG

The Allied territorial commission on Belgium was also entrusted, on 21 February, with the future of the province of Schleswig, which in conjunction with Holstein had been one of the most difficult problems in international law in the mid-nineteenth century. Bismarck's solution to the complex questions of inheritance and the relationship of the two provinces to the Danish crown and to one another, had been to annex both in the course of the 1860s, as a result first of the Austro-Prussian war against Denmark in 1864, and then of the subsequent war between Prussia and Austria in 1866. He had, however, promised, by the terms of the 1867 Treaty of Prague, to conduct a plebiscite in the northern parts of the province of Schleswig. This plebiscite was never held, and now the Danish government sought redress.[53] To their embarrassment, the Danes found that the French wanted to give them more of Schleswig than they deemed it wise to demand, and it was only with some difficulty that they persuaded the Four to reduce the plebiscite area.[54] This was divided in three zones, with voting to occur in the two northernmost – the Danes renounced any interest in the third zone. As they had themselves predicted, the Danes won comfortably in the northern zone (75,413 for Denmark, 25,328 for Germany) and lost even more decisively in the central zone (51,724 to 12,800). A new frontier, based on these results, was recommended in April 1920, and accepted by Germany and Denmark in April 1922.[55]

POLAND

The discussions in Paris about the boundaries of an independent Poland proved to be as bitter and controversial as they were unpredictable, indeed inconceivable, in the early stages of the war. Poland had been destroyed as an independent state in the late eighteenth century, and been swallowed, if not absorbed, by Austria, Russia and Prussia. Poles found themselves, unwillingly, on both sides in 1914, as Clemenceau pointed out, 'We . . . started as allies of the Russian oppressors of Poland, with the Polish soldiers of Silesia and Galicia fighting against us'.[56] Whilst both the Central Powers and Russia had promised a measure of Polish autonomy after the war, realistic Poles could have hoped for no more than the equivalent to a resurrected Grand Duchy of Warsaw, firmly in the orbit of whoever won. Polish territory would become the spoils of war, and Polish autonomy would be an internal matter for the victors. In 1917 the German and Austro-Hungarian empires had defeated Russia but had then themselves collapsed in 1918. It was only this unpredictable coincidence, with its resulting vacuum of power, which made possible the prospect of an independent eastern Europe.

Although sympathetic to Polish sufferings, the pre-war and wartime French governments had taken a cold and realistic attitude: Russia was a vital link in French military planning, Poland was a matter of sentiment, and an independent Poland might become a German client state. When Russia offered support for French ambitions in the Rhineland, France recognised, in return, her 'complete liberty in establishing her Western frontiers'.[57] Poland was sacrificed to strategic and diplomatic advantage but the collapse of Russia and the fear of revolution transformed the situation. Now France could see a strong, independent Poland as the necessary substitute for Russian power on Germany's eastern frontier and as a barrier to bolshevism. Clemenceau admitted that it was 'force of events' which reshaped 'our war of national defence . . . into a war of liberation'[58] but the French now took up the Polish cause with enthusiasm. Any economic or strategic gains which Poland could make at Germany's expense would benefit both the Poles, and, indirectly, the French.

The British attitude to Poland was also determined by an appreciation of the wider considerations of their political objectives.

In a Foreign Office memorandum of August 1916, Ralph Paget and
William Tyrrell had argued that it was in Britain's interest to see a
barrier of states between Russia and Germany but Arthur Balfour
disagreed. In a paper of October 1916, he pointed out that without
the pressure of a mutual frontier, Germany would be freer in western
Europe, and Russia in the Far East. Britain and France might regret
this, thus Balfour favoured an autonomous Poland within the Russian empire.[59] By January 1918 Lenin's success had prodded Lloyd
George into a cautious endorsement of Polish independence: 'We
believe, however, that an independent Poland, comprising all those
genuinely Polish elements who desire to form part of it, is an urgent
necessity for the stability of Western Europe.'[60]

Wilson's thirteenth Point shared Lloyd George's philosophy but
also highlighted problems which would become all too familiar to
the peacemakers:

> An independent Polish state should be erected, which should
> include the territories inhabited by indisputably Polish popula-
> tions, which should be assured a free and secure access to the sea,
> and whose political and economic independence should be guaran-
> teed by international covenant.[61]

Given the ethnographic profile of the area, it would be impossible to
reconcile the linked objectives of access to the sea, and a Poland
inhabited by an indisputably Polish population, even assuming that
it was possible to reach a satisfactory definition of 'indisputably
Polish'. The idea of a guarantee to Poland also carried with it a
whole baggage train of philosophical and political assumptions
about the future regulation of international relations, and the stability of eastern Europe after the peace settlement.

Thus, whilst there appeared to be a close identity of approach
between the Anglo-Americans on the Polish question, and early
contacts between their experts tended to confirm this impression,
Lloyd George proved to have rather different priorities, at first, to
those of the president. The key to Lloyd George's policy towards
Poland during the Paris negotiations lay in his belief that the future
stability of the area, and of Europe as a whole, demanded that the
minimum possible number of Germans be assigned to the new state.
His fear of creating German irredentist dissatisfaction and of provoking a nationalist backlash, perhaps in conjunction with commu-

nist revolution, dominated his approach. Wilson, whether from a romantic wish to redress a great wrong, or for the more prosaic reason that there was a substantial Polish-American vote, tended initially to be more sympathetic to the Polish cause, though his geographical knowledge sometimes left much to be desired.[62]

By the time the peace conference met, however, Poland already existed and was engaged in territorial disputes with all her neighbours. The question for the conference was thus not whether there should be an independent Poland but rather to determine its extent. The Poles were not modest in their ambitions, neither did they make any secret of them. Their spokesman, Roman Dmowski, told the Ten on 29 January that Poland sought her boundaries before the first partition in 1772 as a point of departure. She then wished to reclaim territory in mineral-rich Upper Silesia, lost as far back as the fourteenth century, and to secure her access to the sea via Danzig and parts of East and West Prussia.[63] The Ten set up a commission on Polish affairs on 12 February, but only belatedly referred these territorial claims to it on 26 February, seeking a report by 8 March.[64] The key members of the commission, Jules Cambon of France, Isaiah Bowman of the United States, and William Tyrrell of Great Britain, were all sympathetic to Poland, and their report, delivered to the Ten on 19 March, reflected this bias. Cambon argued that their recommendations were based mainly upon ethnographic grounds, but that given the complexity of the population and the lack of natural frontiers, the commission had also allowed religious, economic, strategic and historical considerations some weight. They had thus assigned to Poland much of the territory she sought, including most of Upper Silesia, Danzig, and both railway lines running from Danzig into the interior, one to Thorn, and the other through Marienwerder to Mlawa, though they did suggest holding a plebiscite in Allenstein, to determine whether it should form part of the 'Polish Corridor' to the sea or remain part of East Prussia.[65]

Clemenceau and Wilson supported the expert report, but Lloyd George, briefed by Headlam-Morley and other disapproving members of the British delegation, began a long campaign to amend it. He argued that the report assigned at least 2,132,000 Germans to Poland, and gave Poland areas like Marienwerder and Danzig where there were clear German majorities. He 'agreed that it was hardly possible to draw any line that would not have Germans on both sides of it, but ... to hand over millions of people to a distasteful allegiance merely because of a railway line was ... a mistake.' This was an exaggeration, the total population of Marienwerder was less than half a million, but Lloyd George's general point remained sound. The experts were asked to think again, but on 22 March they reiterated their previous recommendations.[66] Lloyd George continued his struggle in the Council of Four, on 27 March floating Headlam-Morley's suggestion of Danzig as a free city under the League, linked economically to Poland. Wilson was becoming more receptive, and on 1 April proposed holding a plebiscite in Marienwerder and referring Danzig to a small expert group, consisting of Tardieu, Headlam-Morley and Charles Haskins of the United States.[67] On 9 April the Four agreed that Danzig should become an autonomous state under the League, but incorporated within the Polish customs area, with its external relations handled by Warsaw, and with guaranteed lines of communication to Poland. The Polish premier, Ignacy Paderewski, was dismayed, but neither he nor Clemenceau, who on 12 April tried to bargain Danzig for the abandonment of the Marienwerder plebiscite, had any success in changing the Anglo-American view.[68]

The draft treaty assigned Upper Silesia to Poland, and it was here that Lloyd George had his most striking success in seeking to revise the treaty in June. His argument that there should be a plebiscite in the area, under international supervision, eventually won grudging support from Wilson, who mistrusted Lloyd George's sincerity, particularly in view of his prevarication over the revision of reparations. Clemenceau and Paderewski were again outflanked on the self-determination issue, and the Four approved a plebiscite, to be held within one to two years. In the interim the region was to be administered by an inter-Allied Commission and garrisoned by Allied troops, ostensibly to allow fair play to the Poles, who had not governed the area for hundreds of years.[69]

The treaty ceded the city of Danzig to the League and 260 square miles of German territory to Poland, leaving East Prussia isolated from the rest of Germany by the Polish Corridor. Germany lost 3 million people, although most of these were not German. The fate of a further 2.5 million people would be determined by plebiscites, with nearly 2 million of these living in Upper Silesia. In the end, Marienwerder and Allenstein voted to remain German, and Upper Silesia was divided between Poland and Germany in 1922, after a protracted Anglo-French diplomatic wrangle over the terms of the plebiscite and the interpretation of its results. By 1922, Lloyd George may have come to regret his persistence in 1919.[70]

These losses were the bitterest pill for the Germans to swallow. East Prussia was the heartland of the *Junkers*, who supplied so many of the German decision-makers and their resentment continued to fester. Poland was, in their eyes, a failed nation, without the right to govern Germans. They found an ally in Lloyd George, who found the Poles 'greedy and grasping' and who too doubted the Polish capacity to govern. His sustained opposition to what he saw as exaggerated Polish claims could degenerate into cruel jibes about the Polish war record,[71] but he did convince Wilson that his principles required him to support British rather than French policy on Poland. The key question for Lloyd George concerned future commitments and resolve: 'France would tomorrow fight for Alsace, if her right to it were contested. But would we make war for Danzig?'[72] It was an interesting question.

THE SUDETENLAND AND AUSTRIA

There were two other areas in which there was a possibility of an alteration to the German frontier, and both raised difficult questions about the application of the doctrine of self-determination. The Sudetenland and the small rump republic of Austria were inhabited by people of German speech and cultural and racial origins, though none of them, as citizens of the former Austro-Hungarian empire, had ever, in a political sense, been German. The Sudetenland was part of historic Bohemia and had enormous economic and strategic importance to the new state of Czechoslovakia, but the peacemakers were aware of the problem of a large German population in the area which wished to become part of Germany. 'Masaryk never told me that', claimed Wilson, although his own experts had briefed him earlier.[73] Equally the citizens of the land-locked and bereft Austrian republic wanted permission to merge with Germany. In the end, for reasons which are discussed at greater length in the next chapter, on eastern Europe, neither area was allowed to become part of Germany, and with only infinitesimal changes – the Hultschin district was given to Czechoslovakia – the historic frontiers between Germany and the former Austro-Hungarian empire survived intact.

MEMEL

Germany suffered one further small loss of territory when she was required to surrender the city of Memel in the east of East Prussia to the Allies. Memel was a German city, but was the natural port of Lithuania, to whom the Allies intended to assign it, if the new state survived the uncertainties of the fighting in Russia. Lithuania eventually seized Memel in January 1923 and the Allies abandoned any responsibility for the city.[74]

GERMAN DISARMAMENT

British and American leaders had stressed their intention to curb German militarism and the French had a profound interest in this issue. There was thus no doubt that the German armed forces would be reduced dramatically by the conference, causing further distress to the *Junkers*, the traditional officer-class. There were disagreements as to method, but although sometimes heated, these were rapidly resolved. The Ten established a military commission under Foch on 12 February. It reported on its army recommendations on 3 March, on its naval proposals on 6 March, and by 17 March the disarmament terms were essentially complete.

The military report represented a compromise, both in its effective and recruitment proposals, between the differing views of Foch, Haig and Bliss, the American expert. It recommended a German army of 200,000 and 9000 officers. The officers and NCOs were to be volunteers, serving 25 and 15 years respectively, whilst the men were to be conscripted for one year. Lloyd George favoured a long-term voluntary army, whereas Foch believed a conscript force would be less dangerous. The French accepted the Anglo-American preference for voluntary enlistment (25 years for officers, 12 for other ranks), but Lansing and, with reluctance, Lloyd George, accepted the French case for a reduction to 100,000 men. Germany had to destroy all her fortifications in the west and to demilitarise the west bank of the Rhine, and a 50 kilometre strip paralleling the river on its eastern shore, though the inhabitants of the demilitarised zone could still volunteer for service in the armed forces. She could retain her frontier fortifications in the south and east but was forbidden an airforce, tanks, poison gas, heavy artillery, and a General Staff.

The fate of the German High Seas Fleet, currently interned at the

British naval base of Scapa Flow, created some complex patterns of relationships and proposals, but was essentially settled by the scuttling of 49 warships by their German crews on 21 June, though the legal and diplomatic ramifications lingered into the autumn. The navy, perhaps the most evocative symbol of Wilhelmine Germany, was reduced to little more than a coastal defence force, with only six obsolete battleships, six light cruisers, twelve destroyers and twelve torpedo boats. It was denied submarines and dreadnoughts. Its 15,000 officers and men were to be long-service volunteers and its bases on the islands of Heligoland and Dune were to be dismantled.[75]

Germany and Austria (with an army of 30,000) were disarmed, and the Allies established control commissions to ensure the destruction of surplus equipment and factories, and to monitor their observation of the treaty terms. The remainder of Germany's neighbours were not disarmed. Article 8 of the League Covenant called for 'the reduction of national armaments to the lowest point consistent with national safety', and the Allied reply to the German delegation spoke of the desirability of universal defence cuts,[76] but little tangible progress was made towards world disarmament at Paris, despite Anglo-American aspirations.

'HANGING THE KAISER'

The invasion of Belgium, the sack of Louvain, the mistreatment of civilians and prisoners-of-war, the bombing of British cities, unrestricted submarine warfare and the massacre of the Armenian people – in short, the coming of total war – led to inevitable demands for the punishment of those both directly and indirectly responsible. Such calls were made more by private individuals than by government ministers, whose attitude, throughout the Allied states, tended to be more cautious. The idea of public accountability was an ambiguous weapon, and their enthusiasm waxed and waned with the fortunes of war, but from 1915 onwards, British ministers in particular warned of future justice for enemy miscreants, if only to divert domestic indignation. They gave little thought, however, to the mechanisms by which this policy might be achieved.[77]

On the night of the armistice, Sir Henry Wilson recorded the dinner observations of his companions: 'Lloyd George wants to shoot the Kaiser. F. E. [Smith] agrees. Winston [Churchill] does not.'[78] Lloyd George's enthusiasm was shared by few of his cabinet colleagues, even Curzon thinking in terms of exile not execution, but on 28 November F. E. Smith persuaded them to seek the extradition and trial of the Kaiser, much to the chagrin of his cousin, George V. The public liked the idea, and it proved an important theme in the British election, but Clemenceau was lukewarm, whilst Foch, Sonnino and Wilson, unlikely allies, opposed it. The Ten nonetheless established, on 25 January 1919, a 'Commission on the Responsibility of the Authors of the War and the Enforcement of Penalties'.[79]

The commission agreed that the responsibility for the war 'rests first on Germany and Austria, secondly on Turkey and Bulgaria', and that the Central Powers had fought the war 'by barbarous or illegitimate means', but its chairman, Robert Lansing, the American secretary of state, believed that no basis existed in international law for any prosecution of the Kaiser. He conducted spoiling and delaying tactics on the commission, but was outvoted by his fellow members. On Wilson's instructions, he issued a minority report, accepting the right of Allied powers, either individually or jointly, to try, by military tribunal, individuals accused of violating the laws and customs of war, but denying their right to establish an international court to try a head of state for a crime which, according to him, did not exist. The Japanese delegates, for ideological reasons, concurred, but the European commissioners rejected his legal arguments as 'finespun theories', and demanded the recognition of a law of humanity, against which Germany's leaders had offended. Lansing said they wanted an 'international Lynch law'. The Four would have to decide.[80]

American opinion favoured a trial but Wilson had a consistent record of opposition, which he maintained in the Council of Four on 1 April. Yet between 8 and 10 April, the president bowed to pressure and accepted the principle. James Willis argues that this was, once again, part of the general crisis of the conference, and suggests Wilson may have envisaged it as an extra inducement to the British to accept the exclusion of the Monroe Doctrine from the League Covenant.[81] Nonetheless, he argues, Lansing and Wilson preserved the essence of the American legal position in their drafts of what became Articles 227 to 230 of the treaty. The Dutch were asked to surrender the Kaiser so that he could be tried by a 'special tribunal' of five judges, one each from the major powers, on quasi-criminal charges of 'a supreme offence against international morality and the sanctity of treaties'. Allied military tribunals would try those accused of operational war crimes.[82]

With the addition of Article 231 (the 'War Guilt clause') these articles became the short- and long-term focus of German opposition to the treaty. Aware that they would have to sign something which was unlikely to alter much from the draft they were handed on 7 May, the German delegation and government made strenuous efforts to have these 'shame paragraphs' dropped. The Allied refusal led to the fall of the German government on 19 June, and it was only at the last minute, and under threat of invasion, that the new cabinet capitulated on 23 June.[83]

The idea of trying the Kaiser clearly fulfilled a need to blame someone for the carnage and devastation of the war. It was seductive, but ill-conceived, and the steadfast Dutch refusal to surrender their unwanted guest saved much embarrassment. Later Allied demands for the surrender of major figures such as Tirpitz and Hindenburg as well as those accused of operational crimes or the mistreatment of prisoners-of-war, led to further confusion and recriminations in Anglo-Franco-German relations. The compromise whereby a German court in Leipzig would try cases against non-political offenders degenerated into farce. Yet there was, in the concept of a responsibility to humanity, a nobler side to this question, which linked it to ventures like the League. 'Imperfectly conceived and implemented, marred by vengeful politics and expedient diplomacy, it represented nonetheless in its ideals a desire to establish a world community.'[84]

THE RESULTS

'The Saar basin . . . Poland, Silesia, Oppeln . . . 123 milliards to pay and for all that we are supposed to say "Thank you very much"', an outraged German delegate bellowed down the telephone from Versailles on hearing the peace terms. He might have added (and probably did – he was shouting so loudly that the French listeners could not decipher his words) the destruction of Germany's armed forces, the loss of her empire, and the arraigning of her leaders.[85] Germany lost some 27,000 square miles of territory and between 6.5 and 7 million people, about 13 and 10 per cent respectively of her pre-war resources. Her loss of economic potential was of the same scale – about 13.5 per cent. She paid a high price for losing the war, although had the roles been reversed, the German dictated treaties of Bucharest and Brest-Litovsk suggested that her price would have been higher. Indeed perhaps the hardest thing for Germany to accept was that she had lost a war which she had, from 1914 until the summer of 1918, seemed to be winning.

'Decisive wars', it has been argued, 'are followed by long periods of peace and indecisive wars by the reverse. It was not the superior wisdom of the peacemakers of 1945 which has made their efforts so much more durable than those of their predecessors of 1919 but the more decisive quality of the preceding war.' There is certainly a case that the Germans did not grasp the extent of their defeat in 1918, and hence would probably have resented any settlement based on that premise. Perhaps a continuation of the war for a few more months would have saved countless millions of lives 20 years later. At the time, however, only Pershing of all the Allied generals advocated pursuing the retreating Germans to, and beyond, the Rhine. For Foch and Haig the terms of the armistice sealed their victory and further loss of life was not justified, so there was no invasion of Germany and no Allied victory parade in Berlin. The German generals, aided by politicians like Ebert who needed their support against the Spartacists, could thus claim that they had not been defeated but betrayed; 'stabbed in the back' by communist, socialist and Jewish traitors and knaves.[86]

There is another sense in which a more complete Allied victory and an occupation of the heart of Germany might have aided the process of peacemaking. One of the distinguishing features of 1919, in contrast to either 1815 or 1945, is the lack of the peacemakers' effective control over many of the areas whose future was being considered. This caused problems in eastern Europe in particular, and would continue to plague the process of enforcing the treaty with Germany. An effective Allied force in Berlin could have implemented the terms of the treaty, quickly in many cases, rather than relying on a German government to execute a treaty, of which it did not approve, over a long period. A rapid surgical operation, however brutal, might have proved more successful than the protracted attempt to get Germany to take her medicine. In November 1918, however, few believed they had scotched the snake, not killed it, so the possibility did not arise.[87]

The losses of Alsace-Lorraine and northern Schleswig were predictable, and although unwelcome, not intolerable. The gains made by Belgium and Czechoslovakia were pinpricks, though the fates of Austria, Memel and the Sudetenland were galling. The occupation of the Rhineland raised the spectre of separatism and the danger of a disintegration of the Reich, whilst its demilitarisation left the Ruhr exposed, and discouraged investment in the region until 1936. The uncertainty over the eventual fate of the Saar reinforced Germany's fears in the west but it was the loss of territory to Poland and the forced abandonment of German minorities in eastern Europe which most distressed the Weimar republic about the territorial settlement. The loss of her empire was, comparatively, a minor though painful blow. The war-guilt and war-crime clauses were seen as shameful and insulting, and there were severe doubts as to whether her defence forces would be adequate to protect either her external or internal security. The reparations settlement, incomplete as it was, cast grave uncertainty over German economic and financial prospects.

The future, especially in the short term, was gloomy, but the new map, of eastern Europe in particular, offered some comfort to more farsighted Germans. In 1914 Germany had been hemmed in by three great empires and any attempt to revise her boundaries would have resulted in a major war. France remained, but Austria-Hungary had disintegrated and Russia was in turmoil. Germany's eastern neighbours were now smaller states, with considerable German and other minorities, sandwiched between Germany and Russia, and at odds with one another. Much would depend on Germany's future strength, the situation in the Soviet Union, and the determination of the western powers to preserve the settlement in eastern Europe, but there was great potential for possible later exploitation.

6 The Eastern European Settlement

On 4 April 1919 Robert Lansing, the American secretary of state, wrote:

> Central Europe is aflame with anarchy; the people see no hope; the Red Armies of Russia are marching westward. Hungary is in the clutches of revolutionists; Berlin, Vienna and Munich are turning toward the Bolsheviks. . . . It is time to stop fiddling while the world is on fire, while violence and bestiality consume society. Everybody is clamoring for peace, for an immediate peace.[1]

Always a frustrated onlooker at Paris, Lansing's shrewd comments offer interesting perceptions of the conference, and here he highlighted the many paradoxes of the situation in eastern Europe. The peacemakers knew that here was the area of greatest danger and confusion in Europe, and if Wilson perceived Lenin and revolutionary bolshevism as the main rival to his vision of reformist capitalism, then here was the vital battleground in their shadowy confrontation. It also represented a unique opportunity for the 'new diplomacy' to demonstrate its superiority over the 'old'. Yet the Allied leaders faced pressing and, apparently, more manageable problems nearer home, whereas here was an area of which, with slightly more justification than Neville Chamberlain a generation later, they knew little. Thus the principals tended to neglect or postpone decisions, and to leave much of the negotiations to relatively junior members of the Allied delegations. It was the Council of Five, or the Supreme Council after July 1919, which dealt with most of the east European settlement.[2]

The problems were compounded because the victors had no clear and agreed basis on which to proceed. The exigencies of war had persuaded Britain, Russia and France to purchase the support of new allies in their struggle against the Central Powers. Thus the Treaty of London, signed on 26 April 1915, promised the Italians large tracts of territory currently held by Austria: notably Trentino, the South Tyrol, Trieste, Istria, Dalmatia and a number of islands in the Adriatic. The Treaty of Bucharest, signed on 17 August 1916, offered the Rumanians Bukovina, Transylvania and the Banat of Temesvar. Both agreements cut across the interests of an earlier ally, Serbia, and both presupposed substantial losses of territory by the Austro-Hungarian empire. Yet the British and French remained uncertain whether they wished to destroy or merely reform the Habsburg state, and their policies fluctuated according to the requirements of their current diplomatic manoeuvres.[3]

Wilson refused to countenance these examples of, in his view, the 'old diplomacy' at its worst. Furthermore, his Fourteen Points speech, like that of Lloyd George three days earlier, implied the continued existence of Austria-Hungary. Yet, as late as 24 September, House believed that Wilson 'had no idea of what should be done with Austria, or how the Empire should be broken up, if indeed, it was to be broken up at all', whilst Poincaré wrote, on 30 October, that Clemenceau had 'no plan for the future of Central Europe'. This confusion was reflected in the armistices with the Austro-Hungarian empire which were based on the premise of the continuing authority and political and administrative unity of the empire, despite existing Allied commitments to Serbia, Czechoslovakia and Poland.[4]

There were thus conflicting promises, assumptions and expectations, and the gradual acceptance of the Wilsonian concept of national self-determination by Britain and France was a slow and uncertain process, driven more by the desperate pressures of war, and by rival Bolshevik promises, than by deep-felt conviction. This is hardly surprising, given the revolutionary implications of this secessionist doctrine for their own multinational empires, and even Wilson, as a Southerner, needed no reminding of its relevance to recent American history.[5] It was the disintegration of order in eastern Europe which left the concept as the only prescription beyond force for resolving the conflicting claims of the would-be successor states. Lansing's diary for 22 January 1919 illustrates the urgency of the situation: 'all the races of Central Europe and the Balkans in fact are actually fighting or about to fight with one another . . . the Great War seems to have split up into a lot of little wars'.[6]

Wilson's hope that his principle would bring international peace and internal harmony was founded upon a dangerous paradox, a revolutionary basis for stability. It created at least as many questions as it resolved. The ethnographic map of eastern Europe in 1919 resembled a complicated and irregularly patterned mosaic, reflecting the complex historic interminglings and movements of populations in the region. If national self-determination was to legitimise the new frontiers, what criteria would determine nationality? Language? Culture? Race? Religion? Historical precedent? Geography? Which nationalities should be self-determining, and more importantly, which should not? And how would their self-determination be measured?[7]

Wilson had no clear answers, though he brought the subjective assumptions of a western liberal to these problems. He tended to confuse the concepts of personal and political nationality, to assume that language was the key element, and naturally for an American, to stress the concept of choice. These criteria were not accepted in eastern Europe where race, language and religion were seen as constants determining nationality. An individual could not choose to be Polish, he either was, or he was not. If one added other factors such as economic or defensive viability and communication networks to the equation, then the result was an unstable and shifting pattern which was constant only in its refusal to coincide neatly with the conditions and demands of any given problem. It was, as Robert Lansing predicted, 'a principle loaded with dynamite, raising hopes which can never be realised. . . . What misery it will cause'.[8] Yet it was this principle that the peacemakers were expected to apply.

The prospect was daunting. The difficulties were so great that it was tempting to ignore them, whilst the direct ability of the peacemakers to control events diminished as the distance from Paris increased. There were some Allied forces in eastern and central Europe, but they were mostly French or Italian, they often depended on the goodwill of the new authorities in the area and, although the conference issued warnings 'that possession gained by force will seriously prejudice the claims of those who use such means',[9] subsequent events revealed the emptiness of such statements. The Italians had important direct interests in the area and shared the French perception of eastern Europe as vital to their security and as a potential avenue for the expansion of their influence. Their ambitions were not always compatible, but both resented Anglo-American professions of high-minded principle which lacked the means of enforcement.

Map 2   The peace settlement in Eastern Europe, 1919–23 (Reprinted with permission from C. A. Macartney and A. W. Palmer, *Independent Eastern Europe*, Macmillan, 1962, p. 137.)

THE BALKANS

The steady decline of the Ottoman empire and the intense national rivalries of the emerging Balkan states combined, with the ambitions of their great power sponsors, to create Europe's most persistent international problem in the nineteenth century. It was, as Bismarck had gloomily predicted, 'some damned fool thing in the Balkans' which set Europe ablaze in 1914. Whilst it may distort reality to describe the First World War as the Third Balkan War, the earlier wars in the area certainly influenced the course of the major conflagration which followed. Italian victories over the Turks in 1911 and 1912 paved the way for the smaller powers to wage two wars in the Balkans. In October 1912, Greece, Serbia, Bulgaria and Montenegro declared war on Turkey and succeeded in driving her to the edge of mainland Europe. Of all the vast Ottoman European possessions of the fifteenth and sixteenth centuries only Eastern Thrace was left. But now the victors fell out, and joined by Rumania, Greece and Serbia rapidly defeated Bulgaria in June and July 1913. The resulting division of spoils saw Bulgaria making only small gains at Turkey's expense in Macedonia and Western Thrace, but losing the Southern Dobruja to Rumania, whilst the bulk of Macedonia was divided between Greece and Serbia. Greece gained part of Thrace, and a new independent kingdom of Albania emerged.[10]

In 1914 it was the Austrian attack on Serbia on 28 July which began the fighting in the Great War. In 1915 Bulgaria joined the Central Powers and attacked Serbia in October. Serbia was defeated, a remnant of her army fought its way to the Albanian coast and thence to Corfu, where a government in exile was established. The British and French established a force on Greek soil at Salonika in September 1916 but only after a revolution drove King Constantine from his throne and brought Eleutherios Venizelos to power, did Greece join the *Entente* in June 1917. In August 1916 Rumania also joined the *Entente*, but always under pressure, she was forced to seek an armistice in December 1917 and signed a separate peace with the Central Powers in May 1918. She redeclared war only on 9 November. The Italians also had substantial ambitions in the region and had joined Britain and France in 1915. The *Entente* had, in addition and hesitantly, encouraged the hopes of separatist movements, but the great power in possession of much of the territory that others wanted was Austria-Hungary. It was her collapse which allowed all the competing parties in the Balkans to engage in 'an orgy of claim-jumping' as old and new states did their best to occupy the territories they wished the conference to bestow upon them. The conference had now to create a new order in a region which had been synonymous before 1914 with lawlessness and international anarchy.[11]

Yugoslavia

Yugoslavia[12] was unique amongst the new states of eastern Europe in that it represented a voluntary amalgamation of territories around the nucleus of one existing pre-war state, Serbia, with a second, Montenegro, freely relinquishing its sovereignty to join. Its conception and birth reflected the differing, sometimes diverging, ideas of its progenitors. On the one hand stood Nikola Pašić, a veteran Serbian politician, who consistently envisaged a South Slav state as an enlarged Serbia; on the other stood men like Frano Supilo and Ante Trumbić, who as Croats from Dalmatia, and hence Austrian citizens, campaigned from London for a new state which would include Croats and Slovenes as equal partners. At first the Serbian government was reluctant to recognise the work of Trumbić's Yugoslav Committee but their attitude changed following the disasters of 1915 and the retreat to exile in Corfu. It was, however, the fall of the Tsar and the consequent loss of Russian support that convinced the Serbs of the need to re-establish their position. The Corfu Declaration of 20 July 1917 promised the formation of a Serbo-Croat-Slovene state under the Serbian crown. It did not, however, resolve the issue of whether the new state would be centralised or a federation, as the non-Serbs would have preferred.[13]

Despite the efforts of exiles in London and America, there was little overt international support for the idea of a Yugoslav state. The Poles and Czechs were more successful in promoting their message, but they did not have to contend with Italian ambitions, or the treaty commitments of the British and French. Events, however, proved decisive. In June 1918, Lansing advised Wilson that, since a settlement with Austria-Hungary seemed unattainable, 'primarily as a war measure, but also because it is wise and just for the future, we should encourage in every possible way the national desires of these people', and America thus became a firm supporter of Slav ambitions. On 29 October 1918, as the Austro-Hungarian empire disintegrated, the National Council of Slovenes, Croats and Serbs in Zagreb proclaimed a South Slav state which the Montenegrin parliament voted to join on 26 November. On 1 December 1918, the Serbian Regent, Prince Alexander, accepted the formation of the new state.[14]

Yugoslavia represented the most complex set of problems of all the states in the region. Her internal politics were labyrinthine whilst internationally she had experienced the full force of Allied expediency during the war. In Paris only the Greek of her seven (or eight, counting the Montenegrin) frontiers was not in dispute, and she had the added misfortune to be the only one of the aspiring new states to be in direct confrontation with one of the Big Four. Her whole relationship with the peace conference was coloured by this rivalry with Italy, and the Italians were, for a long time, successful in their attempts to prevent the other powers from recognising the Kingdom of the Serbs, Croats, and Slovenes.[15] Thus, unlike Poland or Czechoslovakia, Yugoslavia was not admitted to the conference in her own right, but instead was represented by Serbia, a state which, to the minds of the Croats and Slovenes and of some, but not all, Serbs, no longer existed. Fortunately, after vigorous protests, Serbia was allocated three, not two, seats at the conference, and thus each of the principal components of the new state could be represented in the Serbian delegation, a vital consideration, given their mutual suspicions and antagonisms.[16]

Yugoslavia claimed a total area of 156,250 square miles including Serbia, Montenegro, Bosnia, Herzegovina, Croatia, Slavonia, Dalmatia, Istria, Southern Styria, Southern Carinthia, Carniola, Trieste, Gorizia and the Banat of Temesvar. Inevitably her ambitions clashed with those of most of her neighbours and the peace conference faced a difficult task in its attempts to reach acceptable solutions to a variety of conflicts. It approached this task in a piecemeal fashion and the results only emerged over a considerable period of time without much thought as to their overall coordination.

The first Yugoslavian issue to come before the Council of Ten, on 31 January, is worth extended consideration because it reveals much about the workings of the conference and of a typical east European problem. Rumania claimed the whole of the Banat (which had previously belonged to Hungary) partly on ethnographic grounds and partly because it had been promised to them by the Treaty of

Bucharest in 1916, though there was doubt as to whether, given the Rumanian surrender in 1916, the treaty remained valid. Their claim to its western, and part of its central regions was disputed by the Yugoslavs (who were summoned to the Ten at four hours notice) for a complex mixture of reasons: ethnic, strategic, historic and economic. The population was hopelessly mixed and there was no possibility of drawing any frontier which did not leave substantial minorities on either side. An earlier attempt by Pašić and Take Ionescu, one of the Rumanian leaders, to reach a compromise had foundered on intransigent Rumanian nationalism, and yet neutral observers believed that common sense and goodwill should have prevented the Banat becoming such a thorn in Yugoslav-Rumanian relations.[17] Here, in microcosm, were most .of the factors of any eastern European frontier dispute, with obligations, communications, nationality, strategy, economics, geography, history and the national pride and prestige of the claimants all pulling in different directions. There was the added complication that both parties had fought on the *Entente* side. Not surprisingly, the Ten passed this parcel to an expert committee![18]

Further typical features emerged during the subsequent negotiations in and around the expert committee. Great power interests were a factor: whereas the British, French and Americans agreed that the Banat should be divided between the two claimants and Hungary, the Italians, who always supported any opponent of Yugoslavia, backed Rumania's full claim. The French, with an eye to a client state, favoured the Yugoslavs, whose ethnic claims had the sympathy of the Americans and British. Rumania raised the spectre of a bolshevik overthrow of her government if her hopes were disappointed, a ploy which soon became too familiar to have much credibility. The statistics available were inaccurate and biased, whilst Rumania and Yugoslavia would accept a plebiscite only if its form was likely to produce a result which supported their respectively incompatible demands. Both parties briefly, at different stages, considered the use of force to resolve the problem.[19] Equally typical was the outcome, which satisfied none of the parties. The Council of Five allowed Hungary to retain the area around Szeged, the bulk of the remainder went to Rumania, but Yugoslavia gained part of the western region with the frontier between them drawn so as to balance the 75,000 Rumanians left in Yugoslavia with the 65,000 Slavs remaining in Rumania. These minorities were to be protected under the auspices of the League, an intrusion resented by both sides.[20]

In general the conference tried not to interfere with surviving pre-war boundaries in the Balkans on the sensible grounds that they had enough problems already, but they did allow the Yugoslavs to make some strategic gains at Bulgaria's expense. She did not obtain the important Dragoman pass but adjustments in the Strumica valley, and in the districts of Vranje, Tsaribrod and Negotin added some 960 square miles (mainly inhabited by Bulgars) to her territory.[21] Her attitude towards Albania was largely determined by the state of play in relations with Italy. An independent Albania could limit Italian ambitions, although the Montenegrins coveted the port of Scutari. Albania threatened to become a pawn in a bigger game, but Wilson resisted this, the Italians withdrew, and a frontier was agreed in 1924 with only minor alterations to that of 1914.[22]

The problem of resolving Yugoslavia's remaining frontiers with Italy and Austria fell into two distinct, but linked, categories: the frontier between Yugoslavia and Italy in Istria and Dalmatia; and the triangular disputes between Austria, Italy and Yugoslavia in the former Austrian provinces of Carniola, Carinthia and Styria. On 18 February the Council of Ten decided that they would deal with any Italian claims, whilst Yugoslavia's demands would be referred to expert committees. With the Italians acting as judges in their own cause, the Yugoslavs felt at a distinct disadvantage, but there was little that they could do. When the Council of Ten split, most of the territorial decisions fell to the Council of Five, but some of the Italian claims, particularly those to Fiume and Dalmatia, were reserved to the Council of Four, thus adding to the complexity of the problems.[23]

'As much as I sympathise with Italy in every way', wrote Charles Hardinge, the British Organising Ambassador, 'they are in my opinion, the most odious colleagues and Allies to have at a Conference . . . and "the beggars of Europe" are well known for their whining alternated by truculence.'[24] Hardinge's opinion was widely shared and Italy won few friends either by the extent of her demands or by her sullen and obstructive negotiating stance. Her claims were based on the Treaty of London, 26 April 1915, in which Britain, France and Russia had promised her Trieste, the Trentino, the Tyrol, Istria, Dalmatia, Valona in Albania, the Dodecanese islands and a share in Asia Minor if it was partitioned. Italy's subsequent fighting performance was disappointing, but she demanded her full bargain – Bismarck's assessment, 'She has such a large appetite and very poor teeth', was much in vogue.

Wilson would not accept the terms of the treaty, and although the British and French governments felt obliged to honour their commitments, it is clear that they did so with reluctance. Balfour commented to Wilson: 'That Treaty ... bears on the face of it evident proof of the anxiety of the Allies to get Italy into the war, and the use to which that anxiety was put by the Italian negotiators. But a treaty is a treaty; and we – I mean England and France (of Russia I say nothing) – are bound to uphold it in letter and spirit.'[25]

The president made one early and significant concession to the Italians when he accepted the strategic argument for the Brenner frontier in Austria. This consigned some 250,000 Germans in the South Tyrol to Italian rule, despite point nine, which had spoken of a 'readjustment of the frontiers of Italy along clearly recognisable lines of nationality'. It is not clear when he made this concession, it may possibly have been as early as 21 December 1918, in Paris. Certainly on 30 January 1919 he told Orlando that 'the Trentino and Trieste had, as far as he was concerned, already been ceded to Italy'. He later admitted that 'It was on the basis of insufficient study that I promised Orlando the Brenner frontier', but Wilson regarded himself as pledged. If he hoped thereby to gain Italian goodwill and, perhaps, concessions over Fiume, he was disappointed.[26]

Wilson began as an instinctive friend of the Slavs, and his resolve hardened as the conference progressed. The Yugoslavs, who were being advised by two Britons, the slavophile academic and propagandist R. W. Seton-Watson and the journalist Henry Wickham Steed, made a shrewd move in offering to submit all their claims to the president's arbitration. In contrast, when Wilson spoke of Sidney Sonnino, the slavophobe Italian foreign minister, he 'clenched his fist and used unparliamentary language'.[27] The Yugoslav case for Istria, Dalmatia and Fiume was mainly ethnic and well-founded, but they did spoil their image by their demand for Trieste. They had general American support, whilst the British and French backed their claim to Fiume, but committed to their treaty obligations, could offer only embarrassed sympathy elsewhere. Gradually the extended negotiations whittled down the areas of dispute, but Fiume refused to disappear. 'If we could get over that hurdle', wrote House, 'the rest would be settled in a canter.'[28]

It is not clear why Fiume became so important to the Italians, but for both them and Wilson it developed an almost mystical significance – an issue upon which, come what may, neither was prepared to budge. Lloyd George commented, 'Wilson was furious at . . . the rape of Fiume. He worked himself to such a pitch of indignation that for some time he concentrated his thoughts and energies upon this comparatively trivial incident to the exclusion of vastly more important subjects which were still awaiting decision.'[29] The Italian frontiers were not discussed until April, when they became entangled with the other issues which combined in the general crisis of the conference. The Americans were ready to concede to Italy half of Istria, and a strategic frontier between Trieste and Fiume, but neither this, nor other proposals for plebiscites, free city status for Fiume, and compromises involving third parties like Albania, proved successful. Lloyd George and Clemenceau tried desperately to extract Orlando (and themselves) from the impasse, but their efforts at mediation failed. Other members of the American delegation were prepared to bargain Dalmatia for Fiume, but not Wilson. Orlando was reduced to tears, Wilson tried to appeal to the Italian people over the heads of their leaders, and the Italian delegation withdrew from the conference on 21 April and left for Rome on 24 April. When they returned, chastened, on 6 May, they reduced, gradually, their demands in Dalmatia to the town of Zara and the coastal strip, but Fiume remained as the stumbling block. Despite the valiant efforts of Tardieu and others, the question was still unresolved when the Treaty of Versailles was signed, and Wilson and Lloyd George left Paris.[30]

Negotiations continued throughout the summer and autumn of 1919, complicated still further by the seizure of Fiume by the Italian adventurer and poet Gabriele D'Annunzio, on 12 September, the very day that a British force was due to replace the largely Italian garrison in the city. Wilson had returned to America and suffered a stroke, but despairing attempts by Clemenceau and Lloyd George to produce a compromise, or even a *diktat*, merely provoked the stricken president into refusing to accept any solution which assigned Fiume to Italy. In January 1920 the Yugoslav leaders thought that they might be forced, by Anglo-French pressure, to abandon Fiume, but once again Wilson came to their rescue. One final flurry of Allied activity, in February and March 1920, ended with another Wilsonian veto, but the president agreed to accept any frontier established by direct negotiation between the Yugoslavs and Italians. With heartfelt relief, Millerand, the new French premier, and Lloyd George relinquished responsibility for this intractable problem.[31]

The Italians and Yugoslavs negotiated the Treaty of Rapallo, signed on 12 November 1920, which gave the Italians Zara, some Adriatic islands and an improved frontier in Istria. Fiume became an independent city, linked territorially to Italy. Yugoslavia gained Susak, a suburb of Fiume, and in a separate and secret agreement, Porto Baros. D'Annunzio was still holding Fiume, but his quixotic gesture in declaring war on Italy on 1 December provoked the Italian premier, Giolitti, into decisive action. Fiume's independence was short-lived and Mussolini forced Yugoslavia to accept Italian annexation of the city in the Treaty of Rome, 27 January 1924. The settlement abandoned perhaps 500,000 Yugoslavs in Italy, for whom, unlike the Italian minority left in Dalmatia, there was to be no special protection. The Yugoslavs had little choice but to accept. Wilson's policies had been defeated, Britain and France, exasperated by his pontifications, wanted the matter settled, and the Italian position was increasingly strong.[32]

The second set of problems related to the borders between Austria, Italy and Yugoslavia. Yugoslavia claimed from Austria, on ethnic grounds, the provinces of Carniola, lower Styria and Carinthia. The majority of their populations were Slovene, and Yugoslav irregulars occupied Carniola and Styria in November 1918, but the issues were complicated by German majorities in the key towns of Marburg, Klagenfurt and Villach; by the important railway links between Austria and the Adriatic passing through Assling and Tarvis; and by considerations of economic integrity. The Italian position was clear throughout. They were anxious to prevent the railway lines between Austria and the coast at Trieste and Fiume from passing through Yugoslav territory and hence argued that the frontier between Austria and Yugoslavia should follow the line of the Karawanken mountains, or even, in the case of Assling, a line to the south of the mountains. They also had a counter-claim to part of Carniola.

Despite outbreaks of serious unrest in the Klagenfurt basin in February and March 1919, these problems did not have a high priority on the conference agenda. The Four and the Five passed the issues back and forth and thus it was not until 9 May that the

Council of Five considered the report of the Yugoslav territorial committee. By this time, Yugoslav forces were pushing into Carinthia, capturing Klagenfurt itself later in May. The Four demanded an armistice on 31 May, but the Yugoslav troops retained possession of Klagenfurt and much of its basin.[33] On 21 June, the Four decided that Klagenfurt's fate would be decided by two plebiscites. If Yugoslavia won in the southern plebiscite area, which had a Slovene majority, then a second vote would be held in the northern, German, zone.[34] The plebiscite of 10 October 1920, despite the arrangements which favoured Yugoslavia, resulted in a victory for Austria by 22,025 to 15,279, a majority of 6746. The ballot in the second zone was therefore not held, and the Klagenfurt basin remained Austrian.[35] Elsewhere the Italians gained part of Carniola and the Yugoslavs gained most of Carniola and lower Styria. The Treaty of Rapallo gave Assling and Tarvis to Yugoslavia, with special arrangements for railway traffic between Austria and Italy.

Yugoslavia emerged from the protracted negotiations as a state half the size of France, with nearly 12 million people, of whom perhaps only 15 per cent were not Slavs, whilst the settlement left 720,000 Slavs beyond her frontiers. Her neighbours collectively resented her success, and internally, the 'one people with three names' continued to experience the tensions between her constituent parts that had been so evident throughout the Paris negotiations, where the Yugoslav delegation and government had lurched from crisis to crisis: What was the name of the state? Was one ethnic group, particularly the Slovenes, sacrificing more of its national aspirations than the rest? Was Yugoslavia only a big Serbia? The unequal and double-standard treatment she had received during the Italian negotiations was galling. Yet, in a remarkably brief period, the dream of a Yugoslav state had been realised, and with reservations, this was a cause for satisfaction.[36]

Bulgaria

Bulgaria's decision to join the Central Powers in 1915 was much influenced by the history of the Balkan wars of 1912–13. A victor in the first war against Turkey, she found herself on the losing side when the victors fell out in 1913, and she suffered substantial territorial losses to Greece and Serbia in Macedonia, and to Rumania in the Dobruja. When the First World War broke out, Bulgaria negotiated with both sides, but the Central Powers were in the stronger position to offer rewards, and Bulgaria, occupying as she did a vital strategic position, proved to be a much larger thorn in the Allied flesh than might have been expected from her size or armed strength. She was perceived as a cruel and treacherous opponent, and 'the Prussia of the Balkans' had few British or French friends at the conference, although the Americans assumed some responsibility for her fate, and the Italians could be counted on for support against Yugoslavia and, perhaps, against Greece.[37]

Uniquely amongst the defeated powers, the Bulgarians approached the conference with the hope of making substantial territorial gains, relying on ethnic arguments to achieve what armed force had not. Neither were they without some grounds for optimism, since the initial American position was that Bulgaria should regain the Southern Dobruja, have her claims in Macedonia impartially investigated, retain Western Thrace and perhaps gain parts of Eastern Thrace from Turkey.[38] Bulgaria did have an ethnic case against Rumania in the Southern Dobruja, where in a population of some 350,000 there were only 7000 Rumanians and 112,000 Bulgarians, but elsewhere the positions were uncertain. Given the Anglo-French perception of Bulgaria, however, and the natural, if not necessarily Wilsonian, assumption that the winners would certainly not lose territory neither, normally, would the losers gain, it was improbable that her hopes would be realised. This was indeed the case, and despite American and Italian objections, the Anglo-French views prevailed. The Rumanians, Yugoslavs and Greeks retained their 1913 spoils and Yugoslavia made some strategic gains at Bulgaria's expense. The Greeks gained Eastern Thrace, and eventually, at the San Remo conference in April 1920, Western Thrace as well. The loss of Western Thrace isolated Bulgaria from the Aegean (she spurned Greek offers of access), and aroused intense anger. The ethnic position was confused, the Turks constituted the majority but there was no question of them regaining the area, and other considerations prevailed. Lloyd George was anxious to strengthen the political hand of the Greek premier Eleutherios Venizelos, whilst there was also the desire to punish Bulgaria, who if she retained Western Thrace, 'alone of enemy powers [would have emerged] from this war with practically no loss of territory'.[39]

The Bulgarian armed forces were limited to 33,000 men, which, trapped by the desire to appear consistent, the conference insisted be recruited on the same long-term basis as in Germany. The Bulgarian claim that few would enlist, though short-term conscription would work, was justified by events. Bulgaria was required to pay some £90m at 5 per cent interest over 38 years in reparations, a figure which had been reduced for political and commercial considerations and of which she paid, eventually, about one-third. Bulgaria resented deeply the outcome of the conference, and did not regard the Treaty of Neuilly, signed 27 November 1919, as a fair or final settlement. Like Hungary, she remained a revisionist power throughout the inter-war period.[40]

Rumania

In 1914 Rumania was an associate of the Triple Alliance but like Italy, she felt absolved from any obligation to her allies by the circumstances in which war had arisen. Her premier, Ioan Bratianu, played a skilful game, awaiting the bribes and inducements of the combatants, and since the Rumanians considered that almost half their brethren were living in various neighbouring states, it was not difficult to imagine what might tempt him. Russian Bessarabia, Austrian Bukovina, oddments of Bulgaria and Serbia, but most of all, Hungary's territories of Transylvania, the Crisana, the Banat and Maramos were on his list. Bratianu was candid enough to admit that Rumania's actions would depend on what she was offered, and the *Entente* could offer more of its opponents' territories. The Treaty of Bucharest, 17 August 1916, promised her Transylvania, Bukovina and the Banat. Rumania declared war on the Central Powers, only to be defeated by December 1917. She was forced to accept an armistice and later the Peace of Bucharest, 7 May 1918, which deprived her of the Dobruja, but she had herself taken advantage of the chaos in Russia to seize Bessarabia, which she annexed formally on 9 April 1918. Thus as the war was ending Rumania was technically at peace with the Central Powers and was not mentioned in the armistices, even after her redeclaration of war on 9 November. This did not prevent her acting as a victorious power, occupying Bukovina and most of Transylvania, nor did it inhibit Bratianu's insistence that the promises made to him in 1916 remained valid.[41]

Rumania's claims were generally accepted by the territorial committee. She was awarded Bessarabia, and most of Bukovina, Transylvania and the Banat, but the committee did admit the possibility of rival claims to parts of the last three. In the Banat, a compromise with Yugoslavia was imposed, whilst, eventually, the scotching of the idea of an independent Ruthenia left all the Bukovina to Rumania. In Transylvania, the Allies were prepared to accept Rumania's economic arguments for enlarging her ethnic case, but not the full 1916 bargain. Meanwhile, however, Rumanian forces had advanced into Hungarian territory beyond the Tisza to stake their claim. This angered the Allies and brought down the Hungarian government, which was replaced, on 21 March, by a coalition led by the Bolshevik Béla Kun. Skilfully exploiting this alarming evidence of the spread of revolution, Bratianu stressed Rumania's anti-bolshevik policy, leaving the Allies in a quandary. The only effective force in the area was the Rumanian army, but to encourage it to put down Kun was likely to leave the Rumanians entrenched in Hungary. Even though the Four approved the new frontiers of Hungary on 12 May, and those of Rumania in Bukovina and the Banat on 21 June, the situation remained obscure. Kun retained power, and Bratianu refused to accept either the frontiers or the imposition of protection for minorities within Rumania, an issue on which he led an unsuccessful revolt by the smaller powers. His troops continued to menace Hungary.[42]

The situation changed after the Four left Paris. The new Supreme Council, the Heads of Delegation, was more favourably disposed to Rumania, whilst in a desperate gamble, Kun attacked her, only to be defeated and forced to flee as Rumanian troops occupied Budapest on 4 August. It was, as they had anticipated, only with the greatest difficulty that the Allies dislodged the Rumanians from Hungary, but the autumn and winter of 1919 saw a gradual settlement of the outstanding problems. In October the threat of war between Yugoslavia and Rumania over the Banat receded, in November the Americans abandoned their fight to return the Dobruja to Bulgaria, in December Rumania was granted more of Bukovina than she had been promised in 1916, and herself accepted the principle of minority protection. In January 1920 it was finally decided that she would retain Bessarabia. Rumania thus more than doubled her pre-war area and population – from 7.5 to 16 million people and from 53,661 to 113,941 square miles of territory. The imposition, by the minorities treaty, of theoretical restrictions on her sovereignty was irksome, even humiliating, but could not obscure her great gains. Rumania was a winner and thus a defender of the

Versailles Settlement, though her Hungarian, Bulgarian and Russian neighbours did not accept her success as final.[43]

Balkan Summary

The Versailles Settlement in the Balkans confirmed and emphasised the results of the 1912–13 wars, and took account of the demise of Austria-Hungary. The winners were the Greeks – whose role is discussed more fully in Chapter 7, on the Turkish settlement – Rumania and Yugoslavia, the losers were Bulgaria, Austria, Hungary and Turkey. Bulgaria's losses of territory and population were small, the real measure of her decline being the consolidation of her rivals around her. Her area in 1914 had been 47,750 square miles, her population 5,500,000. In 1921 the respective figures were 45,000 square miles and 5,200,000 people but the relevant comparison was to Serbia's 33,900 square miles and 4,600,000 people in 1914 and Yugoslavia's 101,250 square miles and 13,635,000 in 1921. Similarly Greece had expanded by 1921, at least temporarily, from 42,000 square miles and 4,800,000 people in 1914 to 60,000 square miles and a population of 7,500,000. Italy and France replaced Austria-Hungary and Russia as the major powers seeking influence in the region, but the Balkan reputation for lawlessness and banditry remained intact. Wilson's definition of Montenegrin self-determination was probably not quite that advanced by a British naval commander: 'their inalienable right to murder each other, as and when they considered it necessary, provided that no inconvenience to the Allies is caused thereby', but the troubled internal politics of the Balkan states did little to alter the outside world's perception of the region.[44]

EASTERN AND CENTRAL EUROPE

It is ironic that a settlement which helped to consolidate the Balkans should be accused of 'balkanising' the remainder of eastern Europe. Yet here the collapse and replacement of the great pre-war empires had a much greater and more direct impact, for it was clear that there could be no reshuffling or adjustment of the old order and that new states must emerge, though it was less clear which states these would be. In fact it was those national groups which most rapidly staked their claim and which were the best organised, both on the ground and abroad, which succeeded. There were no prizes for slow starters in the post-war land rush. Neither was there any sustained attempt to deal with the problems of dissolving the former empires as a whole. Smuts did suggest this on his return from Hungary in April 1919, but nothing came of it, just as nothing came of the British preference for a Central European Federation to fulfil some of the positive roles of the old empire.[45]

Hungary

In October and November 1918 the Austro-Hungarian empire dissolved in a series of coups, revolutions and panic-stricken transfers of power. Emperor Charles renounced all power in Hungary on 13 November and, although he did not abdicate, a republic was proclaimed on 16 November. The new government was led by Count Mihály Károlyi who believed naïvely that, by reconstituting an independent Hungary, he could retain the loyalty of the subject nationalities, defend her historic frontiers and win Allied support. He failed on all three fronts, and Hungary's position was worsened by the enthusiastic pacifism of the war minister, Linder, who disbanded the armed forces, leaving internal and external security at risk. Within weeks two-thirds of Hungary was occupied and administered by Serb, Rumanian and Czech claimants, whose actions were, although contrary to the armistice conditions, tolerated by the Allies.[46] The erosion of Hungarian territory continued throughout January and February 1919. The Károlyi government lost support and, on 21 March, was ousted by a coalition led by the Bolshevik Béla Kun. This confirmation of their worst fears about the communist threat found the Allies, rather strangely, without any firm contingency plan. Smuts, despatched to investigate the new regime, met Kun on 4 April and appeared to be making progress towards an agreement but Kun's attempts to haggle drove the prickly Smuts to quit Budapest the following day, on the train which he had never left throughout his visit. Reluctant to commit their own forces to the area, and equally reluctant to use Rumanian troops to suppress Kun, the Allies tended to let their policy towards Hungary drift.[47]

They did, however, decide the fate of much of the territory disputed between Hungary and her neighbours, rarely to her advantage. She lost most of the Banat to Yugoslavia and Rumania, Transylvania to Rumania, Slovakia and Ruthenia to Czechoslovakia. She even lost territory to Austria, though a later plebiscite cut these losses in the Burgenland to 1500 square miles. By July 1919 most of the Hungarian treaty was complete, but the Hungarian situation remained uncertain, even after the collapse of the Kun regime in August. The final settlement was delayed until 1920, although when the Hungarian delegation led by Count Albert Apponyi arrived in Paris on 7 January, they knew that the essentials of the treaty were established by the treaties already signed with her neighbours. The intermittent negotiations continued until May 1920, with the Hungarians arguing cogently, but mainly ineffectively, against the terms which they were forced to accept in the Treaty of Trianon, signed on 4 June 1920.[48]

Like Germany, Hungary suffered because of the fragmented way in which her settlement was drafted, with the claims against her taken individually and sequentially rather than collectively. She had the added disadvantage that her treaty came later, by which time, as one Hungarian official perceptively remarked, the Allies were 'frightfully bored by the whole Peace Conference' and had 'got into a labyrinth from which they [could not] find a way out'. The new Hungary consisted of the parts her neighbours could not reach. Reduced to one-third of her pre-war territory, with only 41.6 per cent of her former population, Hungary saw one-third of her Magyar population assigned to her neighbours. These Magyar minorities beyond her borders offered a ready source of real or imagined grievances for her to exploit, and feeling that her ethnic case had been ignored, Hungary remained the most bitter and irreconcilable of the revisionist powers throughout the inter-war period.[49]

Czechoslovakia

Czech aspirations before the outbreak of war in 1914 had been confined to a hope of autonomy within the Austro-Hungarian empire. Even when wartime developments encouraged Tomas Masaryk to demand independence for Bohemia, Moravia, part of Austrian Silesia, Slovakia and (after the collapse of Tsarist Russia) Carpatho-Ruthenia, he envisaged the new state cooperating very closely with its neighbours, especially Poland and, hopefully, Yugoslavia. Masaryk spent the war in exile, using his academic contacts in London and Washington to gather support for his proposed union of the Czech and Slovak peoples into a new state, for which there was no exact historical precedent in the territories concerned. He and his colleague, Eduard Beneš, were very successful in projecting a sympathetic image abroad, but the circumstances made it impossible to consult the native populations, and thus, as one authority has remarked:

> To a remarkable extent, Czechoslovakia was manufactured in the West, by Czech refugees under licence from the Allies in cooperation with emigrants out of touch with the opinion of their homeland, and then presented to the indigenous Czech and Slovak populations as a *fait accompli* for their rapturous applause.[50]

The idea of the new state was endorsed by the major Allies during the summer of 1918, and on 28 October the Czech National Council in Prague proclaimed its independence. The next day the Slovene National Council called for a single state and, by the middle of November, a government was formed with Masaryk as president, Karel Kramař as premier and Beneš as foreign minister. Masaryk's visit to London on 29 November, on his way to Prague from the United States, was in sharp contrast to his first arrival as a lonely academic exile in 1915.[51] The new state's demands posed the conference all the usual problems associated with the successor states, but two issues proved to be of note, both in the short and the long term. These were the fate of the German-speaking inhabitants of the Sudetenland, and the quarrel with Poland over the duchy of Teschen, which did so much to destroy Masaryk's vision of a close bond between the two states.

The 3 million German-speaking inhabitants in the Sudeten borderlands, between Germany and the historic kingdom of Bohemia, posed the conference with difficult questions of principle, consistency and the need to create a Czech state that was economically and strategically viable. The ethnic argument lay against the Czechs, but the conference decided that the mineral resources and mountain defences of the Sudetenland were necessary to them, and that the historic frontiers should remain. The French were always firm supporters of the Czech claim, but the problem provoked much heartsearching within the British and American delegations, yet the final decision to maintain Czech control was taken rapidly on 4 April because House thought there were more important issues to settle, and because Lloyd George did not appear to know that there was a problem.[52]

The duchy of Teschen was a rich coal and industrial area, historically part of Bohemia, but where the main ethnic element in the population was Polish. Britain recognised the strength of the Polish case, but in common with France, backed the Czechs because of wider considerations. The Americans, however, supported the Poles. Early hopes of an agreed solution collapsed and in January 1919 the Czechs attempted a coup which misfired both in Teschen, where it provoked fighting with Polish troops, and in Paris, where it sapped Anglo-French support for their claim. The incident revealed the weakness of the Allies in central Europe, both in terms of troops and of an overall plan. They resorted to sending a lightweight Control Commission to supervise a demarcation line which left one-third of Teschen (including the Karvin coalmines) in Czech hands, and control of the important railway linking Bohemia and Moravia with Slovakia divided between the Poles and Czechs. This unsatisfactory state of affairs lasted for over a year.[53]

The Teschen dispute offers further evidence of the confusion and procrastination in Paris in 1919. Three bodies considered the duchy's future: the committees on Czech and Polish frontiers and the commission in Teschen. Each reached different conclusions, although the two Paris committees had only minor differences in the frontiers they recommended. They both awarded Czechoslovakia three of the four administrative districts of Teschen, leaving the other to Poland. The Teschen commission favoured maintaining the area as a small independent state. It was, however, not an issue high on the conference agenda, and no decision was taken, despite continuing unrest and a growing need to restore the region's coal output. It was impossible to adjudicate between the ethnic claims of the Poles and the economic and communications needs of the Czechs and the question really became, in Nicolson's words, 'which of the two states should receive more consideration in the general interest of Europe'.[54]

Here the Czechs lost ground as the conference progressed, their use of force costing them sympathy, whilst the activities of a Slovak separatist group led by Father Hlinka cast doubt upon the validity of the new state. There were also shifts in the attitudes of the major powers, and it appeared in the autumn of 1919 that the Poles might now gain the lion's share of Teschen. Beneš tried to gain support for a frontier along the Olsa river which would give Poland the town of Teschen and the territory to the north, whilst Czechoslovakia would retain the railway and most of the coalfield. He had little success in September 1919, and the Allies resorted to a plebiscite, but did not send a body to conduct it until February 1920, only to find that conditions on the ground and the attitude of the rival claimants made a plebiscite impossible. A further scheme to employ King Albert of the Belgians as an arbitrator also failed, but the Czech position began to improve as Poland became embroiled in her war with the Soviets, and Anglo-French support revived. On 28 July 1920 the Conference of Ambassadors accepted the Olsa line. Once again neither party was satisfied, though the Poles were the major losers and retained the stronger sense of grievance.[55]

Masaryk's vision of a friendly group of successor states cooperating in economic, political and military matters was thus dealt a serious blow. The Teschen dispute poisoned relations with Poland, there was no common frontier with Yugoslavia, and although the Rumanians and Czechs reached an amicable settlement about their frontier in Maramaros in 1921, the former did not abandon their claim for a greater share of the province. The Hungarians were discontented about their frontier. All this did little for French hopes of a solid alliance structure in the region, neither did it bode well for the future. When Hitler destroyed Czech independence there was no shortage of vultures ready to pick at the corpse.[56]

Austria

The rump state of Austria was an embarrassment to the conference. She did not wish to be independent and claimed that the right of self-determination should allow her to join with Germany, a wish shared by the new German state. Britain and America had some sympathy with this view but France refused to countenance such a strengthening of Germany's already large population. The Germans and Austrians were obliged to remove any reference to a union from their constitutions, and the French insisted that such a union could only take place if the League Council approved. They could thus veto any future attempt to merge the two states. Austria was left with a population of 8 million, mostly in or near Vienna, a city now bereft of most of its former *raison d'être* as the banking and financial centre of the old empire. The Treaty of St Germain included both a war-guilt clause and a demand for reparations but this claim soon had to be abandoned when the Allies were forced to come to the reluctant republic's financial rescue in 1921.[57]

Poland

Poland's frontiers in the west with Germany and Czechoslovakia were established, but her frontiers in the east remained undetermined. The situation here was complex and confused because of the uncertain state of Russia, where several groups were battling for power with the Bolsheviks and each other. The conference faced particular difficulties in Eastern Galicia, an area claimed by Poland, the aspiring Ruthene state in the Ukraine, and the White forces in Russia. It agreed to assign the western part of the province to Poland, but there was disagreement between the Anglo-Americans and the French, who wished to give Poland the whole area. In July 1919 the Americans agreed to the French proposal, but Lloyd George continued to resist, not wishing to consign the Ruthene population to the Poles, although Poland was authorised to administer the province for the moment. Meanwhile, in the region itself fighting between the Poles, the Bolsheviks and the Whites ebbed and flowed, although the Whites' position was becoming desperate. Faced with the choice of the Poles or the Bolsheviks, the conference offered Poland a 25-year mandate for Eastern Galicia, which they declined. Only after the Russo-Polish war in 1920, and further fruitless negotiations, did the Conference of Ambassadors, in despair, allow Poland to annex the region in 1923.[58]

The Baltic Provinces

Estonia, Latvia and Lithuania were further beneficiaries of the sequential collapse of first Russia then Germany. Detached from Russia by the Treaty of Brest-Litovsk, their future in 1918 was uncertain and the end of the war did little to clarify the position. The conference did not want Germany to retain control, though their only effective force in the area was the German army, which was required to stand fast by the armistice. This did not prevent the Bolsheviks occupying part of Estonia and all of Latvia. France was anxious to restrict bolshevik influence in the provinces, and although Britain and America were less clear as to their objectives or attitude towards Soviet Russia, Lloyd George had to be mindful of the anti-bolshevik sentiments of his Conservative allies and the vehemence of his Liberal colleague, Winston Churchill. In the circumstances, independence seemed the least unpleasant option, but the volatile situation and the lack of Allied land forces meant that this solution was not rapidly achieved.

A combination of local troops, various volunteers, and German irregulars led by General von der Goltz, drove the Bolsheviks out between February and May 1919, but in April the Latvian government was overthrown by a group of Baltic Germans, supported by von der Goltz, whose ambition was to establish a bridge between Germany and a restored White Russia, and then to defy the Allies. In Lithuania the Poles helped to expel the Bolsheviks, but then themselves seized the port of Vilna. The conference did its best to sort out the confusion and was successful in removing von der Goltz and his forces by December. The Poles retained Vilna. The wider picture was very much dependent on the attitude of the powers to events in Russia, and their thoughts on their future relations with whatever government emerged. They tended to drift and wait upon events, and even when Britain sent aid and a military mission to Latvia and Estonia in the summer of 1919, its leader, Major Gough, was instructed not to endanger relations with any future Russian government – a tall order particularly as it became probable that that government would be bolshevik. Eventually a balance was struck between the forces in the area, and in 1920 the Soviets recognised the independence of the republics, to be followed by Britain and France in 1921. All three republics joined the League in September 1921.[59]

Russia

Nowhere was Jules Cambon's prediction that the result of the peace conference would be 'une improvisation' better fulfilled than in its dealings with Russia. The problem was of such an immense scale, and the uncertainties of the situation so manifest, that it is perhaps not surprising that, in the British diplomat Eyre Crowe's words, their policy was 'a hand to mouth affair'. It seemed unthinkable that the conference should leave unresolved the future of such a vast area of Europe, yet the alternative presupposed an acknowledged and authorised power with which to deal. Given the confusion of Allied interventionist forces, various White and nationalist armies, and the gradual, but by no means inexorable, advance of the Bolsheviks themselves, such a prospect seemed remote. Lloyd George did persuade the Council of Ten in January to invite all the factions to a peace conference on the island of Prinkipo in the Sea of Marmara, but this foundered, despite Lenin's acceptance, when the White forces in Russia refused to attend. Given the scarcely-muted French opposition to the whole plan, this may have been fortunate, but the prospects for future contact were not good.[60]

The Russian problem came in several guises. First there was the question of who would emerge as the governors of territories covering one-sixth of the earth's surface. Then there was the problem of that government's (or those governments') frontiers and relations with its (or their) neighbours, and finally there was an insidious, though ill-defined, ideological threat. Bolshevism meant, for the peacemakers, much more than the precepts of Marxist-Leninism. It meant chaos, despair, fanaticism, famine, anarchy and a threat to all orderly government, hence Lansing's frustration at 'delaying and delaying while the flames of Bolshevism eat their way into Central Europe and threaten the destruction of social order'.[61] Just as the peacemakers at Vienna had had to consider the twin menace of France as a great power and as the source of an ideological contagion, so in 1919, the Soviet state posed a similar dilemma. Unlike France in 1814–15, the Russians were not present in Paris in 1919, though the spectre of revolution was.[62]

It is interesting that Wilson and Lloyd George, despite their firmly held liberal and capitalist principles, were much more flexible in their approach to the question of dealing with the Bolsheviks than was Clemenceau. Yet, if the French were often to the fore in proposing crusades against the Bolsheviks, they did not lack allies in the British government who would prefer to fight rather than 'shake the paw of the hairy baboon'. In February Churchill pressed the conference to back armed intervention against the Bolsheviks. Wilson and Lloyd George were absent from Paris, but both opposed this plan, which was quietly dropped. Instead they tried to establish contact with Lenin, first through a young American diplomat, William Bullitt, whom they sent to Russia, whilst the later Smuts mission to Budapest had, as one of its objectives, the investigation of Kun as a channel of communication. These initiatives were unwelcome to the French and the Whites, and were rendered ambiguous by continued Allied support for anti-Bolshevik forces. Nothing positive came from them, though Lenin did not reject them out of hand. Equally nothing came of the anti-Bolsheviks, and Allied policy drifted whilst other, apparently more manageable, problems claimed the conference's attention.[63]

The Treaty of Versailles dismissed Russia in two brief clauses, requiring Germany to renounce the Treaty of Brest-Litovsk, to recognise the independence of pre-war Russian territory and to respect any new Russian frontiers established by the conference. It protected also the possibility of reparations for Russia.[64] In his Fourteen Points speech Wilson had predicted: 'The treatment accorded Russia by her sister nations in the months to come will be the acid test of their goodwill, of their comprehension of her needs as distinguished from their own interests, and of their intelligent and unselfish sympathy.'[65] If this was so, it could hardly be said that the conference had established the basis for future harmony. On the other hand, it had not sanctioned an all-out attack on the Soviets. Gradually they established their control and Lloyd George ended further assistance to the Whites and began negotiations with Lenin's government. Wilson remained trapped between his instinct that bolshevism would collapse if ignored, and his fear that American withdrawal would open the way for others, notably the Japanese, to step in. The French remained hostile and sought to isolate Russia with a *cordon sanitaire* both to contain the infection and to prevent Germany from taking advantage of Soviet weakness by establishing an informal empire in the east. The results of this haphazard policy were not promising.[66]

National Self-determination, Plebiscites and Minority Protection

The Versailles Settlement reduced by half the number of people in eastern and central Europe living under alien governments. It still left 30,000,000 people in states in which they were not part of the dominant nationality. Short of forcible movements of population – a principle which, on the whole, the conference rejected – it is difficult to see how much more, in total, could have been achieved. Yet the result disappointed some and frustrated others. Wilson told the United States Senate:

When I gave utterance to those words ('that all nations had a right to self-determination'), I said them without the knowledge that nationalities existed, which are coming to us day after day . . . You do not know and cannot appreciate the anxieties that I have experienced as the result of many millions of people having their hopes raised by what I have said.[67]

Wilson tended to confuse the concepts of national self-determination and popular sovereignty, and he had always limited the application of his principle by the caveat:

That all well-defined national aspirations shall be accorded the utmost satisfaction that can be accorded them without introducing new or perpetuating old elements of discord and antagonism that would be likely in time to break up the peace of Europe, and consequently of the world.[68]

It was a reservation which few aspiring national groups chose to notice, and as we have seen, there was an infinite number of 'elements of discord and antagonism' present in eastern and central Europe in 1919. The conference knew that disappointed nationalisms could pose one of the gravest threats to the new international order and it adopted two devices in an attempt to limit the danger: plebiscites and minority protection.

Plebiscites were a double-edged weapon. In theory it seemed good sense to ask the inhabitants of a disputed area for their views, but in practice this led to many complications. Faced with a stark choice between two (or three) options, the wary inhabitant might return an ambiguous answer. As in all such surveys, it depended on the way the question was put, what the question was, how the results were judged – simple overall majority, voting by region, or by district, or by commune – and then how the outcome was interpreted. In cases such as Upper Silesia, a plebiscite could serve further to complicate, rather than to resolve, the issues at stake. The principle itself might prove unfortunate: 'Obviously the conference has nothing to do with territories owned by the allies before the war', noted Hardinge, ' . . . plebiscites taken in countries in our possession . . . might be very inconvenient and certainly should not be encouraged'.[69] Nonetheless it was a ploy to which the conference turned on several occasions, and the results at times cast doubt on some of the assumptions about nationality made by the leaders or their advisers. In Allenstein 46 per cent of the population spoke Polish in 1910, yet only 2 per cent voted for Poland; in Upper Silesia 65 per cent spoke Polish, yet an overall majority voted for Germany; while in Carinthia 68 per cent of the population were Slovenes but only 40 per cent voted for secession from Austria.[70]

The other tool which the conference hoped might square the national self-determination circle was the principle of minority protection. Springing from the established nineteenth-century practice of attempting (often ineffectually) to offer religious protection to minority groups in the new states of eastern Europe, the idea of minority protection was extended in Paris, though the initial concern of the peacemakers was the Jewish communities scattered throughout the region. The hope was that a modest package of guaranteed rights would reconcile populations left on the wrong side of national boundaries to their new states and *vice versa*. It was not to be. The minorities remained firmly unabsorbed, the new states resented both the minorities and the limitations on their national sovereignty imposed by the great powers, and neighbouring kin states exploited the resulting discontent for their own ends.[71]

Conclusion

The problems of eastern Europe and the self-imposed complications which the peacemakers brought to their task were well summarised by the American adviser, Isaiah Bowman:

> In the modern, closely organized, strongly commercialized world it is virtually impossible to make a clean-cut distinction between what is right from the standpoint of ethnography, nationalistic sentiment, and abstract justice, and what is fair from the standpoint of economic advantage. . . . So that if we introduce a new set of conceptions into diplomacy, if we call it, let us say, 'The New Diplomacy', we shall perhaps be able here and there to achieve justice in minor cases, but the great stakes of diplomacy remain the same. We simply discuss them in different terms.[72]

The task of reconciling the irreconcilable was beyond the conference, although it did sketch the broad outlines of the east European states of today. The sardonic comment made by A. J. Balfour may serve as an epitaph, perhaps even as an excuse, for the conference's performance: 'General Plunkett's solution of our eastern European difficulties is that we should put the whole area in charge of a genius. We have no genius's [sic] available.'[73]

7   The Colonial, Near and Middle Eastern Settlements

THE statesmen in Paris faced problems beyond the confines of Europe. The liquidation of the German empire in Africa and Asia, with over 1,000,000 square miles and approximately 14,000,000 people, and the collapse of Ottoman power in the Balkans, Asia Minor and the Middle East meant that their task was much greater than that of any previous peace conference. It was of little consolation to them that a fair measure of their difficulties were the self-inflicted results of their own wartime policies, or that their conflicting promises would now return to dog their footsteps. The loss and gain of imperial territories had been a familiar part of most European settlements in the previous two centuries, but once again, the Paris conference had set itself a higher moral standard than its predecessors and this too would complicate the resolution of an already complex situation. Too often the newly-discovered device of mandates served only to act as a figleaf for the desire of the great powers, and in the British case, of her own empire, to annex territories formerly owned by the defeated powers.[1]

THE MANDATE SYSTEM

The German empire overseas was destroyed by the end of 1916, although in East Africa her forces continued to fight even after the armistice in Europe. Elsewhere British, French, Belgian, Japanese, Australian, New Zealand and South African troops defeated the German forces left isolated by the failure of their expensive navy. The fate of these colonies posed a problem, since the victors, with the exception of Great Britain, made it plain that they intended to annex the territories that they had conquered. Wilson did not object to Germany losing her colonies – indeed that matter was promptly settled in Paris with practically no discussion on 24 January, at the first Council of Ten meeting on the subject[2] – but he was not prepared to accept an old-fashioned colonial readjustment. Instead he pressed for a system of international trusteeship which would apply the principle of self-determination under the auspices of the League of Nations in 'A free, open-minded, and absolutely impartial adjustment of all colonial claims'. His anti-annexationist doctrine, proclaimed also by the Bolsheviks, found a receptive audience amongst radical and socialist circles in Britain who were pressing for international control in the colonial field. This clashed with the perceived needs of the Dominions, particularly Australia, New Zealand and South Africa, whose leaders left the British government in little doubt as to their demand for the outright ownership of neighbouring German colonies which they felt menaced their security. They were supported by a powerful imperial lobby in London which hoped to consolidate the empire into an international organisation with more cohesion and practical value than Wilson's idealistic League. Anxious to avoid the accusation that the war had been fought in the British eighteenth-century tradition of imperial expansion, conscious of the importance of cooperation with the United States, but also aware of the need to ensure imperial security, a concept which apparently had no finite boundaries, the British government found itself under intense pressure.[3]

In typical fashion, admired by some as pragmatic realism and condemned by others as hypocrisy, the British resolved their problem by arguing that it did not exist, and that they could achieve all their major objectives within a framework which would appear to be, nay would be, Wilsonian. Indeed Wilson was merely institutionalising the current good practice of the British empire, therefore by accepting his principles, they might, at little practical cost to themselves, obtain valuable American support in the colonial field. The Americans might even accept a share of 'the white man's burden' by becoming a mandatory power in some difficult area such as Armenia or Constantinople. For these insights they had to thank the astute and flexible minds of Lloyd George and Smuts, the man who conceived the mandate system, though not originally in the context of the German colonies. The potential minefield of self-determination could be avoided if the wishes of the traditional tribal rulers were assumed to be those of their peoples – a formula the British were confident would work in their favour. The Germans were unfit colonial rulers, a concept not in strong evidence before the war but now conveniently discovered, and therefore must lose their possessions, not because they had been defeated but on moral grounds. It was not clear, however, whether the Dominion leaders could be persuaded to substitute this policy of international trusteeship for simple annexation.[4]

Smuts had proposed, in *The League of Nations: A Practical Suggestion*, the idea that the League should act as the trustee for 'territories formerly belonging to Russia, Austria-Hungary and Turkey'. He excluded the German colonies because they were inhabited by 'barbarians' incapable of attaining self-government in the conceivable future. These territories should be annexed outright and for this idea he had the firm backing of the French, the Japanese and the Dominions, with the exception of Canada, acutely aware of a need for good relations with her neighbour. In Paris, where the colonial question was the first major item of discussion, references to Austria-Hungary and Russia were dropped, but a battle-royal ensued over the inclusion of the German colonies. Wilson was insistent that there must be international control, his opponents adamant that there should not. Premier Hughes of Australia, who was especially dismissive of Wilson and his League 'toy', revealed the weakness of the Wilsonian appeal to world opinion and moral justice. Taxed by Wilson as to whether Australia would refuse to accept any German colonies under mandate despite the appeal 'of the whole of the civilised world', Hughes replied 'That's about the size of it, President Wilson'. Hankey commented, 'Hughes and Massey [the New Zealand prime minister] . . . are our principal difficulty, but President Wilson . . . is even more obstinate'.[5]

It was again Smuts and Lloyd George who found a way out of the impasse. Although still anxious to exclude the Pacific islands and South-West Africa from any mandate system, Smuts, supported by Robert Cecil, his colleague on the League commission, proposed to the British delegation on 27 January that the victorious powers should accept responsibility for the government of these territories under three classes of mandate: 'A', where the peoples concerned were near to self-government but needed minimal assistance along that path; 'B', where the mandatory power would be responsible for the administration of the territory, subject to League conditions prohibiting trade in slaves, arms and liquor, and forbidding militarisation; and 'C', which amounted to annexation, subject only to the same safeguards as the 'B' mandates. All mandatories would submit annual reports to the League on their stewardship. Smuts thought that the 'A' mandates would arise in the new states formed from the Turkish empire, the 'B' mandates would occur in the ex-German colonies of Central Africa and the 'C' mandates would apply to ex-German colonies with a neighbouring British Dominion. On 29 January Lloyd George bullied and persuaded his colleagues from Australia, New Zealand and South Africa that the 'C' mandate scheme should apply also to the Pacific islands and South-West Africa. Hughes continued to fight 'like a weasel – which he somewhat resembles – for annexation in the Pacific', until Lloyd George lost his temper and told him that he had no intention of quarrelling with the United States over the Solomon Islands. Hughes finally acquiesced on receiving assurances that, in contrast to the 'B' mandates, he would retain full control over immigration – a matter of great significance to the Pacific powers, which were anxious to exclude the Japanese – and trade. He commented that the terms of the 'C' mandate – the wording of which was drafted by an Australian – achieved his major objectives and differed only 'from full sovereign control as a nine hundred and ninety nine years' lease differs from a fee simple'.[6]

Wilson reacted favourably on first seeing the proposal, but when the Ten discussed it on 30 January he was piqued by a newspaper article Hughes had written, accusing the president of impractical idealism, and this produced unforeseen difficulties. Wilson now argued that the Smuts plan was helpful, but that there could be no final decisions yet as to which states would obtain which mandates; Australia, for example, might not be the mandated power for New Guinea. Hughes was furious, but a dignified intervention by Louis Botha, the South African premier, restored calm and assured the acceptance of the principle. The final text became Article 22 of the Covenant. Although Wilson was anxious to postpone the distribution of mandates as long as possible to avoid the charge 'that the Great Powers first portioned out the helpless parts of the world, and then formed a League of Nations', there was an implicit understanding that, for example, South-West Africa would go to South Africa, and that the Australian and New Zealand wishes would be met. Orlando declared that Italy agreed to the principle and, somewhat anxiously, assured the Council that she would accept responsibilities in this field. Clemenceau was prepared to accept mandates provided that he could use their human resources to defend France in the event of another war. He assured Lloyd George that he had no intention of training 'big nigger armies for the purpose of aggression', but more privately he told Poincaré that the League would have no real authority: 'I can accept the League as a guarantor of peace but not as a colonial power'.[7]

GERMANY'S COLONIES IN AFRICA AND ASIA

The conference decided that since the League was not yet in existence, Germany's colonies, together with all her property in those
colonies, should be surrendered, without compensation, to the five
victorious great powers. The treaty did not specify how the responsibility for governing the colonies would be divided, this being a
matter for decision between the powers themselves. On 6 May,
conveniently in the absence of the Italians who had not yet returned
to the conference, Wilson bowed to the strong pressure of the British
Dominions, the French and Japanese, and agreed to allocate mandates amongst the victors. The outcome was predictable, despite
Wilson's earlier reservations; in general it was the power which had
occupied the territory which gained the mandate, though, as the
Belgians discovered, this was not always the case. Wilson would not
accept any African or Asian mandates for the United States, though
he still toyed with the idea of a mandate for Armenia.[8]

Lloyd George's proposals for the allocation of mandates were
accepted by a brief meeting of the Four as they left the ceremony at
the Trianon to present the draft treaty to the German delegation on
7 May. In Africa, all the mandates fell into the 'B' category. The
Togoland and the Cameroons mandates would be divided between
Britain and France (who were to return to the conference with a
joint proposal) whilst that for German East Africa went to Britain.
South Africa gained the mandate for South-West Africa. Italian
interests were nominally safeguarded, but as Milner commented,
'Ultimately, I presume, Italy will have to be satisfied with what
France and Great Britain are prepared to give up'. This amounted
only to the cession of the Juba valley by Britain and some Saharan
oases by the French. The Belgians, who had occupied much of
German East Africa, were incensed at their exclusion from the
settlement, and the Portuguese also had claims. In August the
conference approved an Anglo-Belgian compromise which granted
the Ruanda-Urundi mandate to Belgium. Portugal was consoled
with a morsel of territory, the Kionga triangle in northern Mozam-
bique, which she gained in full sovereignty. Britain and France
agreed the division of Togoland and the Cameroons in July 1919,
the larger share of each going to France, but the final conditions
were only settled in December 1920.[9]

In the Pacific, Australia received New Guinea, the islands of the
Bismarck Archipelago and islands south of the equator, New Zea-

land received Samoa whilst Japan gained the islands north of the equator. The island of Nauru, which was an important source of phosphates, became the responsibility of the British empire, to allow time for the Australians, British and New Zealanders to work out an acceptable arrangement between themselves. This they did on 2 July, much to the annoyance of Smuts, who argued, unsuccessfully, that the three states could not assume that they were, for this issue, the entire British empire. These territories, apart from the 'B' mandate for Samoa, were all allocated under 'C' mandates and, despite their earlier objections, the two Dominions came to see great advantages in the system in their dealings with the Japanese, of whom they were increasingly distrustful. It enabled them to prevent Japanese immigration into their mandates and, in theory, stopped the Japanese fortifying their mandated territory.[10]

The fate of the German concessions of Kiaochow, Tsingtao and Shantung in China had also to be settled by the conference. The Japanese (with minimal British assistance) had occupied these areas in 1914, and in May 1915 had forced China to accept their 'Twenty-one demands', which included recognition of their hold over Shantung and the granting of extensive economic rights within China. In 1917 Britain sought extra naval assistance from her Japanese allies, in return offering her support for Japanese claims in Shantung and the German islands north of the equator. This represented a mixture of cynicism and wishful thinking. Britain felt the Japanese demands were inevitable and irresistible and hence that she should try to sell her support for the best attainable price. Further, the agreement might make the equator the limit of Japanese expansion. China declared war on Germany in August 1917, but her claim that the former German concessions should return to her was ignored. At the conference Britain, not without misgivings, felt obliged to second the Japanese demands, and she was supported by France. Wilson, who was increasingly suspicious of Japanese ambitions in the Pacific, found himself isolated. When the question came before the conference in April 1919 his position was weakened further by the Italian boycott over Fiume. He could not afford a Japanese walk-out at the same time; hence, reluctantly, on 30 April he accepted the outright transfer of Germany's concessions to Japan. Lloyd George had failed to persuade the Japanese to accept the areas under a 'C' mandate, but they did agree to promise the eventual return of Kiaochow to Chinese sovereignty, although the date was unspecified. Bitterly disappointed, the Chinese refused to sign the treaty.[11]

Not unnaturally, when they arrived in Paris in May 1919, the Germans protested that these decisions were incompatible with Wilson's idea of a free and fair colonial adjustment, but their efforts achieved nothing. The contemporary *History of the Paris Peace Conference* argued that the Allied refusal to contemplate the return of any of the German colonies was justified because of her poor reputation as a colonial power and because 'the burden of miscalculation would fall well-nigh exclusively upon the helpless natives'. This was not a convincing argument. Germany's colonial record had differed little from that of the other imperial powers, and was certainly better than that of Leopold of the Belgians in the Congo, though not, in fairness, of that of the Belgian government once it replaced the king as the responsible party. The fairness of the colonial settlement was, like reparations, an issue which came to trouble commentators and politicians in Britain, and a proposed revision of its terms often formed part of later attempts to appease Hitler, although it is doubtful whether either he, or the Weimar leaders, rated the question as highly as their British counterparts hoped or feared.[12]

THE COLLAPSE OF OTTOMAN POWER

The collapse of the Ottoman empire posed similar problems to the collapse of the Russian, Austro-Hungarian and German empires in eastern Europe and had parallel consequences. What new authority would replace the old regime at the centre, and who would inherit the legacy of the empire in its outlying regions? The confusion of contending candidates seeking to fill the vacuum, and the manner in which their expectations had been raised by contradictory promises from one or more of the great powers, seeking a temporary advantage at times of pressing urgency during the war, were shared experiences. The Middle East had the added refinement that three of the Big Four had direct interests in the region, though the Americans, who were not at war with the Ottomans, tried to act as a restraining force. The Italians had ambitions, which had indeed been recognised and encouraged by the Treaty of London in 1915, but it was the rivalry between France and Britain which assumed a particular importance in the negotiations. As in eastern Europe, the problems of this region were never entirely ignored by the peacemakers, but they did tend to have a lower priority than the German

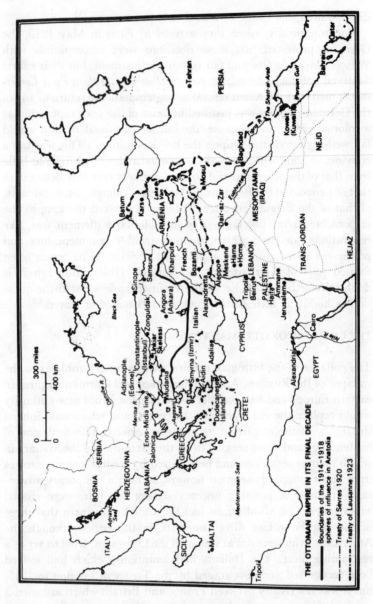

Map 3   The Ottoman Empire in its final decade (Reprinted with permission from Marion Kent (ed.), *The Great Powers and the End of the Ottoman Empire*, George Allen & Unwin, 1984, p. xii.)

settlement, and thus their resolution took a long time. There was a vital difference, however, in that the presence of over 1 million British troops gave the conference a real authority in the Middle East, at least at the outset. The gradual dissipation of that authority, the tragic over-ambition of the Greeks in the Near East and the re-emergence of a revived nationalist force under Mustapha Kemal in Turkey, forced a revision of the first attempt by the conference to establish a new order.

The outbreak of war between the *Entente* and the Turks in November 1914 caused a revolution in British (and, to a lesser extent, in French) attitudes towards the future of the Ottoman empire. Throughout the nineteenth century Britain had a particular interest in Constantinople and the control of the Straits since the implications for her naval supremacy were enormous if the Russians had free access to the Mediterranean from bases in the Black Sea. Thus she tried to limit the erosion of Turkish power in Asia and to preserve, as far as possible, the authority of the Ottomans, particularly *vis-à-vis* the Russians, despite the misgivings which the Turkish treatment of their subject peoples sometimes caused. This seemed to her the best way of safeguarding the approaches to India without herself assuming enormous burdens in Arabia, Afghanistan and Persia. That policy was less clearcut in the twentieth century than it had been in the nineteenth, and certainly less successful: the Ottoman empire lost 32.7 per cent of its population and a fifth of its territory within a generation, whilst its foreign debts were so huge that, by 1914, a quarter of its state revenue was controlled by the Ottoman Public Debt Administration, a body imposed upon the empire by the powers in 1881. Nonetheless the British and French acceptances of Russia's demand for Constantinople and the Straits, on 12 March and 18 April 1915 respectively, signalled a remarkable transformation. This carried important consequences for Britain, which had already annexed Cyprus outright and declared a protectorate over Egypt, abandoning any pretence of a Turkish role. It implied also a reversal of her traditional policy of keeping the Straits closed, and after the Russian collapse created a new dilemma about the future status of Constantinople. In their January 1918 speeches both Lloyd George and Wilson promised the Turks secure sovereignty in the lands 'which are predominantly Turkish in race'. For Lloyd George these lands included Constantinople, provided that the Straits were opened and internationalised, but Wilson was less clear. Elsewhere it seemed unlikely that the Ottoman empire would survive an Allied victory.[13]

That victory was a long time in the making. The Gallipoli and Kut campaigns were failures, which exacted a high toll of men, money and, perhaps most importantly, prestige. Faced with the unexpectedly vigorous opposition of an empire that was supposed to have been ailing throughout the nineteenth century, and with the proof of new Turkish atrocities, most notably of their massacre of over a million Armenians in 1915–16, a consensus hostile to the Turks emerged from the previous divisions within the British political spectrum. Gladstone's policy, that the Turk must be ejected from Europe, 'bag and baggage', was now adopted even by Conservatives erstwhile sympathetic to the empire. The collapse of Russia in 1917, and Ottoman success against the resulting fledgling Transcaucasian republics of Georgia, Armenia and Azerbaijan in 1918, freed the Turks from danger in that quarter. The British, with their Arab allies, gained great victories in the Middle East in 1917 and 1918 but could not hope to menace the Turkish heartlands until 1919. It was only with the long-delayed break-out of the Allied forces at Salonika in September 1918, and their rapid defeat of Bulgaria, that Constantinople was in real and imminent danger. When the collapse came, however, it was sudden and complete. The new Turkish government, which replaced the previous Committee of Union and Progress government, sought an armistice in mid-October, and to British surprise accepted their full list of twenty-four conditions without question. The British negotiator had been instructed that only the first four, including the opening of the Straits, were vital and that the rest were negotiable, or even dispensable. The armistice, signed at Mudros on 30 October 1918, marked a complete Allied, largely British, triumph. As Nicolson boasted, 'The Ottoman Empire lay at our feet dismembered and impotent, its capital and Caliph at the mercy of our guns'. It is thus ironic that the Turkish treaty proved to be the longest and most difficult to finalise, and that, despite this abject surrender, it would be the only negotiated treaty of the entire settlement.[14]

THE PEACE SETTLEMENT IN THE NEAR EAST

It was in part the completeness of the Allied success which was to be their undoing. If they had acted quickly once the conference began, it is probable that they could have forced the compliant government in Constantinople to accept their terms without question. The Allies not only believed that this situation would endure indefinitely, but also, in some cases, came to see even the Turkish portions of the Ottoman empire as available areas in which to compensate the smaller powers, particularly the Greeks and Italians, for disappointments elsewhere. Turkey was unlikely to rate a high priority in peacemaking in any case, but it is probable that Allied complacency had some part in its neglect during the early stages of the negotiations. Indeed not only did the Four do little to advance the settlement in the Near East, they made that settlement much more difficult to achieve. They had sketched the outlines of a possible settlement by the end of June, but this depended upon the American acceptance of mandates for Constantinople and the Straits, and Armenia. This was unlikely, but the uncertainty helped the delay. Meanwhile their decision on 6 May to allow the Greeks to land troops at Izmir (Smyrna) was to unleash a fateful set of consequences which altered the face, not only of the settlement, but also of the entire Near East.[15]

Both the Greeks and the Italians claimed territory in Anatolia. The Italians argued that the Treaty of St Jean de Maurienne entitled them to the Izmir area, whilst the Treaty of London had promised them a share in any break-up of the Ottoman empire. Britain and France accepted, reluctantly, the validity of the London agreement, but held that the lack of Russian ratification invalidated the former. Wilson recognised none of these arrangements. The Greeks had no prior promises, but relied instead upon the charm and personality of their premier, Venizelos, who presented his country's considerable demands to the Ten on 3 and 4 February. He sought Northern Epirus from Albania; the islands of the eastern Mediterranean; western Thrace from Bulgaria and eastern Thrace from Turkey; Izmir (where there was a substantial Greek population) and Aidan and Bursa (where there was not). In the inevitable expert commission the British and French favoured the Greek claims in Anatolia, the Americans objected to foreign sovereignty in Asia Minor, and the Italians, discomfited, largely withdrew from the discussions, and began landing troops in Adalia. It was this action and their wider boycott of the conference over Fiume in April 1919 which clinched the decision in favour of the Greeks.[16]

It has been claimed that 'this diplomatic decision was perhaps one of the least defensible of the twentieth century'. Lloyd George, who had a large hand in it, was consistent in his encouragement of Greek ambitions throughout the prolonged negotiations, though he did not necessarily back his words with practical support. He may have been seeking to substitute an Anglo-Greek understanding in Asia Minor for the more traditional pro-Turkish policy of previous British governments, in the hope of using Greek forces to bolster the British position. He was certainly much impressed with Venizelos, whose vision of a 'Greater Greece' he shared. His Philhellenism, which sometimes went to extreme lengths, was to play a major part in the unfolding tragedy. The ostensible reason for permitting the Greeks to land in Izmir was to prevent the massacre of the local Greek population, but the real motives, shared by Clemenceau, Wilson (who reversed the stance taken by his experts) and Lloyd George were to punish the Italians, to limit their influence in Asia Minor, and (perhaps) to strengthen the Greek hand in Anatolia. The results were disastrous, even if the Greeks and Italians were forced to come to an all-round resolution of their differences in the Tittoni–Venizelos agreement of July 1919. The unsupervised Greek landings on 15 May led not to order but to chaos, and to atrocities against the Turkish inhabitants, which in turn fuelled anti-Greek, anti-Allied and pro-Nationalist sentiment in Turkey.[17]

In an attempt to regain control over dissident Ottoman forces in Anatolia, which were opposing both the Allies and the official government, the Sultan despatched General Mustapha Kemal on 19 May 1919 to restore order. Instead the 38-year-old hero of the Gallipoli campaign began to organise resistance. His dismissal by the government in July was ineffective, and he established a viable national movement with realistic goals, backed by an increasingly strong base in Anatolia, beyond the reach of the Allies or the Sultan. The National Pact, endorsed by congresses at Erzerum and Sivas between July and September, demanded a sovereign, independent and secular Turkish state based upon the principle of self-determination. His astute leadership led to a compromise with the Sultan, but Kemal's position was much improved by elections in January 1920 which returned a Nationalist majority. His movement was misinterpreted and underestimated, particularly by the British who dismissed him as a bandit, and was largely ignored by the Allies as they returned to the Near Eastern problem, in the new situation created by America's rejection of Versailles.[18]

FROM VERSAILLES TO SÈVRES

In late 1919 and early 1920 Britain and France reached agreement upon the shape of a settlement in the Near East. Anatolia would be divided into spheres of Italian and French influence under nominal Turkish sovereignty. The Greeks would gain most of Thrace and be given the opportunity to govern Izmir for the crucial five years before a plebiscite would determine its fate. Initially Lloyd George and Curzon secured Clemenceau's assent to a plan for an indepen-dent state at the Straits and the expulsion of the Turks from Europe, but the British cabinet rejected their scheme, fearing repercussions in India. Instead the Straits would be controlled by an international commission. These decisions were incorporated into the Treaty of Sèvres drafted at the Conference of London, 12 February to 10 April 1920, and finalised at the San Remo meeting on 24 April. The Turkish armed forces were limited to 50,000 men, including 35,000 gendarmes. In addition to the loss of their Arabian territories, Armenia would remain an independent state, although its frontiers had yet to be determined by Wilson, to whom the Allies turned in the vain hope that America might assume the responsibility to the new state which they themselves shirked. The vague possibility of an independent Kurdistan was also mooted. There was to be special protection for minorities and provision for foreign financial control.[19]

Aware that the harsh terms of this imperialist treaty would encourage resistance, the Allies sought to show their resolve by occupying Constantinople on 16 March 1920. They did succeed in forcing the Sultan to sign the treaty on 10 August 1920, but the signature was under protest, and its value was increasingly dubious as events in Turkey gradually sapped the authority of the central government. Kemal, now under sentence of death from the client government in Constantinople, established a new parliament in Ankara (Angora), the Grand National Assembly, which he eventu-ally persuaded, in January 1921, to accept complete responsibility for the affairs of the state and declare him president. His position was far from secure, and an attack on British forces at Ismid in June provoked a successful but limited Greek offensive, which halted in July, when a further advance might have crushed the Nationalists. Thereafter an improving domestic and international atmosphere strengthened Kemal's hand. The fall of Venizelos in Greece, after King Alexander died from the bite of a pet monkey in October, transformed the scene. There were signs that the French and Italians resented being bound by what they saw, not unreasonably, as an essentially British settlement, and would welcome a revision of the treaty. In Britain there was a strong lobby, resisted by Lloyd George and Curzon, which also pressed for more generous treatment for the Turks and the abandonment of support for the Greeks, a policy which grew more attractive when, in December, a referendum endorsed the return of King Constantine, the ex-Kaiser's brother-in-law. Kemal also skilfully exploited a relationship with the Soviet Union, which he kept at arm's length, but which brought substantial aid in 1922.[20]

FROM SÈVRES TO LAUSANNE

By 1921 it was clear that the Sèvres settlement was unworkable, even the Sultan would not ratify it, and Lloyd George's colleagues were pressing for revision. The conference held in London between February and March 1921, which tried to reconcile the demands of the Greeks, the Nationalists and the Constantinople government, ended in failure. Despite Constantine's return Lloyd George remained very supportive of the Greeks and wished to believe their promises that they could enforce the treaty. He undermined the conference decisions by inferring that a Greek attack on Kemal would be welcome, and the intercepted and decoded telegrams containing this information, which the Greek delegation sent home, were highly embarrassing to the British government. So too were the results of the renewed Greek attack, which was repulsed in March, the first serious set-back they had suffered, whilst Kemal's position was strengthened by negotiations with Italy and France. In April the Allies declared their neutrality in the fighting, and alarmed that their troops in Constantinople and the Straits might become involved in a Nationalist backlash, the British offered to mediate. The Greeks refused, and mounted a summer offensive which made good progress until held at Kemal's well-prepared positions before Ankara in August. In September they retreated, and although they did so in good order, their failure was fatal to their hopes of imposing a military solution.[21]

Curzon's attempts to reach a negotiated Greek withdrawal from Asia Minor in return for Thrace remaining Greek dragged into 1922. Even when, in March at a conference in Paris, he secured

Greek acceptance of an unconditional withdrawal and a compromise frontier in Thrace, he could not bring the matter to a peaceful conclusion. The Nationalists demanded an immediate withdrawal, and were bolstered by what Curzon saw as 'treacherous' negotiations by the French and Italians. Already the French had reached an agreement with Kemal, negotiated on 20 October 1921 by the French politician Henri Franklin-Bouillon (irreverently rechristened 'Boiling Frankie' by British diplomats). In return for a French withdrawal from Asia Minor, they gained economic concessions, and recognition of their Syrian frontier. This unilateral declaration of peace enraged the British, but worse was to come in January 1922, after Briand's ill-advised game of golf with Lloyd George. Lloyd George's warning to Briand, that he should not stand in front of the ball whilst it was being driven, otherwise 'Briand couic! et alors . . . Poincaré', proved prophetic when Briand fell from office and Britain's least favourite Frenchman became premier. Now Poincaré let the Turks know that the Paris terms were not necessarily final. Curzon was flabbergasted: 'Here is Poincaré telling the Turks to tear up the agreement on which his signature is still wet. And these are our allies.' Hardinge was not surprised by Poincaré's behaviour: 'I regard him as a dirty dog, a man of very mean character'. All this was not helped by strong British suspicions that the French and Italians were supplying Kemal with arms.[22]

Anglo-French relations reached their nadir in the aftermath of the Greek rout in the summer of 1922. The failure to produce a diplomatic solution was followed by Kemal's August offensive which drove the Greeks out of Izmir and Asia Minor, amid atrocity and counter-atrocity. Kemal's troops took Izmir on 9 September. Their continued advance threatened the British forces guarding the Straits at Chanak, and a new war loomed. Britain's allies made it plain that they would not fight, whilst the only British Dominions to respond positively to Britain's 13 September appeal for help were New Zealand and Newfoundland. Curzon attempted to tell Poincaré a few home truths at an Anglo-French meeting in Paris on 19 September but this rebounded sharply, and he had to be led from the room by Hardinge: '"Charley", he panted, "I can't bear that horrid little man. I can't bear him". He wept.' Curzon withdrew his remarks, Poincaré apologised, the meeting resumed, the Turks were invited to renegotiate the peace settlement, and hostilities were averted at Chanak by a combination of luck and good sense. This outcome was

not helped by an enthusiastic group in the British cabinet, including
Lloyd George, Churchill and Chamberlain, who seemed bent on
war. Following upon the prime minister's dealings with the Soviets,
and the Anglo-Irish treaty, this proved too much for the rank-and-
file Tories, and their revolt destroyed the coalition and drove Lloyd
George permanently from office.[23]

The renewed peace negotiations, held over two phases from 20
November 1922 to 4 February 1923, and from 23 April until 24 July
1923, at Lausanne in Switzerland, were dominated by the two
British representatives, Curzon (who retained the Foreign Office in
the new government) and Sir Horace Rumbold, the High Commissioner at Constantinople. Armed with little more than the two-
edged sword of their knowledge of Turkish intentions gleaned from
their intelligence sources, the two men managed, often against odds
which seemed insuperable, to achieve a settlement which satisfied
everyone sufficiently to make it workable, though the British and
Turks were happier with the outcome than the French and Italians.
Eastern Thrace, Izmir and some of the Aegean islands were returned to Turkey whilst new rules were agreed controlling the
passage of warships through the Straits, under the supervision of an
international commission. The only military restriction placed on
Turkey was a small demilitarised zone along the Straits, whilst all
the financial and extra-territorial privileges enjoyed by the powers
were removed. The destiny of Mosul, disputed between Turkey and
the British mandate of Iraq, became the responsibility of the
League, which awarded it to Iraq in 1925. That part of Armenia
which lay in the former Russian empire was abandoned to the
USSR, and the project to create a new Armenian state from the
former Turkish lands in Anatolia was dropped. There was a rather
brutal exchange of minorities between Greece and Turkey, but more
positively, the Turks joined the League and accepted its minority
guarantees.[24]

The signature of the Treaty of Lausanne on 24 July 1923 was the
last act of a peacemaking process which had taken longer than the
Great War itself. It was by far the most successful and enduring of
the settlements, surviving, in its essentials, though the Straits Convention was modified at Montreux in 1936, until the present. The
Sultanate was abolished, to be followed by the Caliphate in 1924,
and the birth of an independent, strong and relatively homogeneous
Turkish Republic under the presidency of Mustapha Kemal, signalled

the end of the Eastern Question. The fact that the treaty was negotiated rather than imposed is certainly important, but equally significant is the point that the demands of the main parties were realistic,
limited and attainable. It would be dangerous and simplistic to make
too much of the former, and to ignore the latter, when drawing
comparisons between Versailles and Lausanne, nor should the importance of the leadership of Kemal be forgotten. Perhaps the real lesson is
that both sides at Lausanne understood the meaning of defeat as well
as victory and negotiated in that light.

WARTIME DEVELOPMENTS IN THE MIDDLE EAST

Just as it is possible to recognise the current shape of eastern Europe in
the Versailles Settlement, so there is a clear correlation between the
current pattern of states in the Middle East and the map redrawn in
1919 and immediately afterwards. Some of the names have changed:
Mesopotamia (Iraq), Trans-Jordan (Jordan), the Hijaz (Saudi Arabia); some, like Syria and Lebanon, have remained the same. Palestine (Israel) has changed its name but we remain familiar with the
original because it continues to reflect one of the long-term problems
created by the war and its consequences. Nor are the borders exactly as
they were in 1919, but the broad outline of the Middle East of today
may be discerned. The parallel with eastern Europe was not sustained
in one vital respect, however, for only Arabia emerged as an independent state from the conference. The other parts all fell into the ambit,
in varying degrees, of the great powers, whose empires, nominally at
least, were vastly expanded by the conference.[25]

The probability that the Ottoman empire would become part of the
spoils of war encouraged Britain to decide what her aims were, to
reconcile her wishes with those of her allies, particularly the French,
and to ensure that the war was won. It was the conflicting demands of
these pressures which drove the British into a series of complex deals
with a variety of partners, a process aptly described as selling 'the same
horse, or at least parts of the same horse, twice'. The Constantinople
agreement was followed by the Treaty of London, 26 April 1915, which
promised Italy a share in any partition of the German and Turkish
empires. The Sykes–Picot agreement, 16 May 1916, divided the
Ottoman empire between the Russians, the British and the French,
with provision for an independent Arabian state, or confederation of
states. This was amended by the abortive Treaty of St Jean de

Maurienne, 19–21 April 1917, which gave the Italians a stake in Asia Minor. The Russians dropped out of the war without ratifying this treaty, which was substantially amended, to Italy's detriment and the advantage of Greece, in 1919. The Russian claims lapsed, thus leaving the field open for Anglo-French domination. These arrangements between the great powers were supplemented in Britain's case by a series of bargains struck with other forces either in the region or felt to be influential in world opinion.[26]

It is interesting to note that, whereas in eastern Europe, the British were initially reluctant to employ revolutionary tactics against the traditional rulers, they had no such inhibitions when it came to the Turks. In October 1914 Lord Cromer suggested that 'a few officers who could speak Arabic, if sent into Arabia, could raise the whole country against the Turks'. Others had the same idea, and from this, particularly after the failure of the Gallipoli expedition, sprang the negotiations between the British and the Arab leaders which precipi- tated the great revolt in the desert, inextricably linked with the name of T. E. Lawrence, Lawrence of Arabia. In 1915 and 1916 Sir Henry McMahon, the British High Commissioner in Egypt, agreed in princi- ple to the demands of the Sherif of Mecca, Hussein, that as the price of a revolt, Britain would recognise a large and independent Arab Kingdom, subject to certain reservations in territories of direct interest to Britain and France. These were the districts of Mersina and Alexandretta and portions of Syria, together with Baghdad and Basra, where 'special administrative arrangements' would be required to protect Britain's established political and economic interests. The key letter in their correspondence was that of 24 October 1915, later described as 'hopelessly muddle-headed' in its drafting. In particular it disguised the probable extent of French influence within Syria, and it left ambiguous the destiny of Palestine, since the letter referred to areas of Syria 'west of the *vilayets* of Damascus, Homs, Hama and Aleppo'. Since *vilayet* can mean either 'district' or 'province' this loose drafting was to lead to complications, although it seems likely that McMahon meant 'district', and hence did not exclude Palestine from the Arab area. On the other hand, the letter was not a precise agreement, merely a declaration of intent in a continuing correspondence about the possibility of an Arab revolt, though that was not how Hussein perceived it.[27]

Later the British also sought to invoke worldwide Jewish assistance for their cause (not least in revolutionary Russia) by issuing the Balfour

Declaration of 2 November 1917. This stated that 'His Majesty's Government view with favour the establishment in Palestine of a National home for the Jewish people.' Was Palestine now the 'twice-promised land'? Yet, despite all their previous arrangements and agreements, some of which embarrassingly had been published by the Bolsheviks, Britain and France sought to reassure the Arabs with their declaration of 7 November 1918 that they were fighting for 'the complete and definite emancipation of the peoples so long oppressed by the Turks and the establishment of national governments and administrations deriving their authority from the initiative and free choice of the indigenous populations'. To what extent were these undertakings contradictory and mutually incompatible? Further, would they stand the test of the conference and the changes in international circumstances since their creation, most notably the collapse of Russia as a great power and the larger-than-anticipated British share in the victory?[28]

Part of the answer lies in what Britain meant by Arab 'independence' and here Milner's definition during the conference is revealing, 'what we mean by it is that Arabia while being independent herself should be kept out of the sphere of European political intrigue and within the British sphere of influence: in other words that her independent native rulers should have no foreign treaties except with us'. This concept of an area which would continue to need European assistance and protection echoed that of wartime officials and advisers. This deliberately ambiguous approach to the Arabs may help to explain the thinking behind the Sykes–Picot agreement. It would be sensible, from an Anglo-French standpoint, to clarify their mutual spheres of influence in the region, and to exclude ambiguity in their relationship, which was always of much greater mutual importance than any arrangement with the Arabs, which few British or French advisers believed would amount to much. Hence the Sykes–Picot agreement divided the region into sections, with varying degrees of Anglo-French or Allied control. Between Cilicia, coastal Syria and Lebanon, which were to be French, and Baghdad and Basra, which were to be British, they were prepared to recognise an independent Arab state or states, with the proviso that the area was divided into two portions, 'A' (blue) and 'B' (red): 'In the blue area France, and in the red area Great Britain, shall be allowed to establish such direct or indirect control as they may desire and as they may think fit to arrange with the

Arab State or Confederation of Arab States'. Palestine was reserved to an international administration, the form of which was to be decided after consultation with Russia, then the other allies, and Hussein.[29]

Although the Italians were cut in on this deal in 1917 by the treaty of St Jean de Maurienne, the key developments in the Middle East were the collapse of Russia (which left the St Jean treaty unratified) and the striking successes of the British forces in the region. In 1917 Allenby captured Baghdad and Jerusalem and, in 1918, Damascus and Syria. The Russian collapse removed an important player and rival from the game and altered significantly the British perception of the role of France in the region. Whereas before Britain had been anxious to interpose the French between her spheres of influence and the Russians, this no longer seemed so important, and France now appeared more as a rival than as a useful buffer. Further, the fact that the vast majority of Allied forces in the area were British encouraged them to believe that the wartime agreements should be adjusted in their favour, particularly in oil-rich Mosul and in Palestine. Clemenceau, whose main priorities were European and whose interest in, and knowledge of, the Middle East were minimal, was not averse to a readjustment. It is unlikely, however, that his generosity in London in December 1918 was entirely due to emotion at his reception from the cheering crowds. According to Lloyd George, Clemenceau 'asked me what it was I specially wanted from the French. I instantly replied that I wanted Mosul attached to Irak, and Palestine from Dan to Beersheba under British control. Without hesitation he agreed.' Clemenceau clearly believed that this gesture would be reciprocated, probably by British support for France on the Rhine, a share in the oil of Mosul, and the honouring of the remainder of the Sykes–Picot agreement. If so, he was to be disappointed, particularly during the Rhineland debates, whilst there was already a powerful lobby in Britain questioning the wisdom of French control in Syria. The bitterness resulting from this Anglo-French misunderstanding was unfortunate and persistent.[30]

THE MIDDLE EAST AT THE CONFERENCE

The conference did not reach its final decisions on the Middle East until April 1920, by which time many of the conditions prevailing at its outset had dramatically altered. The peacemakers were faced with a complex web of interconnecting problems and aspirations, which led to a series of clashes: between the great powers, most notably Britain and France; between the powers and the representatives of the indigenous populations; between the powers and Zionists; and between Arabs and Zionists. As in eastern Europe, the powers found themselves trying to come to terms with their earlier encouragement of the ideals of self-determination and nationalism, with the added complication of their own aspirations in the area. The principle of mandates helped to present the ambitions of the European powers in a form acceptable to Wilson, but the question of their allocation remained thorny and unresolved. The withdrawal of the Americans, the re-emergence of a Russian threat, in the shape of bolshevism, and the revival of Turkish fortunes under Mustapha Kemal also posed additional problems as time passed, although in the event, the renegotiation of the Sèvres settlement at Lausanne did not greatly affect the arrangements for the non-Turkish parts of the Ottoman empire.

Syria

The single most difficult question which arose in Paris was the future of Syria. The Arab delegation was led by Emir Feisal, Hussein's son. There is no doubt that they added an air of romance to the proceedings, even Robert Lansing was moved to poetic prose when describing Feisal: 'his manner of address and the tones of voice seemed to breathe the perfume of frankincense and to suggest the presence of richly colored divans, green turbans, and the glitter of gold and jewels'. Yet they were also an embarrassing reminder of the difficulties ahead, indeed it was only upon British insistence that the French were moved to grant the delegation official status at the conference. On 6 February Feisal presented his case to the Ten. He argued for the independence, and eventual unification, of the Arab peoples in Asia, and condemned the Sykes–Picot agreement. He did not oppose the idea of assistance from a mandatory power, but he pressed for the right of the population to choose its own mandatory. Arab nationalism now threatened European calculations. The French knew that Feisal had already suggested that whereas Mesopotamia might need a mandatory power, Syria did not. Even if forced to accept a mandatory power, the population would not choose France, yet the French regarded Syria as theirs, whether or not it was mandated to them. Lloyd George's advisers warned him of the importance of Anglo-French cooperation, but he was determined to exploit the Syrian issue to Britain's advantage both in the Middle East and in forcing the French to accept British solutions in Europe, and this led to some acerbic exchanges with the French during a series of unofficial negotiations outside the conference in February and March.[31]

In an attempt to reconcile Arab and French aspirations, the British had proposed various deals to the French which fell far short of the Sykes–Picot arrangements and which weakened French control in Syria to the point of non-existence. In return they offered Lebanon and Alexandretta to France. Clemenceau was outraged: 'Lloyd George is a cheat. He has managed to turn me into a "Syrian".' When the Middle East was discussed at the Council of Four on 20 March Pichon insisted on a French mandate for Syria, whereas Lloyd George, claiming to be the Arab champion, resisted this. Wilson proposed a commission to test opinion in Syria which Clemenceau accepted, provided its terms were to encompass Mesopotamia and the other areas of interest to Britain. Clemenceau believed he had done well, and that his support of Wilson's proposal would, at one stroke, embarrass the British and bring Wilson round to his policy in the Rhineland, but his advisers were appalled. They knew that the commission would reveal the weakness of support for France in Syria, and saw Clemenceau's actions as bordering on the insane. 'They must be drunk the way they are surrendering . . . a total capitulation, a mess, an unimaginable shambles', Paul Cambon expostulated, whilst the *Quai d'Orsay* took the highly unusual step of organising a press campaign against its own government's Middle Eastern policy, the success of which put Clemenceau under pressure from French public opinion.[32]

Other issues dominated the conference throughout much of April and May and, in the event, the commission never really materialised. It was sabotaged, by accident or design, by the continuing Anglo-French confrontation. The European states refused to send representatives on the commission, which became an entirely American affair. The findings, in August, of the King–Crane commission were not officially made known to the conference, but everyone knew they confirmed that the Syrians did not want the French as mandatories, preferring the Americans, or the British. 'A report hardly likely to improve Anglo-French relations', commented one British official, and indeed the Middle East did bring relations between the two states to a very low ebb. The British refusal to evacuate Syria to allow French troops to replace them; the cancellation of the Long–Berenger agreement on the apportioning of oil supplies from Mosul and elsewhere; and what he saw as British avarice and Lloyd George's ill-faith, drove Clemenceau to the point of apparently offering to fight a duel with Lloyd George. The Syrian question continued to drift as the Four finalised the German settlement in May and June, though it became clear that the Americans would not accept a mandate, and that the only possible candidates were the French. Balfour remarked that the inhabitants could indeed 'freely choose; but it is Hobson's choice after all'.[33]

Palestine

The future of Palestine was an added complication, inextricably linked to the Syrian issue, not least because the Arabs claimed Palestine as part of Syria. Lloyd George and Balfour were deeply committed to the Zionist cause and to the idea of a British mandate in Palestine. Quite why is not clear; there were certain strategic advantages to Britain, but British control in Palestine was not dependent upon the success of the Zionist cause. British and French observers shared the view that if the Jews were given a special position, the Palestinian mandate would become a poisoned chalice, with the mandatory merely acting to keep Jews and Arabs from killing each other.[34] Sir Mark Sykes discovered, in a two-month visit to Palestine and Syria in late 1918 and early 1919, that there was strong local opposition both to the Zionists and to the Sykes–Picot agreement, but he died of influenza shortly after his return to Paris, before he could convince others of the need for a reappraisal of policy. Nonetheless Balfour knew that Britain was in a difficult position since she was supporting Arab self-determination in Syria against French interests, but had to argue for its suspension in Palestine, where 'If the present inhabitants were consulted they would unquestionably give an anti-Jewish verdict', a judgement which the King–Crane commission confirmed.[35]

The Ten heard the Zionist case on 27 February when Dr Chaim Weizmann, a Jewish scientist who enjoyed a very close relationship with Lloyd George and Balfour, argued that the empty spaces of Palestine could accommodate at least 4 to 5 million Jews 'without encroaching on the legitimate interests of the people already there'. Eventually, after some years of immigration, when they 'formed the large majority, they would be ripe to establish such a Government as would answer to the state of development of the country and to their ideals'. Although Weizmann and Feisal enjoyed amicable relations in Paris, there was no doubt that Arab and Jewish aspirations were incompatible, and that Britain's association with the Zionist cause must affect her relationship with the Arabs. Curzon, who was not noted for his willingness to give up British influence, feared that British support of the Zionist claim to a homeland would develop into support for a Jewish state, and looked to Wilson's Middle East commission to extricate Britain from this situation. This did not happen, and Britain became entangled in a labyrinth from which she has still not entirely escaped.[36]

FROM VERSAILLES TO SAN REMO

The Four proved unable to reach a settlement in the former Ottoman territories and it was left to their successors to complete the task. The broader consequences of the continuing Anglo-French acrimony, particularly in dealings with Turkey, aided by the pressure on Britain's military and financial resources imposed by her worldwide commitments, convinced Lloyd George that an accommodation must be reached with France in the Middle East. At Deauville on 15 September Lloyd George accepted that British forces would evacuate Syria and Cilicia and be replaced by the French. By November this had occurred, whilst in October Feisal was told to reach the best deal he could with France. Trapped between the powers and the rising tide of Arab nationalism, Feisal felt betrayed by the British, but there was little doubt that Britain's relationship with France was of paramount importance. If forced to choose between French demands for control in Syria and Arab aspirations, particularly at a time when Hussein and Feisal were being eclipsed as Arab leaders by the formidable Ibn Saud, Britain would have no option but to support France. This policy was dictated by the need for French assistance in the enforcement of the wider settlement, and by an underlying community of interests in the Middle East, despite their bitter quarrels. Balfour was quite candid: 'Neither of us wants much less than supreme economic and political control, to be exercised no doubt (at least in our case) in friendly and unostentatious cooperation with the Arabs – but nevertheless, in the last resort, to be exercised.'[37]

This control was threatened in late 1919 by the possibility of links between increasing Arab unrest and the Kemalist movement in Turkey, creating the danger of a great anti-European crusade. Feisal, reluctantly, tried to make terms with the French, but since their aim was little short of total control, he found this very difficult. His attempts to enlist the support of Syrian nationalism merely left him squeezed between two implacable forces. Feisal was offered the throne of an independent Greater Syria, including Lebanon and Palestine, by an assembly in Damascus on 8 March 1920. Simultaneously, a group of Iraqi officers present in Damascus proclaimed the independence of Iraq, with Feisal's brother Abdullah as king, and announced their common cause with the Syrians. Neither Britain nor France was prepared to make concessions to this movement, and at an inter-Allied conference at San Remo in April 1920, they finalised the details of the Middle Eastern settlement, largely ignoring the Arabs, despite Curzon's complaints of harassment: 'Syrians, Zionists, Armenians. . . . They take rooms in the same hotels as we are in and they dog our footsteps wherever we go.' Feisal's Syrian subjects refused to accept the reality of French control, even after their forces were defeated and Damascus occupied in late July. Feisal abandoned his hopeless task and left Syria on 1 August. In 1921 the British made him king of Mesopotamia.[38]

The British and French had already reached agreement, at the London conference in February 1920, on the frontier between Palestine and Syria, which gave Lloyd George his line from Dan to Beersheba, and on the French proposal for the frontier between Syria and Turkey. A new oil agreement, which was very similar to the Long–Berenger agreement dropped the previous year, was concluded at San Remo on 26 April. The mandates for Syria and Lebanon went to France, those for Palestine and Mesopotamia to Britain, under terms which they themselves proposed. The boundaries between the British and French mandates were not finalised until December 1920, and the whole arrangement was only sanctioned by the League on 24 July 1922.[39]

The American withdrawal, and the Italian role as ineffective spectators, reduced the question of the future of the Middle East to an Anglo-French affair. It is generally agreed that their response to the challenge was in the worst traditions of pre-war imperialism, despite their wartime promises. Yet, ironically, this part of the overall settlement contributed little to Anglo-French goodwill, with Lloyd George and Clemenceau exchanging artillery barrages throughout the negotiations, and reaching agreement only grudgingly and under pressure. The settlement paid little attention to the needs of the native populations, but was determined by the requirements of the two powers. Their actions, and their disregard for Arab nationalism, did damage both to the region, and to their own relations with its peoples. Britain managed to keep most of Arabia free from the influence of other powers, but this was about the limit of her success. Her attempts to retain control through client rulers fell apart as they fell out, and she found herself subsidising several sides in a Middle Eastern muddle. France gained control of Syria and Lebanon, but her quarrel with Britain and her bad relations with her new subjects made her grasp insecure and her position always difficult. Curzon had predicted, accurately, that the French 'do not realize what they are in for'. Serious uprisings in Syria, Palestine and Iraq during 1920 revealed the depth of Arab resentment at this imposed settlement, a resentment which has continued to play a part in the troubled history of the region since the end of the Great War.[40]

Conclusion

'We are digging up the foundations of a very old world.'

ANYONE who has served on a committee will, upon reflection, appreciate the overwhelming nature of the task facing the peacemakers
in 1919. It is so often the complex inter-relationships between
decisions either taken, or not yet taken but which should have been,
which cause even relatively simple problems to become the subject
of endless, frequently fruitless, discussion. There is, apparently,
rarely an ideal time at which to decide any issue, and certainly no
ideal point of departure. Yet in Paris the problem was hardly simple;
it was nothing less than to reshape the world, the nature of states
and international relations in a new image. Promises had been
made, expectations and aspirations raised, either deliberately or by
accident, and now these pledges had to be redeemed. This study has
arranged the questions and dilemmas facing the statesmen and
diplomats into relatively neat packages, but this was not how they
reached the conference, and many were either insoluble or raised
agonising issues of principle or practicality, and frequently both.
Everything was happening at once, worldwide, and on a massive
scale, the sheer enormity and responsibility of the task were awe-
some. The Four and their colleagues did not need to be told by the
Germans that their decisions could cause the death of millions, they
were aware constantly of that possibility. Yet, as for books and
student essays, there was a deadline; decisions had to be taken, on
countless individual occasions, with imperfect information, under
pressure, frequently when those responsible were both mentally and
physically exhausted. And then the next decision had to be taken,
probably on a new, apparently unrelated topic, and this went on day
after day in an unremitting round, whilst the rest of the world
refused to stand still to allow them a breathing space.

James Joll's speculation as to how the pressure of the 1914 July
crisis may have forced the key decision-makers to rely upon their
inner resources of upbringing and character, their 'unspoken as-

sumptions', seems equally appropriate when considering the experience of the peace conference. Indeed ever since Keynes' classic polemic, the conference has been seen in terms of the personalities and influence of the major figures of Orlando, Clemenceau, Wilson and Lloyd George, and of the interplay between them. This approach is open to the criticism that the process of peacemaking took much longer than the first six months of 1919, that none of the Four was still in office by the end of it, and that it gives a false impression of the real authority of the conference, particularly as the distance from Paris increased. Yet to deny the influence of these men upon the shape and tone of the settlement would itself be a distortion.[1]

Orlando was the least effective member of the group, reflecting both the relative weight of Italy and his own inability to speak English. He was absent more often than the rest and fell from office before the treaty was signed. It would be unwise, however, to discount his influence, not least because Italy's claims were so large and caused some of the bitterest and most difficult negotiations of the conference, leaving an indelible mark on the crisis of April 1919. A lawyer, with a good sense of humour but also a temper which Clemenceau enjoyed provoking, Orlando was, in Lansing's view, 'a statesman rather than a politician. . . . As an opportunist he was a failure.'[2]

Clemenceau was a formidable character, a born survivor with a remarkable political instinct, an amazing constitution, a malicious sense of humour, and few inhibitions about his methods when engaged in a contest – attributes which earned him his nickname, the Tiger. 'He had', wrote Keynes, 'one illusion – France; and one disillusion – mankind, including Frenchmen, and his colleagues not least.' He dominated the conference, reducing the Plenary Sessions to a rubber stamp, and forcing committees to take decisions, whilst his influence in the Four was immense – Lansing declared him 'the strongest man of the many strong men who participated in the negotiations in Paris'. He had little time for Wilson's idealistic schemes, preferring more tangible guarantees of security for a France which he saw as threatened by the overwhelming potential of her neighbour. His integrity and skill as a negotiator were widely recognised, though his detractors pointed to his fiercely dictatorial and individualistic streak, and accused him of neglecting France's wider interests.[3]

Wilson believed he had a great mission to accomplish, he felt 'the dumb eyes of the people' upon him, demanding miracles: an end to war, justice for all, national self-determination, and a world safe for democracy. Men of the intelligence, education and experience of Keynes and Nicolson had similar expectations. When he disappointed them, they turned on him with a startling ferocity: Keynes accused him of being incapable of being 'de-bamboozled' once Lloyd George and Clemenceau had bamboozled him, whilst Nicolson wrote: 'We ceased from that moment to believe that President Wilson was the Prophet whom we had followed. From that moment we saw in him no more than a presbyterian dominie.' Yet, as Wilson pointed out, with belated insight, 'What is expected of me only God could perform'. Wilson fought hard but collapsed under the pressure of the crisis of the conference and compromised his principles. Perhaps the saddest aspect of Wilson's performance was that he refused to accept that he had compromised, and convinced himself that the treaty conformed entirely to his ideals. Thus, both in Paris and in Washington, he became stubborn and unbending at precisely the wrong moments.[4]

Lloyd George is the most fascinating and elusive figure. He had vision, incomparable powers of persuasion and enormous charm, coupled with a cruel and bullying nature. There was an essential and fatal gap between his capacity to set admirable long-term goals and his delight in short-term manipulation. If it was Wilson who went to Paris expecting an 'intellectual treat', it was Lloyd George who came away having had 'a wonderful time'; the game was often more important than the result. His ability to reconcile the irreconcilable was legendary, but it was achieved too often at the price of deceit, and his faith that this would not be discovered was ill-founded. The resulting distrust meant that his immediate successes were often the root of his long-term difficulties. The universal description of Lloyd George is that of 'liar', though this could be expressed in more or less picturesque terms. He was not without principles, though he was not fastidious in their observance, and many of his contributions, in terms of debate and of decisions, were sensible and fair. His feel for compromise, his command of language, the extraordinary quickness of his mind under pressure, his ability to manipulate facts and figures, all are beyond question. And yet . . . The problem with Lloyd George is that one is always left with an 'And yet . . .'[5]

The Four found themselves thrown together, needing to make

decisions, engaged in a race between anarchy and peace. Each had also to pursue long-term goals within the context of domestic democratic structures which often put a premium on short-term issues. The inevitable result was a series of compromises reached under pressure, a situation in which the strongest characters were likely to win: 'We are making headway', Lloyd George told Frances Stevenson, 'which means that I am getting my own way.' To an extent he was right but the final treaty reflected something of each of the Four. It was thus an unhappy mixture of understandable, but not necessarily compatible, motives in which the needs of security, economic and political stability, nationalism and justice all vied with each other.[6]

The central issue in Paris, as it had been before and during the war, and would continue to be after the peace, was Germany. Could this industrial, economic and military giant be accommodated peacefully into a European structure which would allow it a reasonable, but not an overwhelming, role? Wilson hoped that the new Germany would demonstrate the virtues and advantages of his democratic and reformist capitalism, and provide both an advertisement for his system and a trading partner for the United States. Germany could become the dynamo of the new Europe, and her prosperity would encourage peace and stability, a view which Lloyd George came to share, especially after Germany was removed as a naval and colonial threat to the British empire. He also saw Germany as a vital counter to the threat of bolshevism and as a crucial element in the European balance of power which some British decision-makers believed was menaced by France. Clemenceau was more pessimistic; France faced a young, vigorous and expanding German population of over 60 millions, backed by an industrial economy remarkably unscathed by the war. Her own mines, factories and farms in northern France had been wrecked and she could afford her losses of manpower much less than the Germans. Her population of 40 millions was ageing, her birthrate was alarmingly low, and there seemed little prospect of reversing her comparative decline of the later nineteenth century. He was profoundly depressed by the British attitude towards France and by her desire to distance herself from Europe. Twice in his lifetime he had seen German armies in France, and he was determined to ensure that this costly victory brought security to France.

The Anglo-Americans determined that Germany might be reduced but not dismembered. Instead they relied upon a combination of measures to reduce her capacity for mischief, and the hope that the new, democratic, Germany, set in the context of a new, fairer, Europe and in the new, more rational, international structures of the League, would accept a more peaceful and stable role. They resisted, as far as possible, French efforts to build penalties and sanctions for its enforcement into the text of the treaty. Thus, for all its 440 articles there were remarkably few provisions to ensure its enforcement, and those there were tended to be vague or of limited immediate value. Clemenceau doubted the wisdom or effectiveness of this policy. His strategy in Paris aimed at achieving French security and was based upon two main premises: the need for a continuation, in some form, of the wartime cooperation with Britain and America; and an attempt to reduce Germany's potential for expansion and domination. He concentrated on tangible factors such as frontiers, especially in the Rhineland, disarmament and reparations, but also pursued his objectives with a wider variety of methods than previously assumed.[7]

Foch was not pleased with the outcome of the Paris negotiations, 'This is not Peace. It is an Armistice for twenty years', he declared. His prediction proved uncannily accurate, though the outbreak of a second major European war, particularly one of the scale and intensity which came with the expansion of hostilities in 1941, was neither inevitable nor entirely the responsibility of the peacemakers of 1919. In the first place the problems which had caused Europe to explode in 1914 persisted, secondly the exigencies of total war had created new complications and exacerbated old ones. Finally, as Clemenceau and Lloyd George forcefully pointed out, the peace itself was only the starting point. It had to be enforced and kept, what later decision-makers chose to make of it was not their responsibility.[8]

The Four were rapidly removed from office, all, to varying degrees, the victims of the settlement. Orlando went in June 1919, destroyed by Fiume, Wilson lingered until 1920, but his physical exertions, in Paris and on his return to the United States, brought about the stroke in September 1919 which left both himself and the presidency in a curious limbo. Clemenceau's bid for the French presidency was thwarted in January 1920 by the intrigues of jealous rivals seeking revenge. They preferred a nonentity of doubtful mental stability to the powerful Tiger, who was perceived to have delivered less than he had promised, and whose style of leadership left him isolated when the whispering campaign against him in the chamber began. He retired from the premiership to contemplate the efforts of his successors with a sardonic eye. Lloyd George survived longest, though with increasing difficulty, as his Tory partners watched his policies on Ireland and the Soviet Union with gathering distrust. There were growing signs of a Tory backbench revolt which would demand an end to the coalition, whilst liberal opinion was alienated by its dislike of the peace settlement and subsequent developments. Kemal was the straw that broke his back in October 1922. He never returned to office, although only 59, but even his photograph at Chequers terrified those who followed him: Baldwin defaced it and Ramsay MacDonald hid it in a drawer. It was thus other men who had to maintain the settlement and adapt it to changing conditions.[9]

The events of 1917 to 1919 ushered in a strange set of inter-national circumstances in Europe. Russia, Austria-Hungary, the Ottoman empire and Germany were all defeated and temporarily, at least in some cases, destitute. Whereas in 1914 there had been five great European powers (not counting Italy or the Ottomans) in 1919 there were only two, Britain and France (and, perhaps, Italy), but the United States was now an important factor. The vacuum of power in central and eastern Europe was the necessary precondition for the new order there, and enabled Poland, Czechoslovakia and the smaller Baltic states to establish their independence. Austria-Hungary had vanished, but the treaty preserved the independence and essential integrity of Germany, and to an increasing degree, the powers left Russia to work out its own destiny. Could the settlement survive the revival of either German or Russian power, or the revival of both? Could it survive the defection of the United States, which had played such a vital part in winning the war and shaping the peace? It is just possible that, if Britain and France had agreed upon their policies and then cooperated closely to carry them out, they could have imposed their will upon this curiously weakened Europe, but this was not to be. Instead their differing approaches and philosophies served only to cancel out any merit either might have had on its own.

They were divided over their definition of a reasonable role for Germany, and over their attitudes to treaty enforcement. Geography played a major part and the view from Paris was different from that from London. France feared Germany and sought to impose as many restraints upon her as possible, the weaker Germany was the better. Critics of Versailles argued that Germany should have been dismembered and France's frontier moved to the Rhine. Imperfect though the settlement was, however, it still represented the success-ful outcome of a war which France felt fortunate to have won. If, as they reluctantly accepted, it was the best Clemenceau could achieve in the circumstances, then it must be executed line by line, clause by clause; a policy which came to be synonymous with the name of Raymond Poincaré.

If France feared that Europe could not live with Germany, Britain feared that it could not live without her. Britain's view of Germany was shaped by two main considerations: her estimation of the future role and ambitions of France, and her assessment of her own position in the world. 'I am seriously afraid', wrote Curzon on 2 December 1918, 'that the great power from whom we have most to fear in future is France.' He was expressing an opinion widely held by British decision-makers, who for a variety of reasons – tra-ditional emnity, colonial rivalry, a concern for the balance of power – tended to believe that German militarism was dead, but that the French still harboured ambitions of a Napoleonic domination of Europe. Whereas for France Europe was central, for the British the hope was that it could revert to that marginal status which many of the political elite, who had grown up in late Victorian times, believed to be the norm. Britain could then concentrate once more upon her main concerns which were Indian and colonial. She would not commit herself to an alliance with France, despite her unre-deemed promise given in the abortive Anglo-American Treaty of Guarantee. The resistance, in 1919 and 1920, to plans to build a Channel Tunnel, was symbolic of a wish to distance herself from the continent.[10]

Britain's main objectives in Paris were to eliminate Germany as a colonial and naval rival and to gain a reasonable share in any reparations. Once these had been achieved, as they were early in the conference, new factors gradually came to dominate her view of Germany's role. The first was trade; in 1913 Britain sold more to Germany than to anyone except India and bought more from Germany than from anyone except the United States. Where the French saw a military threat, the British saw a commercial oppor-tunity, and they came to associate the persistence of unemployment in Britain after 1920 with the collapse of the central European market. Secondly Germany could act as a bulwark against bolshevism, an aim which could be respectably proclaimed, and finally she could act as a counter to French domination, something which was more difficult to publicise in the light of their recent common struggle – there were too many graves in France to suggest that cooperation would not continue.[11]

In the course of one of his most moving speeches in the Council of Four Clemenceau told Wilson, 'You wish to do justice to the Germans. Do not believe that they will ever forgive us; they will merely seek the opportunity for revenge.' Reflecting Clemenceau's profound pessimism, this also reminds us that the definition of justice is a matter of perspective. In the short term there was wide acceptance in the Allied states that Germany had provoked a war in 1914 for her own aggressive ends, that she had fought that war in a wanton and cruel manner, and that she had lost. It would not be just if she profited from her wickedness. Hence the exclusion of the Sudetenland and the rump of Austria from the new Germany even though this ran counter to Wilson's precept of national self-determination. Hence Wilson's acceptance of the Allied definition of reparations because he thought it just that Germany should pay, and of the inclusion of pensions because he believed Britain would get a fairer share of the receipts. The Germans accepted none of these premises, and hence rejected the Allied reasoning as special pleading, and the treaty as hypocritical and unjust.[12]

Britain's attitude to the settlement was increasingly shaped by doubts as to its justice and its practicality. It was reparations, and Keynes' stinging attack on the treaty, which gave the British a bad conscience about Versailles, although it could be argued that British revisionism began in June 1919, before Keynes had launched his polemic, and that many saw the failure of that attempt to modify the treaty as only temporary. British attempts to revise the settlement were not always consistent nor, arguably, were they bold enough, but the roots of interwar appeasement, though not necessarily Neville Chamberlain's version of it, have been traced back to 1919 itself. The feelings of many British delegates were summed up by Smuts when he told Lloyd George: 'This Treaty breathes a poisonous spirit of revenge, which may yet scorch the fair face – not of a corner of Europe, but of Europe.' When problems of enforcement arose whereas the French thought Germany would not execute the

treaty, the British believed she could not. This fundamental difference of approach dominated the troubled relations between the two
states in the crucial early years of treaty enforcement, and as we
have seen, those relations were not improved by imperial rivalries in
the Near and Middle East. The British also became alarmed at
French aircraft and submarine production. Even when British
decision-makers sympathised with French fears they were exasperated at what they saw as French intransigence and unnecessary
insistence on the details of treaty execution. 'They are so dreadfully
afraid of being swallowed up by the tiger, that they spend all their
time poking it', complained Balfour.[13]

The French quest for security led them into eastern Europe.
There was a firm belief that the miracle of the Marne in 1914 had
only been made possible because of Russian pressure upon Germany
in the east. For many the ideal would have been the continuation of
an alliance with a Russia which still shared a long land frontier with
Germany, but events in Russia and eastern Europe eliminated this
option. Instead the French turned to the successor states to provide
them with a threat to Germany's east. A strong Poland and Czechoslovakia were therefore, for France, an extension of her own security,
and in the early 1920s she concluded a series of east European
alliances. This was a double-edged sword, for the eastern states saw
France as a supplier, not a receiver, of security, and in the 1930s
these alliances increasingly became hostages to fortune, particularly
once the Rhineland had been evacuated and the Maginot mentality
dominated French military planning. From the beginning French
leaders tried to convince the British that the security of eastern
Europe was vital to the west, and that any German attempt to
undermine the settlement would begin there. There would be a new
Sadowa before any new Sedan. French attempts to include eastern
Europe in any Anglo-French security pact were firmly resisted by
Britain, which was not prepared to commit herself east of the Rhine.
Few diplomats or politicians in Britain were as perceptive on this
issue as James Headlam-Morley, and thus Neville Chamberlain's
interest in the affairs of 'a faraway country . . . of [which] we know
nothing' came as a sudden shock in 1938.[14]

Comparing the tasks of Vienna and Versailles, Lloyd George
declared, in April 1919:

You then had to settle the affairs of Europe. It took eleven months.

But the problems at the Congress of Vienna, great as they were, sink into insignificance compared with those which we have had to attempt to settle at the Paris Conference. It is not one continent that is engaged – every continent is affected.

It was indeed a formidable undertaking. In 1914 there had been sufficient dissatisfaction with the existing system to occasion a war; that war had brought death, destruction, famine, disease and revolution to Europe and the world on an unprecedented scale. It had distorted economies, destroyed patterns of trade, toppled thrones and dynasties, removed old certainties. It is not surprising that the cry in 1919 was for a return to 'normalcy' – except that 'normalcy' was what had caused the whole mess.[15]

If the French had been the 1919 villains of *The Economic Consequences of the Peace* for their desire for a Carthaginian peace, by 1922 it was the Americans whom Keynes blamed in *A Revision of the Treaty* for their lack of an economic masterplan. It is true that there was no Marshall aid for Europe in 1919, and that it was difficult to persuade America to take anything but a commercial attitude to the problem of inter-Allied debts. On the other hand the United States did attempt to assist in the reparations field with the Dawes and Young plans, and Hoover's relief work in eastern Europe was both valuable and generous. The Versailles Settlement relied too much on liberal economic doctrine whilst doing little to implement it. Yet, once again, the days were already numbered of Keynes' idyllic pre-war world of commerce and capitalism, and the distortions which the war forced upon the economic and financial arrangements of the combatants could not easily be corrected. The encouragement of declining staples such as steel production and shipbuilding and the stimulation of agriculture to a level which could not be profitably maintained in peacetime, all helped to create economic and political problems in the inter-war period. Markets lost to native industries or to American and Japanese competitors could not be recaptured. It was thus not entirely the responsibility of the settlement that the end of the war failed to bring lasting and solid prosperity.[16]

More by luck than judgement the settlement in the Near East (though not in the Middle East) proved to be a success, but the prescriptions which the peacemakers brought for Europe's ills proved to be inadequate. The settlement left too many powers dissatisfied, too many powers who were revisionist rather than *status quo* in their outlook. As the 1920s moved into the 1930s the support for the settlement waned further, and hence its survival seemed unlikely. Clearly the Germans, accepting neither the verdict nor the sentence of 1919, sought to break the new order. They condemned Versailles as a *diktat*, which it was, and a slave treaty, which it was not. Reparations and disarmament were persistent reminders of the irksome treaty, and the lost lands of the east were never forgotten, even in the heady days of Locarno. The Hungarians were equally opposed, but lacked the potential for revision that Germany's innate power gave her. The Soviets did not consider themselves bound by Versailles, to which they had not been party but which had deprived them of territory. These were the losers, but even the winners were not satisfied. Italy, which upon any objective reading had done well out of Versailles, did not see things that way, and considered herself cheated of rewards in Africa, Asia Minor and the Adriatic. Even though there was now no major power on her new strategic Brenner frontier, and the Balkans seemed open to penetration, she was still, in so far as she dared to be, a revisionist power, and condemned the peace as 'mutilated'. In eastern Europe the successor states, which should have been working closely together to guard against being picked off by Russia or Germany should either of these potential giants be restored, instead bickered and quarrelled, driving their French ally to despair.[17]

Many of these differences were the result of disappointments arising from attempts to apply the elusive doctrine of national self-determination, which had raised so many hopes in war-torn Europe. It is difficult to see how, in the prevailing circumstances, the doctrine could have been more fully applied, or how it could have been ignored, but bitterness and frustration were inevitable. Each of the new states of eastern and central Europe was left with minorities which might prove useful levers for powerful kin states to exploit against the settlement. The application of economic nationalism in the fragmented former empires highlighted the weakness of Allied policy on this issue, exacerbated the effects of the enduring interwar depression, and drove further wedges between the new states. It is interesting to note how many of these problems have already re-emerged in the wake of events so astounding to a generation brought up with the apparent certainties of the Cold War and a monolithic Eastern bloc.

The deficiencies of the settlement, and of those who sought to interpret it, were exposed in the 1920s and played a major role in the eventual collapse of the system in the 1930s. The central decision to leave Germany as a unified state, still possessing, in essence, the necessary resources to become, with Russia, one of the giants of the continent, had been taken quite deliberately. Yet at the same time, the Allies did little to foster the new democratic Germany which they hoped would ensure peace. It is unlikely that Germany would ever have become reconciled to the Versailles Settlement, but Allied insistence on German war guilt and reparations, upon the stringent disarmament of a state which had always attached great value to its army, and on the demands for the surrender and trial of war criminals proved fatal to some German leaders, such as Matthias Erzberger and Walther Rathenau, assassinated by right-wing death squads, and perhaps to German democracy itself. Thus the treaty has been accused, with some justice, as being 'too severe where it should have been lenient' and *vice versa*. Germany felt humiliated by the treaty, but it had not crippled her, and now surrounded, except on her French border, by minor powers, the startling paradox that she might actually be in a stronger position than in 1914 left the medium- to long-term future of the settlement in doubt.[18]

Yet the peacemakers were as much the victims of their virtues as their vices. They might not have allowed Germany to expand, but they did not destroy her. They tried, often in vain, to draw their maps around people, rather than move the people to fit the maps. The League was less successful than its founders would have wished, but in 1945 few suggested that a new experiment along similar lines was not necessary. Faced with an overwhelming task, they struggled to produce a settlement which would guarantee peace and stability; they failed, but any explanation of their failure has to take into account the war, its causes and its effects and the decisions taken by those who followed them. If the Versailles Settlement 'balkanised' Europe (and what was the alternative?) then it might be reasonable to suppose that it might provoke the sort of wars that the Balkans had experienced before 1914, but the outbreak of a second Great War cannot be explained without Hitler and National Socialism. 1919 cannot, of itself, explain 1939, but has a vital role to play in explaining how the Europe of 1914 became the ruin of 1945. Perhaps it will provide important lessons for Europe in the 1990s as its leaders seek to create another new order; the Four may be watching with interest.[19]

Abbreviations

AHR	*American Historical Review*
AJPH	*Australian Journal of Politics and History*
BLP	Bonar Law Papers, House of Lords Record Office
CAB	Cabinet Papers, Public Record Office, Kew
DBFP	*Documents on British Foreign Policy, 1919–1939* (First Series, 1947 onwards) ed. E. L. Woodward and R. Butler
FC	Fonds Clemenceau, Service Historique de l'Armée de Terre, Vincennes, Paris
FO	Foreign Office Papers, Public Record Office
FRUS	*Papers Relating to the Foreign Relations of the United States: The Paris Peace Conference of 1919* (13 vols, Washington, 1943 onwards)
HJ	*Historical Journal*
JCH	*Journal of Contemporary History*
JMH	*Journal of Modern History*
LGP	Lloyd George Papers, House of Lords Record Office
Temperley	H. W. V. Temperley (ed.), *A History of the Peace Conference of Paris* (6 vols, 1920)

Notes

(Place of publication is London unless otherwise noted.)

1. THE OLD WORLD FALLS APART

1. Gerhard Schulz, *Revolutions and Peace Treaties, 1917–1920* (1967, 1972 translation), p. 223.

2. F. R. Bridge and R. Bullen, *The Great Powers and the European States System 1815–1914* (1980), pp. 142–63. Salisbury, 4.5.98, see J. A. S. Grenville, *Lord Salisbury and Foreign Policy: The Close of the Nineteenth Century* (1964, 1970 paperback), pp. 165–6, 434–40. H. W. Koch, 'Social Darwinism as a Factor in the "New Imperialism"', in H. W. Koch, *The Origins of the First World War: Great Power Rivalry and German War Aims* (1972 edn), pp. 329–54, reprinted in the 1984 2nd edn, pp. 319–42.

3. Paul Kennedy, *The Rise and Fall of the Great Powers: Economic Change and Military Conflict from 1500 to 2000* (1989 paperback), pp. 270–1. The following section is mainly based on Kennedy, pp. 249–330.

4. Ibid., pp. 299–312. There are extracts from historians expressing different viewpoints conveniently assembled in the section on 'the Origins of the Russian Revolution' in Clive Emsley, *Conflict and Stability* (1979), pp. 193–258.

5. Michael Howard, *The Continental Commitment: The Dilemma of British Defence Policy in the Era of Two World Wars* (1972 paperback), pp. 9–30; Zara Steiner, *Britain and the Origins of the First World War* (1977), pp. 15–21; Kennedy, *Rise and Fall*, pp. 290–9; G. W. Monger, *The End of Isolation: British Foreign Policy 1900–1907* (1963), pp. 1–20; Steiner, *Britain, passim.*

6. Kennedy, *Rise and Fall*, pp. 128, 314, 261–5, 277–90.

7. V. R. Berghahn, *Germany and the Approach of War in 1914* (1973), *passim.*

8. Kennedy, *Rise and Fall*, pp. 277–82; Ken Ward, *Mass Communications and the Modern World* (1989), pp. 58–61.

9. Bernard Porter, *The Lion's Share* (1975 paperback), pp. 74–232.

10. Coral Bell, *The Conventions of Crisis: A Study in Diplomatic Management* (1971), pp. 17–19.

11. Bridge and Bullen, *The Great Powers*, pp. 142–79.

12. Monger, *End of Isolation, passim*; Howard, *Continental Commitment*, pp. 31–51; Jonathan Steinberg, *Tirpitz and the Birth of the German Battle Fleet* (1965), pp. 31–60.

13. There is an immense literature on the origins of the war and the July crisis but the salient features are well summarised by Ruth Henig, *The Origins of the First World War* (1989). Fritz Fischer's two seminal studies, *Germany's War Aims in*

the *First World War* (1967 translation of 1961 original) and *The War of Illusions* (1973 translation of 1969 original), have provoked a new flood of books attacking, supporting or qualifying his ideas: Berghahn, *Approach of War*; Koch, *Origins*; Steiner, *Britain*; F. R. Bridge, *From Sadowa to Sarajevo* (1972); Richard Bosworth, *Italy and the Approach of the First World War* (1983); D. C. B. Lieven, *Russia and the Origins of the First World War* (1983); John Keiger, *France and the Origins of the First World War* (1983); James Joll, *The Origins of the First World War* (1984).

14. See P. H. S. Hatton, 'Britain and Germany in 1914: The July Crisis and War Aims', in Koch, *Origins* (1st edn), pp. 30–5. British war aims and policy are well covered in V. H. Rothwell, *British War Aims and Peace Diplomacy 1914–1918* (Oxford, 1971) and Kenneth Calder, *Britain and the Origins of the New Europe 1914–1918* (Cambridge, 1976). David Stevenson, *French War Aims against Germany 1914–1919* (Oxford, 1982) reveals much about French planning for peace. See Porter, *Lion's Share*, pp. 233–47 and Christopher Andrew and A. S. Kanya-Forstner, *France Overseas: The Great War and the Climax of French Imperial Expansion* (1981) on imperial developments.

15. Montagu to Balfour, 28.12.18, FO 800/215.

16. Wartime developments may be followed in Z. A. B. Zeman, *A Diplomatic History of the First World War* (1971), *passim*. He quotes Lloyd George's message via Page, the American ambassador in London, 8.2.17, p. 202. There is a good general summary in C. J. Bartlett, *The Global Conflict 1880–1970: The International Rivalry between the Great Powers* (1984), pp. 82–106. See also Kennedy, *Rise and Fall*, pp. 330–54.

17. See L. E. Gelfand, *The Inquiry* (Yale, 1963); Stevenson, *French War Aims*; M. L. Dockrill and J. D. Goold, *Peace Without Promise: Britain and the Paris Peace Conferences 1919–1923* (1981), pp. 17–29; H. Elcock, *Portrait of a Decision: The Council of Four and the Treaty of Versailles* (1972), pp. 22–4; Schulz, *Revolutions and Peace Treaties* pp. 95–104.

18. The Rapallo conference in November 1917 had established the Supreme War Council, comprising a monthly meeting of the political leaders of France, Britain and Italy, with an American observer, and a permanent military and naval committee at Versailles. H. Rudin, *Armistice, 1918* (Yale, 1944), pp. 89–96; D. Lloyd George, *War Memoirs* (2 vols, ed. 1938), vol. 2, pp. 1954–6; Balfour Papers, FO 800/206; S. P. Tillman, *Anglo-American Relations at the Paris Peace Conference of 1919* (Princeton, 1961), p. 41. C. Seymour, *The Intimate Papers of Colonel House* (4 vols, 1928), vol. 4, pp. 87–8.

19. Ibid., pp. 83–5. Tillman, *Anglo-American Relations*, p. 44.

20. Seymour, *Intimate Papers*, vol. 4, p. 167.

21. Ibid., vol. 3, p. 341.

22. Elcock, *Portrait of a Decision*, p. 33. J. M. Keynes, *The Economic Consequences of the Peace* (New York, 1920 edn), pp. 38–9. Stevenson, *French War Aims*, p. 101 quotes the French postal censors' report for 15 Jan.–15 Feb. 1918: 'While criticisms of our own diplomacy . . . are frequent, the approbation given President Wilson is without reserve.'

23. K. N. Waltz, *Man, the State and War: A Theoretical Analysis* (Columbia, 1959), pp. 1–15.

24. The text of the Fourteen Points and relevant extracts of Wilson's other 1918 speeches are reproduced in Temperley, vol. 1, pp. 431–48.

25. Principle 2 of the Four Principles (11.2.18); Particulars 4 and 5 of the Five Particulars (27.9.18); End 1 of the Four Ends (4.7.18); Particular 1 echoing Principle 1 and End 4.

26. Tillman, *Anglo-American Relations*, pp. 44–51.

27. Seymour, *Intimate Papers*, vol. 4, pp. 184–93. See also Sir William Wiseman's comment: 'The "Freedom of the Seas" nearly broke up the Conference', ibid., p. 171n. Tillman, *Anglo-American Relations*, pp. 48–51; C. K. Webster, 'The Congress of Vienna 1814–15 and the Conference of Paris 1919: A Comparison of their Organisation and Results', in W. N. Medlicott (ed.), *From Metternich to Hitler* (1963), p. 9.

28. Tillman, *Anglo-American Relations*, p. 52.

29. D. R. Watson, *Georges Clemenceau: A Political Biography* (1974), p. 335; S. Weintraub, *A Stillness Heard Round the World* (New York, 1985), pp. 43–166; P. Renouvin, *L'Armistice de Rethondes* (Paris, 1968), *passim.*; Lloyd George, *Memoirs*, vol. 2, pp. 1980–5. Temperley, vol. 1, pp. 459–76.

30. Seymour, *Intimate Papers*, vol. 4, p. 194; D. Lloyd George, *The Truth about the Peace Treaties* (2 vols, 1938), vol. 1, p. 80. Sir Eyre Crowe minuted in the Foreign Office 30.11.18, 'I do not believe President Wilson has thought out his nebulous proposals, FO371/4353.

2. THE PARIS PEACE CONFERENCE

1. P. Cambon, *Correspondance* (3 vols, Paris, 1946), vol. 3, p. 311; Lord Percy of Newcastle, *Some Memories* (1958), pp. 60–1. In general see F. S. Marston, *The Peace Conference of 1919: Organisation and Procedure* (Oxford, 1944); Temperley, vol. 1, pp. 236–78; Harold Nicolson, *Peacemaking 1919* (1933); A. Headlam-Morley (ed.), *Sir James Headlam-Morley: A Memoir of the Paris Peace Conference 1919* (1972); Tillman, *Anglo-American Relations*; Elcock, *Portrait of a Decision*; Sally Marks, 'Behind the Scenes at the Paris Peace Conference of 1919'; *Journal of British Studies*, ix, No. 2 (1970), 154–80.

2. The French estimated that at the height of the conference there were 1037 delegates and 70 plenipotentiaries (104 with substitutes). The British delegation numbered 200, and was housed in 5 hotels. Temperley, vol. 1, pp. 243–4; Nicolson, *Peacemaking*, p. 76; Seymour, *Intimate Papers*, vol. 4, p. 226 and pp. 229–30.

3. Ibid., pp. 215–24; Tillman, *Anglo-American Relations*, pp. 56–7.

4. Lord Hankey, *The Supreme Control at the Paris Peace Conference 1919* (1963), pp. 11–13.

5. R. S. Baker, *Woodrow Wilson and the World Settlement* (3 vols, 1922), vol. 3, pp. 56–65.

6. Seymour, *Intimate Papers*, vol. 4, pp. 224, 245–7.

7. Ibid., pp. 257–60; Lloyd George, *The Truth*, vol. 1, pp. 131–47 and vol. 2, p. 1038.

8. Seymour, *Intimate Papers*, vol. 4, pp. 218–23; Nicolson, *Peacemaking*, pp. 69–76; S. Bonsal, *Unfinished Business* (1944), pp. 17–22.

9. Lloyd George, *The Truth*, vol. 1, p. 182. Wilson chose House, Lansing, General Tasker Bliss and Henry White to accompany him as the American plenipotentiaries. The choice of a more prominent Republican than White,

perhaps ex-President Taft, might have eased the later passage of the treaty.

10. Nicolson, *Peacemaking*, p. 241.

11. Ibid., p. 241; *FRUS*, vol. 3, p. 196; Marston, *Peace Conference*, pp. 62ff.

12. Ibid., pp. 84ff.

13. Ibid., pp. 65–6.

14. A. E. Alcock, *History of the International Labor Organization* (New York, 1971), pp. 18–37; A. Walworth, *Wilson and his Peacemakers: American Diplomacy at the Paris Peace Conference, 1919* (1986), pp. 315–20. The Treaty established some ambitious principles like the eight-hour day and equal pay for equal work for women (Article 427) but these were rarely observed. *Treaty*, pp. 718–19.

15. Temperley, vol. 2, pp. 21–9; Tillman, *Anglo-American Relations*, pp. 101–33.

16. Marston, *Peace Conference*, pp. 106–7.

17. Ibid., pp. 111–19; Isaiah Bowman, in E. House and C. Seymour, *What Really Happened at Paris* (1921), pp. 158–9.

18. Tillman, *Anglo-American Relations*, pp. 96–110.

19. Nicolson, *Peacemaking*, pp. 122–3, 128–9.

20. Seymour, *Intimate Papers*, vol. 4, pp. 363–4; Baker, *Woodrow Wilson*, vol. 1, pp. 310–11.

21. Hankey, *The Supreme Control*, pp. 97–106; S. Roskill, *Hankey: Man of Secrets* (3 vols, 1970 onwards), vol. 2, pp. 73–80.

22. Marston, *Peace Conference*, pp. 165–71; On Orlando's command of English see the Earl of Crawford's diary 5.1.20, John Vincent (ed.), *The Crawford Papers* (Manchester, 1984), p. 405. F. Stevenson (ed. A. J. P. Taylor), *Lloyd George: A Diary* (1971), p. 182.

23. G. Clemenceau, *Grandeur and Misery of Victory* (1930 translation), p. 138.

24. Nicolson, *Peacemaking*, p. 339.

25. Marston, *Peace Conference*, pp. 171–6.

26. Keynes, *Economic Consequences*, pp. 27–55.

27. *FRUS*, vol. 5, pp. 112–48. Cf. Keynes' record of a meeting, 29.4.19, in Roskill, *Hankey*, vol. 2, pp. 84–7.

28. Ibid., pp. 70–3. Lloyd George, *Truth*, vol. 1, pp. 404–16.

29. H. I. Nelson, *Land and Power: British and Allied Policy on Germany's Frontiers, 1916–1919* (1963), pp. 198–248; Watson, *Clemenceau*, pp. 348–53; Tillman, *Anglo-American Relations*, pp. 176–93.

30. Tillman, ibid., pp. 184–93; Nelson, *Land and Power*, pp. 249–81.

31. Tillman, *Anglo-American Relations*, pp. 202–9; Nelson, *Land and Power*, pp. 176–97.

32. Tillman, *Anglo-American Relations*, pp. 229–59.

33. Nelson, *Land and Power*, p. 261.

34. Clemenceau, *Grandeur and Misery*, pp. 122–6; Marston, *Peace Conference*, pp. 189–90.

35. Tillman, *Anglo-American Relations*, pp. 316–33; Dockrill and Goold, *Peace Without Promise*, pp. 190–9.

36. Dockrill and Goold, ibid., pp. 333–43.

37. Headlam-Morley, *Memoir*, pp. 103–5; A. Lentin, *Guilt at Versailles: Lloyd George and the Pre-history of Appeasement* (1984), pp. 83–4. Keynes himself resigned from the British delegation on 5 June.

38. A. Luckau, *The German Delegation at the Paris Peace Conference* (New York, 1941), pp. 118–21; Nicolson, *Peacemaking*, p. 330.

39. Luckau, *German Delegation*, pp. 84–5; Marston, *Peace Conference*, pp. 192–4.

40. Lloyd George, *The Truth*, vol. 1, pp. 688–720.

41. Marston, *Peace Conference*, p. 193; Alan Sharp, ' "Quelqu'un nous écoute": French Interception of German Telegraphic and Telephonic Communications during the Paris Peace Conference, 1919', *Intelligence and National Security*, 3, no. 4 (1988), 124–7.

42. Lloyd George, *The Truth*, vol. 1, pp. 720–8.

43. Dockrill and Goold, *Peace Without Promise*, pp. 79–80; Marston, *Peace Conference*, pp. 198–9.

44. Cambon, *Correspondance*, vol. 3, p. 281; Headlam-Morley, *Memoir*, pp. 178–9; F. Stevenson, *Lloyd George*, p. 187; Nicolson, *Peacemaking*, pp. 365–71.

45. Walworth, *Wilson and his Peacemakers*, pp. 528–46.

46. See Alan Sharp, Britain, France, Germany and the Execution of the Treaty of Versailles 1919–1923, with particular reference to Reparations and Disarmament. (Unpublished PhD thesis, Nottingham, 1975).

3.   THE LEAGUE OF NATIONS

1. F. P. Walters, *A History of the League of Nations* (Oxford 1952, 1967 edn), pp. 4–14; A. Zimmern, *The League of Nations and the Rule of Law, 1918–1935* (1939), pp. 13–133.

2. Grey to House, letters of 10.8 and 26.8.15 and 22.9.15, Seymour, *Intimate Papers*, vol. 2, pp. 87–9.

3. There was an embarrassing moment in the League commission when Venizelos claimed not to have heard of the body. Bourgeois was not amused. Bonsal, *Unfinished Business*, p. 59.

4. See F. R. Bridge and R. Bullen, *The Great Powers, passim*; D. Armstrong, *The Rise of the International Organisation: A Short History* (1982), pp. 1–6.

5. G. W. Egerton, *Great Britain and the Creation of the League of Nations: Strategy, Politics, and International Organisation, 1914–1919* (1979), pp. 3–80 [all references to Egerton are to this book unless otherwise stated]; Armstrong, *Short History*, pp. 1–7; Walters, *A History . . . League of Nations*, pp. 15–24; Zimmern, *League of Nations*, pp. 160–79.

6. Egerton, p. 31.

7. Ibid., pp. 57–62.

8. David Hunter Miller, *The Drafting of the Covenant* (New York, 1969 reprint of 1928 original, 2 vols), vol. 1, pp. 3–7.

9. Ibid., vol. 2, p. 3; Egerton, pp. 65–9. I am grateful to Dr Ruth Henig for information about the timing of the Phillimore Commission meetings.

10. Miller, *Covenant*, vol. 1, pp. 6–7 and vol. 2, p. 4.

11. Hankey wanted the League to resemble the present Supreme War Council, and Lloyd George, whilst favouring a 'league of some kind' was anxious not to commit himself to extreme schemes. Roskill, *Hankey*, vol. 1, pp. 471, 482, 593–4; Egerton, pp. 47–8; Peter Yearwood, ' "On the Safe and Right Lines":

The Lloyd George Government and the Origins of the League of Nations 1916–1918', *HJ*, 32, no. 1 (1989), 131–55.

12. Miller, *Covenant*, vol. 1, pp. 10–12; Zimmern, *League of Nations*, pp. 180–9.

13. Miller, *Covenant*, vol. 1, pp. 12–15, vol. 2, pp. 7–11.

14. Ibid., vol. 2, pp. 12–15.

15. P. Raffo, 'The Anglo-American Preliminary Negotiations for a League of Nations', *JCH*, 9 (1974), 153–76; Egerton, pp. 106, 92–4.

16. Miller, *Covenant*, vol. 1, pp. 35–6, Zimmern, *League of Nations*, pp. 210–15; Walters, *A History . . . League of Nations*, pp. 27–30; Walworth, *Wilson and his Peacemakers*, p. 107n.

17. Miller, *Covenant*, vol. 1, pp. 38–9; Egerton, pp. 99–101.

18. Miller, *Covenant*, vol. 1, pp. 40–1; Tillman, *Anglo-American Relations*, pp. 115–18; P. Raffo, 'The League of Nations Philosophy of Lord Robert Cecil', *AJPH*, 20, no. 2 (1974), 186–96.

19. Egerton, pp. 98, 115–16; Nicolson, *Peacemaking*, pp. 104–8.

20. Miller, *Covenant*, vol. 1, pp. 45–8.

21. Ibid., pp. 48–50.

22. Ibid., pp. 51–2; J. Barros, *Office Without Power: Secretary General Sir Eric Drummond, 1919–1933* (Oxford, 1979), p. 1; Egerton, pp. 115–17.

23. Miller, *Covenant*, vol. 1, pp. 52–61, vol. 2, pp. 131–41; Egerton, pp. 118–19.

24. *FRUS*, vol. 3, pp. 179–200; Walworth, *Wilson and his Peacemakers*, p. 113.

25. Egerton, pp. 121–5.

26. Ibid., pp. 125–6; Miller, *Covenant*, vol. 1, pp. 65–7; Seymour, *Intimate Papers*, vol. 4, pp. 299–300.

27. Miller, *Covenant*, vol. 1, pp. 72–3; Egerton, pp. 127–9; Seymour, *Intimate Papers*, vol. 4, pp. 300–3; Walworth, *Wilson and his Peacemakers*, pp. 114–15.

28. Miller, *Covenant*, vol. 2, pp. 231–7.

29. Ibid., vol. 1, pp. 83–5, vol. 2, pp. 255–60.

30. Ibid., vol. 1, p. 118, vol. 2, p. 231 and pp. 238–56 for the French and Italian proposals; Tillman, *Anglo-American Relations*, p. 123; Egerton, pp. 129–30; Walworth, *Wilson and his Peacemakers*, pp. 115–16.

31. Miller, *Covenant*, vol. 1, p. 450, vol. 2, pp. 123–6, 143.

32. Ibid., vol. 1, pp. 140–53, 158–63, vol. 2, pp. 256–63; Bonsal, *Unfinished Business*, p. 61; Egerton, pp. 130–1.

33. Miller, *Covenant*, vol. 1, pp. 168–9, vol. 2, p. 264; Tillman, *Anglo-American Relations*, pp. 125–6; Percy, *Memories*, p. 69; Egerton, pp. 131–2.

34. Miller, *Covenant*, vol. 1, pp. 202–3, vol. 2, pp. 288–9.

35. Ibid., vol. 2, pp. 264–5; Egerton, p. 132.

36. Miller, *Covenant*, vol. 2, pp. 265–70; Egerton, pp. 132–3.

37. Ibid., pp. 134–8; Miller, *Covenant*, vol. 1, pp. 209–10, 216–17; Tillman, *Anglo-American Relations*, pp. 129–31; Walworth, *Wilson and his Peacemakers*, p. 118n.

38. Miller, *Covenant*, vol. 2, p. 302; Barros, *Office Without Power*, pp. 1–14; Egerton, pp. 167–8. Hankey decided in April 1919 that the post was not for him, Roskill, *Hankey*, vol. 2, pp. 64–7, 79–80; Hankey, *The Supreme Control*, pp. 104–5.

204   THE VERSAILLES SETTLEMENT

39. Egerton, pp. 139–47; Tillman, *Anglo-American Relations*, pp. 132–3; *FRUS*, vol. 3, pp. 209–30; Walworth, *Wilson and his Peacemakers*, pp. 119–20.

40. Egerton, pp. 147–9; Miller, *Covenant*, vol. 1, pp. 276–7; Walworth, *Wilson and his Peacemakers*, pp. 181–8, 191–2.

41. Miller, *Covenant*, vol. 2, pp. 336–60; Egerton, pp. 152–6; Walworth, *Wilson and his Peacemakers*, pp. 195–6.

42. Egerton, pp. 160–3; Tillman, *Anglo-American Relations*, pp. 281–97; Miller, *Covenant*, vol. 2, pp. 370–2; Walworth, *Wilson and his Peacemakers*, pp. 307–9.

43. Miller, *Covenant*, vol. 2, pp. 387–92; Egerton, p. 164; Tillman, *Anglo-American Relations*, p. 300–4. Walworth, *Wilson and his Peacemakers*, pp. 309–11; I. H. Nish, *Alliance in Decline: A Study in Anglo-Japanese Relations, 1908–23* (1972), pp. 269–74.

44. Egerton, p. 168; Tillman, *Anglo-American Relations*, pp. 298–9; *FRUS*, vol. 3, pp. 286–315; Walworth, *Wilson and his Peacemakers*, pp. 311–12.

45. Cecil to the House of Commons, 21.7.19, *Hansard*, vol. 118, cols. 990–2; Bonsal, *Unfinished Business*, p. 49.

46. Walworth, *Wilson and his Peacemakers*, p. 315; Walters, *A History . . . League of Nations*, pp. 63–74, 258–9; G. W. Egerton, 'Britain and the "Great Betrayal": Anglo-American Relations and the Struggle for United States Ratification of the Treaty of Versailles, 1919–1920', *HJ*, 21, no. 4 (1978), 885–911.

47. On 2.5.19 Wilson wrote to Cecil: 'I feel, as I am sure all the other members of the commission feel, that the laboring oar fell to you and that it is chiefly due to you that the Covenant has come out of the confusion of debate in its original integrity.' Lord Robert Cecil, *A Great Experiment: An Autobiography* (1941), p. 100. See Egerton, pp. 200–5, Armstrong, *Short History*, pp. 22–3, and Ruth Henig (ed.), *The League of Nations* (1973), pp. 1–15 for realistic, yet sympathetic, analyses of the League as drafted.

4.   REPARATIONS

1. A. Bowley, *Some Economic Consequences of the Great War* (1930); A. Sauvy, *Histoire économique de la France* (2 vols, Paris, 1965); D. Lloyd George, *The Truth about Reparations and War Debts [Reparations]* (1932).

2. Keynes, *Economic Consequences*; A. J. P. Taylor, *The Origins of the Second World War* (1961, 1964 paperback), pp. 69–70; R. A. C. Parker, *Europe 1919–1945* (1969), pp. 6–9. J. M. Roberts, *Europe 1880–1945* (1967), p. 310; M. Kitchen, *Europe between the Wars: A Political History* (1988), pp. 10–12.

3. Temperley, vol. 2, p. 40; Kerr to Lloyd George 25.2.19, LGP F/89/2/32; Marc Trachtenburg, *Reparation in World Politics: France and European Economic Diplomacy 1916–1923* (New York, 1980), pp. 41–2. Bonar Law told W. Lane-Mitchell 8.11.18 that an indemnity was precluded by the Fourteen Points but 'under the term reparation . . . a far larger sum can be claimed than Germany can ever pay', BLP 95/4. Lloyd George warned his colleagues that the repair of the French damage alone 'would probably absorb the whole of the amount it was possible to obtain from Germany', 19.2.19, CAB 23/9.

4. Seymour, *Intimate Papers*, vol. 4, p. 161; WC491A in CAB 23/14; Temperley, vol. 1, pp. 457–8.

5. Temperley, vol. 1, p. 465, vol. 2, p. 44; Note 19.10.18 in FC 6N73, 'Armistice'; *FRUS*, vol. 6, p. 480.

6. R. E. Bunselmeyer, *The Cost of the War of 1914–1919: British Economic War Aims and the Origins of Reparation* (Connecticut, 1975), chs 5–8 *passim*; W. S. Churchill, *The World Crisis – The Aftermath* (1929), pp. 20–1; Lentin, *Guilt at Versailles*, pp. 11–24. Bruce Kent, *The Spoils of War: The Politics, Economics, and Diplomacy of Reparations 1918–1932* (Oxford, 1989), pp. 23–4 argues that the wording was mainly incorporated to protect the interests of the French *sinistrés*, those people displaced by the war.

7. Bunselmeyer, *Cost of War*, p. 88.

8. A figure reached apparently either by divine inspiration or entrepreneurial whim: Hankey to Lloyd George 21.2.19 Lothian Papers GD40,17,64. Lloyd George later dismissed it as 'a wild and fantastic chimera', Lloyd George, *The Truth*, vol. 1, p. 461. Bunselmeyer, *Cost of War*, p. 101.

9. Respectively George Barnes at Nettleton 29.11.18, and Eric Geddes at Cambridge 9.12.18

10. See Lentin's masterly analysis of Lloyd George's personality and policies, *Guilt at Versailles*, pp. 107–22. Kent, *Spoils of War*, argues that: 'The idea of an immense reparations claim only really took hold when it was touted by men of property and dominion statesmen as a solution to the British Empire's post-war budgetary and commercial problems', p. 33. He makes a similar case against the French leadership, pp. 24–8.

11. Dockrill and Goold, *Peace Without Promise*, p. 48; P. Renouvin, *Histoire des rélations internationales; les crises du XXe siècle:* 1 *de 1914 à 1929* (Paris, 1969), p. 167.

12. Trachtenberg, *Reparation . . . Politics*, pp. 38–46.

13. Ibid., p. 7.

14. Ibid., pp. 7–18.

15. Ibid., pp. 20–7.

16. Ibid., pp. 35–9.

17. Ibid., p. 46.

18. Lentin, *Guilt at Versailles*, p. 33; Tillman, *Anglo-American Relations*, pp. 234–5.

19. Meeting 29.3.19, P. Mantoux, *Paris Peace Conference 1919: Proceedings of the Council of Four (March 24–April 19)* [Mantoux, *Proceedings*] (Paris, 1964), p. 57. Meeting 5.4.19, ibid., p. 117.

20. Treaty references are taken from *The Treaty of Versailles and After; Annotations of the Text of the Treaty* (1968 reprint of 1944 US Government original) [*Treaty*], pp. 413, 425. Fontainebleau Memorandum 25.3.19 printed in Cmd 2169, *Negotiations for an Anglo-French Pact, 1919–1924* (1924), pp. 86–7.

21. Trachtenberg, *Reparation . . . Politics*, pp. 62–6, 70–1.

22. *FRUS*, vol. 5, pp. 54–5; T. Lamont, 'Reparations' in House and Seymour, *What Really Happened*, p. 272.

23. Letter to Bonar Law 30.3.19, BLP 97/1/17. See Davis' views 5.4.19, *FRUS*, vol. 5, pp. 23–4.

24. Figures discussed 22.2.19, Trachtenberg, *Reparation . . . Politics*, pp. 59–60.

25. Loucheur told his colleagues that he would deny his agreement if the figure became public. P. Birdsall, *Versailles Twenty Years After* (1941), pp. 246–7.

Clemenceau had apparently approved the figure. L. Loucheur, *Carnets secrets de Louis Loucheur* (Brussels, 1962), p. 71.

26. Cmd 2169 pp. 79, 77; Tillman, *Anglo-American Relations*, p. 241; Kent, *Spoils of War*, pp. 72–3.

27. P. Mantoux, *Les Délibérations du Conseil des Quatre* (2 vols, Paris, 1955), vol. 1, pp. 58–62.

28. *FRUS*, vol. 5, p. 28.

29. Ibid., pp. 22–7.

30. Mantoux, *Délibérations*, vol. 1, pp. 161–2.

31. *FRUS*, vol. 5, pp. 35–7; Lloyd George, *The Truth*, vol. 2, pp. 374–84.

32. Decision of 23.4.19, modified 29.4.19, *FRUS*, vol. 5, pp. 155–7, 359–60; Article 248, *Treaty*, pp. 530–1; *FRUS*, vol. 5, pp. 156–7.

33. Ibid., p. 76.

34. Mantoux, *Délibérations*, vol. 1, p. 236.

35. See Trachtenberg, *Reparation . . . Politics*, pp. 84–5; Tillman, *Anglo-American Relations*, pp. 253–4.

36. *FRUS*, vol. 5, p. 161. See J. F. Dulles' opinion, Treasury memo., 18.8.22 in FO 371/7484.

37. Annex IV to Part VIII, *Treaty*, pp. 506–7.

38. Article 246, ibid., p. 523; Brockdorff-Rantzau to Clemenceau 13.5.19, *FRUS*, vol. 5, p. 740; German reply 29.5.19, ibid., vol. 6, pp. 797–8. See Trachtenberg, *Reparation . . . Politics*, pp. 86–7; Kent, *Spoils of War*, pp. 80–2.

39. Lloyd George, *The Truth*, vol. 1, pp. 480–1.

40. Mantoux, *Délibérations*, vol. 2, p. 267; *FRUS*, vol. 6, pp. 261–9.

41. *FRUS*, vol. 2, p. 222; ibid., vol. 6, pp. 262–3, 273–80.

42. Trachtenberg, *Reparation . . . Politics*, pp. 66–8.

43. Ibid., p. 94.

44. Lloyd George, *Reparations*, p. 14.

45. Mantoux, *Délibérations*, vol. 1, p. 47.

46. Quoted by Lentin, *Guilt at Versailles*, p. 96.

47. CAB 491B 26.10.18 in CAB 23/14.

48. Sauvy, *Histoire économique*, vol. 1, p. 169. The United States had sequestered £85,000,000 worth of German property; Kent, *Spoils of War*, pp. 67, 76–8.

49. Trachtenberg, *Reparation . . . Politics*; S. Schuker, *The End of French Predominance in Europe: The Financial Crisis of 1924 and the Adoption of the Dawes Plan* (North Carolina, 1976); J. Bariéty, *Les Rélations Franco-Allemandes après la Première Guerre Mondiale: 10 Novembre 1918–10 Janvier 1925. De l'exécution à la négociation* (Paris, 1977).

50. *FRUS*, vol. 6, p. 799.

51. See the Reparation Commission's assessment of the claims against Germany, February 1921, *Treaty*, pp. 471–5.

52. Fischer, *Germany's War Aims* and *War of Illusions*; Berghahn, *Approach of War*.

53. *Treaty*, p. 60.

54. 3.3.21, *DBFP*, vol. xv, pp. 258–9.

55. See J. Joll, *The Origins of the First World War* (1984); J. Droz, *Les Causes de la Première Guerre Mondiale* (Paris, 1973).

5. THE GERMAN SETTLEMENT

1. For details see Tillman, *Anglo-American Relations*, Temperley, vol. 2, Nelson, *Land and Power*, and Elcock, *Portrait of a Decision*. There is an interesting and balanced account from a German perspective in Erich Eyck, *A History of the Weimar Republic: Volume 1, From the Collapse of the Empire to Hindenburg's Election* (New York, 1962), pp. 80–128. Headlam-Morley's memo., 15.4.19, illustrates the complexity of the issues: Headlam-Morley, *Memoir*, p. 76.

2. Stevenson, *French War Aims*, pp. 11–12, 23ff, 17, and 79; J. J. Becker, *1914: Comment les Français sont entrés dans la Guerre* (Paris, 1977), p. 580.

3. Stevenson, *French War Aims*, pp. 78–9, 101.

4. Ibid., pp. 22, 118–19, 140; Watson, *Clemenceau*, pp. 332, 336–7; *FRUS*, vol. 5, pp. 376–86; Article 51, *Treaty*, p. 183.

5. On continuing Franco-German relations over Alsace-Lorraine see Bariéty, *Rélations Franco-Allemandes*, pp. 5–22; Walter A. McDougall, *France's Rhineland Diplomacy, 1914–1924: the Last Bid for a Balance of Power in Europe* (Princeton, 1978), p. 104.

6. Ibid., pp. 15–25; Stevenson, *French War Aims, passim*; J. C. King, *Foch versus Clemenceau: France and German Dismemberment, 1918–1919* (Harvard, 1960), pp. 1–27.

7. See King, ibid., pp. 3–10, on wartime literature and propaganda; A. Aulard, *La Paix future d'après la Révolution Française et Kant* (Paris, 1916), quoted King, p. 8; McDougall, *France's Rhineland Diplomacy*, pp. 16–32; Stevenson, *French War Aims, passim*.

8. A. Ribot (ed.), *Journal d'Alexandre Ribot et correspondances inédites, 1914–1922* (Paris, 1936), p. 93; Cmd.2169, pp. 2–3, 4–5.

9. Lloyd George, *The Truth*, vol. 1, pp. 132–47; Watson, *Clemenceau*, p. 353; Nelson, *Land and Power*, pp. 206–9; King, *Foch versus Clemenceau*, preface; R. McCrum, 'French Rhineland Policy at the Paris Peace Conference, 1919', *HJ*, 21, no. 3 (1978), 623–48.

10. Text of Foch's note in Cmd.2169, pp. 20–6; Lloyd George's remark, 7.3.19, LGP F/147/1/1; Curzon's speech, E4 in CAB 32/2. See also McCrum, 'French Rhineland Policy', p. 625.

11. There are a number of identical statues representing the major French towns in the Place de la Concorde. From 1871 until 1918, that symbolising Strasbourg (and hence the lost provinces) was covered in black. There was a moving ceremony, 17.11.18, in the Place, to celebrate their return. E. Bonnefous, *Histoire Politique de la Troisième République* (7 vols, Paris, 1967 edn), vol. 2, p. 424; A. Tardieu, *The Truth about the Treaty* (1921), p. 171; Mantoux, *Proceedings*, p. 28.

12. Seymour, *Intimate Papers*, vol. 4, p. 345.

13. Ibid., p. 344; Clemenceau, *Grandeur and Misery*, p. 220; Mantoux, *Délibérations*, vol. 2, p. 271.

14. Cmd.2169, pp. 42–57.

15. See McCrum, 'French Rhineland Policy', pp. 627–8.

16. Lloyd George, *The Truth*, vol. 1, p. 260.

17. Cmd.2169, pp. 61–5.

18. Cab 23/15/541A.

19. Lloyd George, *The Truth*, vol. 1, p. 403.

20. Tardieu, *Truth about the Treaty*, pp. 197–201; Cmd.2169, pp. 71–4.

21. Nelson, *Land and Power*, pp. 233–40.

22. R. Poincaré, *Au Service de la France* (11 vols, Paris, 1928–74), vol. 11, p. 337.

23. Mantoux, *Délibérations*, vol. 1, pp. 318–19.

24. *FRUS*, vol. 5, pp. 112–14, 117–18; Nelson, *Land and Power*, pp. 238–243.

25. *FRUS*, vol. 5, p. 357; Nelson, *Land and Power*, pp. 243–5.

26. McDougall, *France's Rhineland Diplomacy*, pp. 67–9; McCrum, 'French Rhineland Policy', pp. 637–42; Watson, *Clemenceau*, pp. 351–2.

27. Stevenson, *French War Aims*, p. 177, cf. Watson, *Clemenceau*, p. 352.

28. McCrum, 'French Rhineland Policy', p. 624.

29. Dockrill and Goold, *Peace Without Promise*, p. 35.

30. Nelson, *Land and Power*, p. 229.

31. Ibid., pp. 249–52.

32. Letters to Hurst and Kerr, 7.2.19, Headlam-Morley, *Memoir*, pp. 23–4.

33. Stevenson, *French War Aims*, p. 177; Tardieu, *Truth about the Treaty*, pp. 251–62.

34. Mantoux, *Délibérations*, vol. 1, pp. 74, 69–71.

35. Stevenson, *French War Aims*, pp. 177–8; Nelson, *Land and Power*, p. 256–8.

36. Headlam-Morley, *Memoir*, p. 67. He had suggested three possibilities to the Four, 31.3.19, *FRUS*, vol. 5, pp. 66–70. See also pp. 60–1.

37. Headlam-Morley, *Memoir*, pp. 74, 78. The crucial debates occurred from 9 to 13 April; Nelson, *Land and Power*, pp. 272–81.

38. Headlam-Morley, *Memoir*, pp. 100–3.

39. Temperley, vol. 2, p. 176; Part VIII, Annex V, *Treaty*, p. 512–13.

40. Temperley, vol. 2, p. 180.

41. Bariéty, *Rélations Franco-Allemandes*, p. 139.

42. Stevenson, *French War Aims*, p. 179.

43. See Sally Marks, *Innocent Abroad: Belgium at the Paris Peace Conference of 1919* (Chapel Hill, 1981), pp. 137–54, 206–306, 339–402.

44. Minute, 28.2.19, quoted by Dockrill and Goold, *Peace Without Promise*, p. 41.

45. Meetings of 16 April and 4 June, Mantoux, *Délibérations*, vol. 1, pp. 261–3 and *FRUS*, vol. 4, pp. 800–1.

46. Headlam-Morley, *Memoir*, pp. 164–5; Stevenson, *French War Aims*, p. 170, Marks, *Innocent Abroad*, pp. 144–53.

47. Ibid., p. 153; Temperley, vol. 2, pp. 190–1.

48. The area was technically under American occupation but Foch ensured the presence of French troops by making the city his headquarters. Marks, *Innocent Abroad*, pp. 206–20; Stevenson, *French War Aims*, pp. 82–3, 183–4.

49. Minute April 1919, quoted by Marks, *Innocent Abroad*, p. 231.

50. See Marks, ibid., p. 229, for possible explanations.

51. Ibid., pp. 230–54.

52. Ibid., pp. 274–97; Dockrill and Goold, *Peace Without Promise*, pp. 39–43.

53. Temperley, vol. 2, pp. 197–203.

54. Stevenson, *French War Aims*, pp. 170, 183; Mantoux, *Délibérations*, vol. 2, p. 424.

55. *Treaty*, pp. 262–9; Temperley, vol. 2, pp. 203–6.

56. Clemenceau, *Grandeur and Misery*, p. 180. For an authoritative account of Polish affairs at the conference see K. Lundgreen-Nielsen, *The Polish Problem at the Paris Peace Conference: A Study of the Policies of the Great Powers and the Poles, 1918–1919* (Odense, 1979), *passim*.

57. Stevenson, *French War Aims*, p. 86, Tel. 11.3.17, Russian ambassador in Paris to St Petersburg, Cmd. 2169, p. 8.

58. Clemenceau, *Grandeur and Misery*, p. 180.

59. Lloyd George, *The Truth*, vol. 1, p. 13 and *War Memoirs*, vol. 1, pp. 525–6.

60. Ibid., vol. 2, p. 1514.

61. *FRUS*, vol. 6, pp. 153–4.

62. 'It sounds like a joke that although President Wilson had been talking privately and publicly for months for the restoration of a modified Poland he is reported to have believed when he arrived in Paris that Prague was the capital of that already informally organised state. It was more excusable that he thought Bagdad to be in Persia and Sarajevo in Serbia.' W. H. Dawson, *Germany under the Treaty* (1933), p. 31.

63. *FRUS*, vol. 3, pp. 773–81.

64. Ibid., pp. 1007, 1014.

65. See Nelson, *Land and Power*, pp. 145–75; *FRUS*, vol. 4, pp. 413–14.

66. *FRUS*, vol. 4, pp. 415, 419, 449–50.

67. Mantoux, *Proceedings*, pp. 29, 79–82.

68. Ibid., pp. 154–7, 181; Nelson, *Land and Power*, pp. 176–97.

69. Lloyd George, *The Truth*, vol. 1, p. 480; *FRUS*, vol. 6, pp. 139–43, 149–54, 196–7, 303–4, 316–18; Nelson, *Land and Power*, pp. 346–58.

70. Piotr Wandycz suggests that there were only 585,000 Germans in the border areas ceded to Poland. German sources claimed over a million Germans, but they included all Germans living in Poland. Polish sources suggest between 740,000 and 780,000. P. Wandycz, 'Poland between East and West', in G. Martel (ed.), *The Origins of the Second World War Reconsidered: The A. J. P. Taylor Debate After Twenty-Five Years* (1986), pp. 195, 207n. See F. Gregory Campbell, 'the Struggle for Upper Silesia, 1919–1922', *JMH*, 42, no. 3 (1970), on the subsequent history of the Upper Silesian dispute.

71. *FRUS*, vol. 6, pp. 196–7.

72. Mantoux, *Proceedings*, p. 82.

73. Percy, *Memories*, p. 68; Walworth, *Wilson and his Peacemakers*, p. 263.

74. C. A. Macartney and A. W. Palmer, *Independent Eastern Europe* (1962), pp. 109, 115.

75. *Treaty*, Articles 159–210, pp. 301–59. The conference debates can be followed in *FRUS*, vol. 4, pp. 183–360. See also Tillman, *Anglo-American Relations*, pp. 161–75, Dockrill and Goold, *Peace Without Promise*, pp. 43–5, and Lloyd George, *The Truth*, vol. 1, pp. 581–603. Lorna Jaffe, *The Decision to Disarm Germany* (New York, 1985) covers the issue and the earlier debates about policy very thoroughly. The naval issues are well covered in S. Roskill, *Naval Policy between the Wars: Volume 1, The Period of Anglo-American Antagonism, 1919–1929* (2 vols, 1968 and 1976), vol. 1, pp. 71–101.

76. *FRUS*, vol. 6, p. 954.

77. J. F. Willis, *Prologue to Nuremberg: The Politics and Diplomacy of Punishing War*

Criminals of the First World War (Connecticut, 1982), pp. 3–48. I have based this section mainly on Willis' authoritative study. See also Tillman, *Anglo-American Relations*, pp. 311–14; Lentin, *Guilt at Versailles*, pp. 24–9.

78. Sir C. E. Callwell, *Field Marshal Sir Henry Wilson: His Life and Diaries* (2 vols, 1927), vol. 2, p. 149.

79. Willis, *Prologue*, pp. 49–68.

80. Ibid., pp. 68–77.

81. Ibid., pp. 78–9. For an alternative view see I. Floto, *Colonel House in Paris: A Study of American Policy at the Paris Peace Conference, 1919* (Aarhus, 1973), pp. 205–8. The debates may be followed in Mantoux, *Proceedings*, pp. 80, 90–3, 144–54.

82. Willis, *Prologue*, pp. 80–1. I am grateful to Dr Tony Lentin for the clarification of some legal technicalities on this issue.

83. Willis, *Prologue*, pp. 82–5.

84. Ibid., pp. 176, 98–147.

85. FC 6N72 7.5.19.

86. T. C. W. Blanning, *The Origins of the French Revolutionary Wars* (1986), p. 27. F. Foch, *The Memoirs of Marshal Foch* (1931), pp. 536–41, 574–7.

87. See Taylor, *Origins of Second World War*, pp. 51–2, and the critique by Sally Marks in Martel, *Origins*, pp. 26–7.

6. THE EASTERN EUROPEAN SETTLEMENT

1. Quoted by D. Perman, *The Shaping of the Czechoslovak State* (Leiden, 1962), p. 169.

2. N. G. Levin, *Woodrow Wilson and World Politics* (New York, 1968), pp. 13–49 and *passim*. 'What a funny shape Austria must be', commented Lord Robert Cecil, the British minister responsible for enforcing the Allied blockade: Rothwell, *British War Aims*, p. 17. See also the acerbic comments of Dawson, *Germany under the Treaty*, p. 31; Nicolson, *Peacemaking*, pp. 24–5 and *passim*.

3. See W. Fest, *Peace or Partition: The Habsburg Monarchy and British Policy 1914–1918* (New York, 1978), *passim*. Stevenson, *French War Aims*, *passim*.

4. Perman, *Czechoslovak State*, pp. 50, 62; Poincaré, *Service*, vol. 10, p. 399.

5. See Calder, *Britain*, Rothwell, *British War Aims* and Stevenson, *French War Aims*, all *passim*.

6. Perman, *Czechoslovak State*, p. 105.

7. See P. Alter, *Nationalism* (1989), pp. 4–23, 109–10.

8. R. Lansing, *The Peace Negotiations, a Personal Narrative* (New York, 1921), pp. 97–8.

9. Temperley, vol. 4, p. 132.

10. J. Remak, '1914 – The Third Balkan War: Origins Reconsidered', *JMH*, 43, no. 3 (1971), 353–66; C. Macartney and A. Palmer, *Independent Eastern Europe* (1962), pp. 30–4.

11. Ibid., p. 117. For details of the wartime manoeuvrings see pp. 39–96.

12. Until 1929 the official title was the Kingdom of the Serbs, Croats and Slovenes, but as Eyre Crowe remarked, 9.5.19, 'It is a national calamity for a new state to be burdened with such an elephantine designation. Perhaps some national poet can invent a single nation word to meet the case.' FO 608/42.

13. See H. and C. Seton-Watson, *The New Europe*, *passim*; Barbara Jelavich, *History of the Balkans* (2 vols, Cambridge, 1983), vol. 2, pp. 143–6; I. J. Lederer, *Yugoslavia at the Paris Peace Conference: a Study in Frontiermaking* (Yale, 1963), pp. 3–26.

14. Memo. 25.6.18, quoted by Lederer, ibid., p. 35, see also pp. 36–45. Jelavich, ibid., vol. 2, pp. 146–7; Temperley, vol. 4, pp. 171–207.

15. The Italians did not accept Montenegro's decision to join Yugoslavia and insisted that a seat be reserved for her at the conference. They refused to recognise Yugoslavia. Wilson did so, 7.2.19, and the Allied exchange of credentials with the Germans, 1.5.19, named her. Britain and France announced their recognition, 2.6.19 and 6.6.19.

16. Marston, *Peace Conference*, p. 61. The Serbian plenipotentiaries were Nikola Pašić from Serbia, Ante Trumbić, a Croat, and Ivan Žolger, a Slovene, and until recently an Austro-Hungarian minister.

17. Temperley, vol. 4, pp. 222–4; Nicolson, *Peacemaking*, pp. 135–6; R. Albrecht-Carrié, *Italy at the Paris Peace Conference* (New York, 1938, 1966 Archon reprint), p. 94. H. and C. Seton-Watson quoting R. Seton-Watson in *The New Europe*, 13.2.19, p. 342.

18. Meetings of 31.1.19 and 1.2.18 in *FRUS*, vol. 3, pp. 822–34, 840–55. See Lederer, *Yugoslavia*, pp. 94–101 for details of the Yugoslav case.

19. The Yugoslavs in February, the Rumanians in August 1919. Lederer, ibid., pp. 143–5, 165, 173–7, 235; Temperley, vol. 4, pp. 222–3, 229.

20. Temperley, vol. 4, p. 229; Lederer, *Yugoslavia*, p. 181; Meeting 23.5.19, *FRUS*, vol. 4, pp. 749–51; S. D. Spector, *Rumania at the Paris Peace Conference: A Study of the Diplomacy of Ioan I. C. Bratianu* (New York, 1962), pp. 123–6.

21. Lederer, *Yugoslavia*, pp. 256–7; Temperley, vol. 4, pp. 455–6.

22. Lederer, *Yugoslavia*, p. 96, p. 291.

23. Ibid., pp. 156–63; *FRUS*, vol. 4, p. 55.

24. Hardinge to Rodd 19.5.19, quoted by Dockrill and Goold, *Peace Without Promise*, p. 110. Hardinge had hoped for a larger role for himself (and the Foreign Office) at the conference but was left with only a grandiose, but meaningless, title. See Nicolson, *Peacemaking*, pp. 26, 46.

25. Letter, 30.1.18, Seymour, *Intimate Papers*, vol. 3, pp. 52–3. See also Lloyd George, *The Truth*, vol. 2, pp. 791–4.

26. Albrecht-Carrié, *Italy*, pp. 80–1, 102. See also A. E. Alcock, *The History of the South Tyrol Question* (1970), pp. 19–26.

27. H. and C. Seton-Watson, *The New Europe*, pp. 345–50; Lederer, *Yugoslavia*, pp. 152–3; H. Wickham Steed, *Through Thirty Years* (2 vols, 1924), vol. 2, p. 273.

28. Diary 15.4.19, Seymour, *Intimate Papers*, vol. 4, p. 457.

29. Lloyd George, *The Truth*, vol. 2, p. 809.

30. For details see Albrecht-Carrié, *Italy*, pp. 114–83; Lederer, *Yugoslavia*, pp. 184–217. The negotiations in the Council of Four can be followed in *FRUS*, vols 5 and 6.

31. Lederer, *Yugoslavia*, pp. 246–75; Albrecht-Carrié, *Italy*, pp. 231–89.

32. For details see Lederer, *Yugoslavia*, pp. 276–308 and Albrecht-Carrié, *Italy*, pp. 293–326; Temperley, vol. 4, pp. 307–37.

33. Lederer, *Yugoslavia*, pp. 219–24; Temperley, vol. 4, pp. 367–71.

34. *FRUS*, vol. 6, pp. 581–6.

35. Temperley, vol. 4, pp. 371–81.

36. See Lederer, *Yugoslavia*, pp. 309–12; R. Pearson, *National Minorities in Eastern Europe 1848–1945* (1983), pp. 155–60.

37. Nicolson, *Peacemaking*, pp. 34–5, 347; Temperley, vol. 4, pp. 1–28, 444–6; Albrecht-Carrié, *Italy*, p. 134.

38. Temperley, vol. 4, pp. 449–50; Seymour, *Intimate Papers*, vol. 4, p. 208.

39. Nicolson memo. 15.7.19 quoted by Dockrill and Goold, *Peace Without Promise*, p. 96 and generally pp. 93–101. Temperley, vol. 4, pp. 453–9.

40. Temperley, vol. 4, pp. 454–5, vol. 5, pp. 39–50. Dockrill and Goold, *Peace Without Promise*, pp. 99–101.

41. Spector, *Rumania*, pp. 15–66. The Allies admitted Rumania as an ally at the outset of the conference. Ibid., p. 75; Temperley, vol. 4, pp. 211–24.

42. Spector, *Rumania*, pp. 73–154; Temperley, vol. 4, pp. 224–30; Dockrill and Goold, *Peace Without Promise*, pp. 101–5.

43. Spector, *Rumania*, pp. 155–237; Temperley, vol. 4, pp. 230–6; Pearson, *National Minorities*, pp. 166–9.

44. Admiralty to F.O. 15.1.19 quoted by Dockrill and Goold, *Peace Without Promise*, p. 108; Temperley, vol. 4, p. 454.

45. Perman, *Czechoslovak State*, p. 188; Bonsal, *Unfinished Business*, pp. 131–2; Dockrill and Goold, *Peace Without Promise*, pp. 90–1.

46. F. Deak, *Hungary at the Paris Peace Conference: The Diplomatic History of the Treaty of Trianon* (New York, 1942), pp. 4–14; Temperley, vol. 4, pp. 89–125; Perman, *Czechoslovak State*, p. 80.

47. Deak, *Hungary*, pp. 61–3; Temperley, vol. 4, pp. 487–9; Dockrill and Goold, *Peace Without Promise*, pp. 103–5.

48. For details see Deak, *Hungary*, *passim*; Dockrill and Goold, *Peace Without Promise*, pp. 125–7; Temperley, vol. 4, pp. 488–92.

49. Deak, *Hungary*, p. 237n; Pearson, *National Minorities*, pp. 170–4.

50. Pearson, ibid., p. 151; Perman, *Czechoslovak State*, pp. 1–9.

51. He was greeted by the band of the Grenadier Guards (which did not risk the new national anthem) and an official car which did not have enough seats for himself, his colleague, and his two main British supporters, Seton-Watson and Wickham Steed. Undaunted, the two Czechs took their friends on their knees and drove off in state: Seton-Watson, *The New Europe*, pp. 324–5. See also Temperley, vol. 4, pp. 237–67 and Perman, *Czechoslovak State*, pp. 9–70.

52. Balfour summarised the dilemma of justifying different outcomes to apparently similar problems: 'It is perfectly true that a pedantic striving after consistency is always a blunder and sometimes a crime . . . whatever our decisions they are sure to be violently attacked; we cannot be popular, our only chance is to be just, and we shall not be thought just unless we can make it clear that our different treatment of *apparently* similar cases is really capable of a justification which the plain man can be made to understand.' Minute, 1.4.19 FO 608/5. Perman, *Czechoslovak State*, pp. 169–75; Mantoux, *Délibérations*, vol. 1, p. 149.

53. Perman, *Czechoslovak State*, pp. 95–120.

54. Ibid., pp. 228–42.

55. Ibid., pp. 242–57, 266–75; Temperley, vol. 4, pp. 348–63; S. Bonsal,

Suitors and Suppliants: The Little Nations at Versailles (New York, 1946), pp. 156–66.

56. Perman, *Czechoslovak State*, pp. 273–5; Spector, *Rumania*, p. 222; Temperley, vol. 4, pp. 267–77; Lundgreen-Nielsen, *Polish Problem*, pp. 400–1.

57. K. S. Stadler, *The Birth of the Austrian Republic 1918–1921* (Leyden, 1968); Temperley, vol. 4, pp. 389–411; Stevenson, *French War Aims*, pp. 182–3.

58. Macartney and Palmer, *Independent Eastern Europe*, pp. 111–15; Temperley, vol. 6, pp. 266–78; Dockrill and Goold, *Peace Without Promise*, pp. 117–18; Lundgreen-Nielsen, *Polish Problem*, pp. 385–99.

59. Macartney and Palmer, *Independent Eastern Europe*, pp. 73–115; J. Hiden, *The Baltic States and Weimar Ostpolitik* (1985), pp. 1–35.

60. For details see J. M. Thompson, *Russia, Bolshevism and the Versailles Peace* (Princeton, 1966), pp. 82–130; Tillman, *Anglo-American Relations*, pp. 135–9.

61. Memo. 22.1.19, quoted by Thompson, *Russia*, p. 389.

62. See A. J. Mayer, *Politics and Diplomacy of Peacemaking; Containment and Counter-Revolution at Versailles 1918–1919* (1968 edn) for an interesting, but exaggerated, account of the centrality of the Russian/Bolshevik issue in Paris.

63. Churchill's phrase during the negotiations for an Anglo-Soviet trade agreement in 1921. Krassin was the 'baboon'. Lord Beaverbrook, *The Decline and Fall of Lloyd George* (1966), p. 292. Thompson, *Russia*, covers the Bullitt mission in detail, pp. 131–77, and the military schemes pp. 178–221. See also Mayer, *Politics and Diplomacy*, pp. 411–603.

64. *Treaty*, pp. 272–4.

65. Temperley, vol. 1, p. 434.

66. See S. White, *Britain and the Bolshevik Revolution: A Study in the Politics of Diplomacy, 1920–1924* (1979), pp. 3–26; Thompson, *Russia*, pp. 382–3 and generally pp. 376–98; Watson, *Clemenceau*, pp. 372–9.

67. Pearson, *National Minorities*, p. 136; Temperley, vol. 4, p. 429.

68. Principle Four of the Four Principles, 11.2.18, Temperley, vol. 1, p. 439; A. Cobban, *The National State and National Self Determination* (1969), p. 50.

69. Telegram 2.2.19 in FO 608/33.

70. K. J. Newman, *European Democracy between the Wars* (1970), p. 148.

71. C. A. Macartney, *National States and National Minorities* (1934), *passim*; J. W. Headlam-Morley in Temperley, vol. 5, pp. 112–19. Alan Sharp, 'Britain and the Protection of Minorities at the Paris Peace Conference, 1919', in A. C. Hepburn (ed.), *Minorities in History* (1978), pp. 170–88.

72. House and Seymour, *What Really Happened*, p. 154.

73. Minute c.19.3.19 in FO 608/51.

7.   THE COLONIAL, NEAR AND MIDDLE EASTERN SETTLEMENTS

1. See Tillman, *Anglo-American Relations*, pp. 69–70, 85–98 and 219–28; Dockrill and Goold, *Peace Without Promise*, pp. 64–8, 131–79; W. R. Louis, *Great Britain and Germany's Lost Colonies 1914–1919* (Oxford, 1967), pp. 117–60.

2. *FRUS*, vol. 3, p. 718.

3. Louis, *Great Britain*, pp. 1–10; Temperley, vol. 2, pp. 223–6; H. D. Hall, 'The British Commonwealth and the Founding of the League Mandate System',

in K. Bourne and D. C. Watt (eds), *Studies in International History* (1967), pp.
345–68. Balfour commented, 9.12.18: 'Every time I come to a discussion – at
intervals of, say, five years – I find there is a new sphere which we have got to
guard, which is supposed to protect the gateways of India. Those gateways are
getting farther and farther from India.' Eastern Committee minutes, CAB
27/24.

4. Louis, *Great Britain*, pp. 7–10, 117–21; Temperley, vol. 2, pp. 220–2.
Leo Amery commented: 'I do not think that the Mandate is likely to impose
upon us any conditions which we would not impose upon ourselves or which we
have not been in the habit of imposing upon ourselves whenever we dealt with
subject peoples.' Porter, *Lion's Share*, p. 245.

5. Tillman, *Anglo-American Relations*, pp. 85–93; Louis, *Great Britain*, pp.
128–32; Lloyd George, *The Truth*, vol. 1, p. 542; Hankey, *The Supreme Control*,
letter of 29.1.19, p. 60.

6. Tillman, *Anglo-American Relations*, pp. 92–4; Louis, *Great Britain*, pp.
132–6, the quotations come from the Colonial Office papers and the Hughes
papers and are cited by Louis. Hughes preferred to see himself as 'a Welsh
tribesman', Hall in Bourne and Watt, *International History*, p. 355n and pp.
359–61.

7. Hall, ibid., pp. 134–9. The terms and conditions of the different classes of
mandate were established, with some difficulty, particularly in the case of the 'A'
mandates, by a committee chaired by Lord Milner, the British colonial secretary. Ibid., pp. 144–5; *FRUS*, vol. 3, pp. 797–809; Temperley, vol. 2, pp.
237–40; Hankey, *The Supreme Control*, pp. 55–66; Lloyd George, *The Truth*, vol.
1, pp. 543–8; Andrew and Kanya-Forstner, *France Overseas*, pp. 182–3; Poincaré, *Service*, vol. 11, pp. 104–5.

8. *Treaty*, pp. 276–83; *FRUS*, vol. 5, pp. 492–3; Lloyd George, *The Truth*,
vol. 2, pp. 1254–66.

9. *FRUS*, vol. 5, p. 508; Louis, *Great Britain*, pp. 152–4; Lloyd George, *The
Truth*, vol. 1, pp. 550–3; Albrecht-Carrié, *Italy*, pp. 225–30; Marks, *Innocent
Abroad*, pp. 316–21; Andrew and Kanya-Forstner, *France Overseas*, pp. 232–3.

10. *FRUS*, vol. 5, p. 508; Hall in Bourne and Watt, *International History*, pp.
364–7; Nish, *Alliance in Decline*, pp. 267–9. See also A. J. Crozier, 'The
Establishment of the Mandates System 1918–25: Some problems created by the
Paris Peace Conference', *JCH*, 14 (1979), 483–513.

11. Nish, ibid., *passim*, but in particular pp. 132–40, 202–11, 272–6; Dockrill and Goold, *Peace Without Promise*, pp. 67–8; Louis, *Great Britain*,
pp. 146–7. See also Louis's *British Strategy in the Far East 1919–1939* (Oxford,
1971), pp. 17–49; Temperley, vol. 6, pp. 368–90.

12. German observations on the draft treaty, 29.5.19 *FRUS*, vol. 6,
pp. 841–4; Temperley, vol. 2, p. 236. A. L. Kennedy, *Britain Faces Germany*
(1937), pp. 164–74; G. M. Gathorne-Hardy, *The Fourteen Points and the Treaty of
Versailles* (Oxford, 1939), pp. 21–6.

13. Elizabeth Monroe, *Britain's Moment in the Middle East 1914–1956* (1963,
1965 paperback), pp. 23–6. I have drawn heavily upon chapters 5 and 6 of
Dockrill and Goold, *Peace Without Promise*, in the preparation of this section,
specifically here pp. 131–4. M. E. Yapp, *The Making of the Modern Near East
1792–1923* (1987), pp. 179–277; Marian Kent (ed.), *The Great Powers and the End*

of the Ottoman Empire (1984) pp. 24–6, 100–2, 165–6, 185–9; Andrew and Kanya-Forstner, *France Overseas*, pp. 83–115. Temperley, vol. 6, pp. 23–4. Those seeking further details from a Turkish perspective should consult S. R. Sonyel, *Turkish Diplomacy 1918–1923: Mustafa Kemal and the Nationalist Movement* (Beverley Hills, 1975), *passim*.

14. Paul Helmreich, *From Paris to Sèvres: The Partition of the Ottoman Empire at the Paris Peace Conference of 1919–1920* (Ohio, 1974), pp. 3–5; Yapp, *Modern Near East*, pp. 297–300; Dockrill and Goold, *Peace Without Promise*, pp. 181–6; H. Nicolson, *Curzon: The Last Phase, 1919–1925. A Study in Post-War Diplomacy* (1934), p. 3.

15. M. L. Smith, *Ionian Vision: Greece in Asia Minor 1919–1922* (1973), pp. 62–101; Yapp, *Modern Near East*, pp. 301–7; *FRUS*, vol. 5, pp. 483–4; Temperley, vol. 6, pp. 26–8.

16. *FRUS*, vol. 3, pp. 859–66, 868–75; Dockrill and Goold, *Peace Without Promise*, pp. 186–90; Yapp, *Modern Near East*, pp. 307–8; Helmreich, *Paris to Sèvres*, pp. 38–46; Temperley, vol. 6, p. 25; Albrecht-Carrié, *Italy*, pp. 201–30; Walworth, *Wilson and his Peacemakers*, pp. 351–5; N. Petsalis-Diomidis, *Greece at the Paris Peace Conference, 1919* (Thessalonika, 1978), *passim*; Harry J. Psomiades, *The Eastern Question: The Last Phase* (Salonika, 1968), *passim*.

17. Dockrill and Goold, *Peace Without Promise*, p. 195 and generally pp. 190–7; Yapp, *Modern Near East*, pp. 307–8; Macartney and Palmer, *Independent Eastern Europe*, pp. 131–2; Albrecht-Carrié, *Italy*, pp. 242–3.

18. See E. Goldstein, 'Great Britain and the Greater Greece 1917–1920', *HJ*, 32, no. 2 (1989), 339–56 for a detailed analysis of British policies and the attitudes of key decision-makers. Yapp, *Modern Near East*, pp. 308–10; Dockrill and Goold, *Peace Without Promise*, pp. 202–4; Smith, *Ionian Vision*, pp. 103–4, 118–123.

19. Temperley, vol. 6, pp. 26–31; Helmreich, *Paris to Sèvres*, pp. 242–61, 291–309, 314–22; Dockrill and Goold, *Peace Without Promise*, pp. 204–9; Yapp, *Modern Near East*, pp. 310–13; Smith, *Ionian Vision*, pp. 135–59.

20. Dockrill and Goold, *Peace Without Promise*, pp. 214–16; Yapp, *Modern Near East*, pp. 313–17.

21. Dockrill and Goold, *Peace Without Promise*, pp. 216–21; Yapp, *Modern Near East*, pp. 317–18; Smith, *Ionian Vision*, pp. 180–236. Keith Jeffery and Alan Sharp, 'Lord Curzon and Secret Intelligence', in C. Andrew and J. Noakes (eds), *Intelligence and International Relations 1900–1945* (Exeter, 1987), pp. 108–9.

22. Ibid., pp. 110–15. For the golf match incident see J. Laroche, *Au Quai d'Orsay avec Briand et Poincaré* (Paris, 1957), pp. 152–3, 146–7. Smith, *Ionian Vision*, pp. 266–83; Dockrill and Goold, *Peace Without Promise*, pp. 221–6; Yapp, *Modern Near East*, pp. 318–19.

23. Sir Henry Wilson had feared a confrontation between Kemal and General Harington's British force at Constantinople, as he wrote to Henry Rawlinson, the Indian Commander-in-Chief, 5.4.21: 'Tim [Harington] will find himself sitting in Constantinople with our friend Kemal facing him with a few odd guns stuck in the bushes, having a shot at Tim, or anything from a battleship to a jampot, from behind some bushes and therefore quite invisible . . . the sooner we clear out of those places that do not belong to us and hang on to those that do the better for England.' Keith Jeffery (ed.), *The Military Correspondence of Field*

Marshal Sir Henry Wilson 1918–1922 (1985), p. 252. Dockrill and Goold, *Peace Without Promise*, pp. 228–36; Yapp, *Modern Near East*, pp. 319–20; Nicolson, *Curzon*, p. 274; Smith, *Ionian Vision*, pp. 284–311; Lord Hardinge of Penshurst, *Old Diplomacy* (1947), pp. 271–4; David Walder, *The Chanak Affair* (1969), *passim*.

24. Jeffery and Sharp, 'Lord Curzon', pp. 114–22; Dockrill and Goold, *Peace Without Promise*, pp. 236–46; Nicolson, *Curzon*, pp. 290–350; Sonyel, *Turkish Diplomacy*, pp. 185–226; Martin Gilbert, *Sir Horace Rumbold: Portrait of a Diplomat 1869–1941* (1973), pp. 280–98.

25. Monroe, *Britain's Moment*, pp. 11–70; John Darwin, *Britain, Egypt and the Middle East: Imperial Policy in the Aftermath of War 1918–1922* (1981), pp. 3–46; M. Kent, *Oil and Empire: British Policy and Mesopotamian Oil, 1900–1920* (1976), pp. 117–57. See also Kent, *The Great Powers, passim*; J. Nevakivi, *Britain, France and the Arab Middle East 1914–1920* (1969), *passim*; Yapp, *Modern Near East*, pp. 266–351; Temperley, vol. 6, pp. 1–117.

26. Temperley, ibid., pp. 185–7; Dockrill and Goold, *Peace Without Promise*, p. 141; Darwin, *Imperial Policy*, pp. 141–2.

27. Monroe, *Britain's Moment*, pp. 26–45; Dockrill and Goold, *Peace Without Promise*, pp. 135–9; Isaiah Friedman, 'The McMahon–Hussein Correspondence', *JCH*, 5, no. 2 (1970), 83–122. The phrase is Arnold Toynbee's, *JCH*, 5, no. 4 (1970), 193. Yapp, *Modern Near East*, pp. 281–4; E. Kedourie, *In the Anglo–Arab Labyrinth: The McMahon–Husayn Correspondence and its Interpretations 1914–1939* (Cambridge, 1976), pp. 65–137; G. Antonius, *The Arab Awakening* (Beirut, 1969), pp. 164–83.

28. Yapp, *Modern Near East*, pp. 288–300; Nevakivi, *Arab Middle East*, pp. 45–103; Friedman, 'McMahon–Hussein Correspondence', pp. 98–103.

29. Letter to Lloyd George, 26.5.19, LGP F/39/1/21. (I am grateful to my colleague Keith Jeffery for this reference.) Friedman, 'McMahon–Hussein Correspondence', pp. 84–7. Grey thought the Arab state 'a castle in the air', Picot believed 'Such a state will never materialise. You cannot turn a myriad of tribes into a viable whole', whilst Clayton, the director of military intelligence in Egypt, did not 'consider it within the bounds of practical politics.' Andrew and Kanya-Forstner, *France Overseas*, pp. 90–7. For the text of the Sykes–Picot agreement see *DBFP*, vol. 4, pp. 245–7.

30. Darwin, *Imperial Policy*, pp. 143–61; Helmreich, *Paris to Sèvres*, pp. 17–18; Yapp, *Modern Near East*, pp. 304–6; Dockrill and Goold, *Peace Without Promise*, pp. 143–50; Andrew and Kanya-Forstner, *France Overseas*, pp. 174–6; Watson, *Clemenceau*, pp. 368–9; Lloyd George, *The Truth*, vol. 2, p. 1038.

31. R. Lansing, *The Big Four and Others of the Paris Peace Conference* (1922), p. 169; Antonius, *Arab Awakening*, pp. 286–7; *FRUS*, vol. 3, pp. 889–94; Andrew and Kanya-Forstner, *France Overseas*, pp. 186–9; Dockrill and Goold, *Peace Without Promise*, pp. 150–5; Darwin, *Imperial Policy*, pp. 162–5; Nevakivi, *Arab Middle East*, pp. 148–9; Helmreich, *Paris to Sèvres*, pp. 51–6.

32. *FRUS*, vol. 5, pp. 1–14; Andrew and Kanya-Forstner, *France Overseas*, pp. 193–4; Helmreich, *Paris to Sèvres*, pp. 64–79.

33. Dockrill and Goold, *Peace Without Promise*, pp. 162–4; Andrew and Kanya-Forstner, *France Overseas*, pp. 196–9; Kent, *Oil and Empire*, pp. 140–50; Nevakivi, *Arab Middle East*, pp. 151–71.

34. Cecil remarked 'we shall simply keep the peace between the Arabs and the Jews. We are not going to get anything out of it. Whoever goes there will have a poor time.' Lloyd George, *The Truth*, vol. 2, p. 1150. Robert de Caix, a temporary French foreign office official, confirmed this view: 'Any mandate there is likely to be extremely thorny. . . . The Mandatory . . . will be subjected to criticisms, to obstacles and to obligations of all sorts.' Andrew and Kanya-Forstner, *France Overseas*, p. 170. Dockrill and Goold, *Peace Without Promise*, pp. 161–2; Yapp, *Modern Near East*, pp. 327–30.

35. Antonius, *Arab Awakening*, pp. 290–1; Helmreich, *Paris to Sèvres*, pp. 56–9. On being told, at the start of a meeting, of Sykes' death, Balfour pettishly remarked 'Dear, dear, it seem as though we shall never get on with the problem.' Bonsal, *Suitors and Suppliants*, p. 42. Dockrill and Goold, *Peace Without Promise*, pp. 159, 164.

36. *FRUS*, vol. 4, pp. 161–70; Dockrill and Goold, *Peace Without Promise*, pp. 158–64.

37. Nevakivi, *Arab Middle East*, pp. 172–96; Yapp, *Modern Near East*, pp. 322–5; Dockrill and Goold, *Peace Without Promise*, p. 167.

38. Yapp, *Modern Near East*, pp. 325–7; Dockrill and Goold, *Peace Without Promise*, pp. 169–73; Andrew and Kanya-Forstner, *France Overseas*, pp. 205–7; Nevakivi, *Arab Middle East*, pp. 220–42.

39. Kent, *Oil and Empire*, pp. 148–9; Dockrill and Goold, *Peace Without Promise*, pp. 173–4; Nevakivi, *Arab Middle East*, pp. 241–50.

40. Nevakivi, ibid., pp. 251–60; Dockrill and Goold, *Peace Without Promise*, pp. 168, 174–9; Andrew and Kanya-Forstner, *France Overseas*, pp. 207–8; Antonius, *Arab Awakening*, pp. 305–16.

CONCLUSION

The quotation is from Lloyd George: F. Stevenson, *Diary*, 10.4.19, p. 179.

1. James Joll, '1914: The Unspoken Assumptions'. His 1968 inaugural lecture reprinted in Koch, *Origins*, (first edn), pp. 307–28. Elcock, *Portrait of a Decision*, pp. 298–324.

2. Lansing, *The Big Four*, p. 107.

3. Keynes, *Economic Consequences*, p. 32; Lansing, *Big Four*, p. 10; Cambon, *Correspondance*, vol. 3, p. 303; Watson, *Clemenceau*, pp. 277–8, 397–407.

4. Keynes, *Economic Consequences*, pp. 54–5; Nicolson, *Peacemaking*, p. 164; Lentin, *Guilt at Versailles*, p. 138.

5. Hussein spoke scathingly of 'Luweed Jurj'. 'The English, my son, are an honourable kind, in word and in deed, in fortune and in adversity. . . . Only his Excellency the estimable, energetic Luweed Jurj is something of an acrobat and a fox. I say a fox, saving your presence.' Antonius, *Arab Awakening*, p. 183. Henri Jaspar, the Belgian statesman, was direct in his notes for an article, 'menteur', but more circumspect in the text: 'Et le culte de la veracité comme la suite dans les idées n'obsédèrent jamais Lloyd George.' Papiers Jaspar, Archives du Royaume, Brussels, Dossier 209. Martin Pugh paints a perceptive and sympathetic picture in *Lloyd George* (1988), *passim*. Lentin, *Guilt at Versailles*, pp. 111–23; Lord Riddell, *Intimate Diary of the Peace Conference and After, 1918–1923* (1933), p. 101.

6. F. Stevenson, *Diary*, 5.4.19, p. 178.

7. See the discussion of Paragraph 18 of Annex II of the reparation section in Chapter 4. Article 430 authorised the reoccupation of territory in the Rhineland evacuated under the terms of Article 429 – essentially, therefore, a sanction with little value until at least the first section of the occupied zone was due for evacuation, or not before 1925. Article 213 authorised the League to investigate breaches of the disarmament clauses by Germany, after the Allied Control Commissions had completed their tasks, but specified no penalties. See W. M. Jordan, *Great Britain, France, and the German Problem 1918–1939* (1943, 1971 edn), pp. 66–84.

8. W. S. Churchill, *The Gathering Storm* (1949 edn), p. 6; Clemenceau, *Grandeur and Misery*, pp. 355–67; Lloyd George, *The Truth*, vol. 1, p. 6.

9. Pugh, *Lloyd George*, p. 164.

10. Eastern Committee minutes, CAB 24/27. Kerr to Lloyd George, 2.9.20 F/90/1/18 LGP. Nicolson CID paper 251–B, 10.7.20 in Cab 4/7. Alan Sharp, 'Britain and the Channel Tunnel 1919–1920', *AJPH*, 25, no. 2 (1979), 210–15.

11. See, for example, Lord D'Abernon, 20.8.23: 'Anyone who supposes that a French Government dominating the Continent as Napoleon dominated it after Tilsit will remain friendly to England must be a poor judge of national psychology. . . . Desiring the maintenance of the Anglo–French Entente, I am compelled to desire the existence of a strong Germany.' *An Ambassador of Peace* (3 vols, 1929), vol. 2, pp. 238–9.

12. Mantoux, *Délibérations*, vol. 1, p. 70.

13. Lentin, *Guilt at Versailles*, *passim*. See also the same author's forthcoming Historical Association pamphlet *The Versailles Peace Settlement 1919*; Martin Gilbert, *The Roots of Appeasement* (1966), *passim*. Robert Vansittart wrote, 'We all blamed France . . . for being vindictive, when her real motive was funk.' *The Mist Procession* (1958), p. 206. Kitchen, *Europe between the Wars*, p. 59.

14. P. Wandycz, *France and her Eastern Allies 1919–1925* (Minneapolis, 1962), *passim*. Headlam-Morley pointed out, in 1925, that the main danger points in Europe were no longer the Rhine and Alsace-Lorraine, but the Vistula and Danzig. He then speculated on the possibility of an *Anschluss* and a Sudetenland crisis: J. W. Headlam-Morley, *Studies in Diplomatic History* (1930), p. 182. Broadcast 27.9.38, Neville Chamberlain *The Struggle for Peace* (n.d.), p. 275.

15. Andrew and Kanya-Forstner, *France Overseas*, p. 180.

16. Keynes, *Economic Consequences*, pp. 10–12; Kennedy, *Rise and Fall*, pp. 358–66. Kent, *Spoils of War*, *passim*.

17. A French official wrote, 30.6.36: 'Among the five countries of which each has a treaty known as an "alliance" with France there are few who regard themselves as allies of one another. There is no need to dwell on the relations between the USSR and Poland, between Poland and Czechoslovakia, on the mutual distrust of Poland and Rumania, born of Polish–Russian hostility, and which makes the Polish–Rumanian alliance a figment of the imagination, the absence of an undertaking of assistance between the three states of the Little Entente, except against Hungary . . . without mentioning less apparent but persistent rivalries and differences.' Anthony Adamthwaite, *The Making of the Second World War* (1977), pp. 159–60.

18. Jacques Bardoux, *Action Française*, 8.5.19.

19. For future developments see Ruth Henig's two pamphlets, *Versailles and After 1919–1933* (1984) and *The Origins of the Second World War 1933–1939* (1985). Kennedy, *Rise and Fall*, pp. 355–444; Sally Marks, *The Illusion of Peace: International Relations in Europe 1918–1933* (1976). P. M. H. Bell, *The Origins of the Second World War in Europe* (1986).

Bibliographical Note

THERE is such an array of literature on the peace settlement that students may be grateful for some preliminary guidance as to further reading, particularly concerning the more recent publications. The starting point for any deeper research remains the remarkable *History of the Paris Peace Conference*, edited by H. W. V. Temperley in 1920 and largely written by participants. It is still an invaluable source of information on all aspects of the treaties, providing maps, statistics and document extracts, as well as an account of the decisions. Other contemporary sources include the memoirs and diaries of the politicians and diplomats, notably Bonsal, Clemenceau, Headlam-Morley, House, Lansing, Lloyd George (though written somewhat later), Loucheur, Nicolson, Poincaré and Tardieu. No student should miss the pleasure of reading J. M. Keynes's vitriolic attack on the settlement and its authors in his *Economic Consequences of the Peace* supplemented by his essay on Lloyd George in *Essays in Biography* and somewhat tempered by *A Revision of the Treaty* which he wrote in 1922. The best text of the Treaty of Versailles is the annotated edition *The Treaty of Versailles and After*, published by the United States government in 1944 and reprinted in 1968. It contains helpful commentaries and information on the execution of the various clauses.

Two short surveys of the settlement are excellent sources of ideas and approaches. R. B. Henig, *Versailles and After* (1984) and A. Lentin, *The Versailles Peace Settlement 1919* (1990) both manage to pack a great deal into a limited space. A rapid perusal of the footnotes will reveal how useful I found M. L. Dockrill and J. D. Goold, *Peace Without Promise. Britain and the Peace Conferences 1919–1923* (1981) as a general guide to British policy, whilst S. P. Tillman, *Anglo-American Relations at the Paris Peace Conference of 1919* (1961) is also helpful over a wide range of treaty issues. There are an increasing number of specialised studies of aspects of the settlement. Reparations have been hotly debated both in the scholarly journals and in three recent monographs: R. E. Bunselmeyer, *The Cost of the War of 1914–1919. British Economic War Aims and the Origins of Reparation* (1975); M. Trachtenberg, *Reparation in World Politics. France and European Economic Diplomacy 1916–1923* (1980); and B. Kent, *The Spoils of War. The Politics, Economics and Diplomacy of Reparations 1918–1932* (1989). L. S. Jaffe, *The Decision to Disarm Germany* (1985) provides a thorough study of the disarmament issue. George Egerton, *Great Britain and the Creation of the League of Nations: Strategy, Politics, and International Organization, 1914–1919* (1979) covers the background and League negotiations very well. The development of the idea of war crimes and war criminals forms the basis of an interesting study by J. F. Willis, *Prologue to Nuremburg. The Politics and Diplomacy of Punishing War Criminals of the First World War* (1982). French territorial ambitions are well covered by D. Stevenson,

French War Aims against Germany 1914–1919 (1982) and W. A. McDougall, *France's Rhineland Diplomacy 1914–1924. The Last Bid for a Balance of Power in Europe* (1978). Most of the standard studies of individual countries at the conference were written before the mid-1960s but K. Lundgreen-Nielsen, *The Polish Problem at the Paris Peace Conference* (1979), S. Marks, *Innocent Abroad: Belgium and the Paris Peace Conference of 1919* (1981), N. Petsalis-Diomidis, *Greece at the Paris Peace Conference 1919* (1978) and M. Kent (ed.), *The Great Powers and the End of the Ottoman Empire* (1984) are notable exceptions. There is also a good summary of events in Turkey and Arabia in M. E. Yapp, *The Making of the Modern Middle East 1792–1923* (1987).

Those seeking to investigate the personalities involved in the negotiations should begin with A. Lentin's, *Guilt at Versailles. Lloyd George and the Pre-History of Appeasement* (1985) which presents a stimulating and elegant view of some of the main and secondary figures at the conference. Woodrow Wilson is thoroughly investigated by K. Schwabe, *Woodrow Wilson, Revolutionary Germany and Peacemaking 1918–1919* (1985) and A. Walworth, *Wilson and his Peacemakers* (1986). D. R. Watson, *Georges Clemenceau. A Political Biography* (1974) remains the standard English work though C. M. Andrew and A. S. Kanya-Forstner present a less sympathetic picture of the French leader in *France Overseas. The Great War and the Climax of French Imperial Expansion* (1981). Their views on the colonial settlement may be supplemented by those of W. R. Louis, *Great Britain and Germany's Lost Colonies 1914–1919* (1967).

It is always worth investigating the journals, particularly in anniversary years. The *Journal of Modern History* devoted one issue in 1979 to reappraisals of various aspects of the treaty debate and although 1789 rather overshadowed 1919 in 1989 there was a thoughtful retrospective by C. Seton-Watson in the *Review of International Studies* (15, no. 4, October 1989). For those seeking to put 1919 into a wider context of international politics P. Kennedy, *The Rise and Fall of the Great Powers. Economic Change and Military Conflict from 1500 to 2000* (1989) offers a splendid and provocative analysis whilst S. Marks, *The Illusion of Peace. International Relations in Europe 1918–1933* (1976) provides some interesting insights from a continental perspective. She also contributes a useful essay on the Versailles debate in G. Martel (ed.), *The Origins of the Second World War Reconsidered. The A. J. P. Taylor Debate after Twenty-Five Years* (1986). Finally, P. M. H. Bell's brilliant *The Origins of the Second World War in Europe* (1986) skilfully analyses the events and ideas which influenced decision-making in the 1920s and 1930s, carrying the story forward to the outbreak of another major European conflict.

Bibliography

UNPRINTED DOCUMENTS

This study makes no claim to be a piece of original research but it has utilised
some manuscript sources.

The Foreign Office (FO 371), Cabinet Office (CAB 23 and 24), and Peace
  Conference papers (FO 608) are all held in the Public Record Office at Kew,
  as are certain papers of Foreign Office personnel (FO 800).
The Lloyd George and Bonar Law papers are kept in the House of Lords Record
  Office.
The Lothian papers are kept in the National Library of Scotland.
The Hardinge papers are kept in Cambridge University Library.
The Clemenceau papers (FC) are held by the Service Historique de l'Armée de
  Terre at Vincennes.

PRINTED DOCUMENTS

*British Documents on Foreign Affairs: Reports and papers from the Foreign Office
  Confidential Print*, general editors K. Bourne and D. C. Watt. *Part II. From the
  First to the Second World War. Series I.*
The Paris Peace Conference of 1919, vols 1–7, Dockrill, M. (ed.) (Maryland, 1989).
MANTOUX, P., *Les Délibérations du Conseil des Quatre* (2 vols, Paris, 1955).
——, *Paris Peace Conference 1919: Proceedings of the Council of Four (March 24–April
  18)* (Geneva, 1964).
*Papers Relating to the Foreign Relations of the United States: The Paris Peace Conference of
  1919* (13 vols, Washington, 1943 onwards). *The Treaty of Versailles and After:
  Annotations of the Text of the Treaty* (Washington, 1944, 1968 reprint).
WOODWARD, E. L. and BUTLER, R. (eds), *Documents on British Foreign Policy,
  1919–1939* (First Series, 1947 onwards).

BOOKS AND ARTICLES

ADAMTHWAITE, ANTHONY, *The Making of the Second World War* (1977).
ALBRECHT-CARRIÉ, R., *Italy at the Paris Peace Conference* (New York, 1938, 1966
  reprint).
ALCOCK, A. E., *History of the International Labor Organization* (New York, 1971).
——, *The History of the South Tyrol Question* (1970).
ALTER, P., *Nationalism* (1989 translation).
AMBROSIUS, LLOYD E., *Woodrow Wilson and the American Diplomatic Tradition. The
  Treaty Fight in Perspective* (Cambridge, 1987).

ANDREW, CHRISTOPHER and KANYA-FORSTNER, A. S., *France Overseas: The Great War and the Climax of French Imperial Expansion* (1981).

ANDREW, CHRISTOPHER and NOAKES, JEREMY, *Intelligence and International Relations* (Exeter, 1987).

ANTONIUS, G., *The Arab Awakening* (Beirut, 1969).

ARMSTRONG, D., *The Rise of the International Organisation: A Short History* (1982).

AULARD, A., *La Paix future d'après la Révolution française et Kant* (Paris, 1916).

BAKER, R. S., *Woodrow Wilson and the World Settlement* (3 vols, 1922).

BARDOUX, J., *De Paris à Spa: la bataille diplomatique pour la paix française* (Paris, 1921).

——, *Lloyd George et la France* (Paris, 1923).

BARIÉTY, J., *Les Relations franco–allemandes après la Première Guerre Mondiale: 10 Novembre 1918–10 Janvier 1925. De l'Exécution à la Négociation* (Paris, 1977).

BARROS, J., *Office Without Power: Secretary General Sir Eric Drummond, 1919–1933* (Oxford, 1979).

BARTLETT, C. J., *The Global Conflict 1880–1970: The International Rivalry between the Great Powers* (1984).

BARUCH, BERNARD M., *The Making of the Reparation and Economic Sections of the Treaty* (1920).

BEAVERBROOK, LORD, *The Decline and Fall of Lloyd George* (1966).

BECKER, J. J., *1914: Comment les Français sont entrés dans la guerre* (Paris, 1977).

BELL, CORAL, *The Conventions of Crisis: A Study in Diplomatic Management* (1971).

BELL, P. M. H., *The Origins of the Second World War in Europe* (1986).

BIRDSALL, P., *Versailles Twenty Years After* (1941).

BLAKE, R., *The Unknown Prime Minister: The Life and Times of Andrew Bonar Law, 1858–1923* (1955).

BLANNING, T. C. W., *The Origins of the French Revolutionary Wars* (1986).

BONNEFOUS, E., *Histoire politique de la Troisième République* (7 vols, Paris, 1967 edn).

BONSAL, S., *Suitors and Suppliants: The Little Nations at Versailles* (New York, 1946).

——, *Unfinished Business* (1944).

BOSWORTH, RICHARD, *Italy and the Approach of the First World War* (1983).

BOURNE, K. and WATT, D. C. (eds), *Studies in International History* (1967).

BOWLEY, A. L., *Some Economic Consequences of the Great War* (1930).

BRIDGE, F. R., *From Sadowa to Sarajevo* (1972).

BRIDGE, F. R. and BULLEN, R., *The Great Powers and the European States System 1815–1914* (1980).

BUNSELMEYER, R. E., *The Cost of the War of 1914–1919: British Economic War Aims and the Origins of Reparation* (Connecticut, 1975).

BUTLER, J. R. M., *Lord Lothian, Philip Kerr: 1882–1940* (1960).

CALDER, KENNETH J., *Britain and the Origins of the New Europe 1914–1918* (Cambridge, 1976).

CALLWELL, SIR C. E., *Field Marshal Sir Henry Wilson: His Life and Diaries* (2 vols, 1927).

CAMBON, PAUL, *Correspondance* (3 vols, Paris, 1946).

CAMPBELL, F. GREGORY, 'The Struggle for Upper Silesia, 1919–1922', *JMH*, 42, no. 3 (1970), 361–85.

CECIL, LORD ROBERT, *A Great Experiment: An Autobiography* (1941).

CHAMBERLAIN, NEVILLE, *The Struggle for Peace* (n.d.).

CHURCHILL, W. S., *The Gathering Storm* (1949 edn).

——, *The World Crisis – The Aftermath* (1929).

CLEMENCEAU, GEORGES, *Grandeur and Misery of Victory* (1930 translation).

COBBAN, A., *The Nation State and National Self Determination* (1969, paperback).

COUPE, W. A., 'German Cartoonists and the Treaty of Versailles', *History Today*, 32 (January 1982), 46–52.

CRAIG, G. A. and GILBERT, F., *The Diplomats: 1919–1939* (Princeton, 1953).

CROZIER, A. J., 'The Establishment of the Mandates System 1919–25; Some problems created by the Paris Peace Conference', *JCH*, 14 (1979), 483–513.

D'ABERNON, LORD, *An Ambassador of Peace: Pages from the Diary of Viscount D'Abernon (Berlin 1920–1926)* (3 vols, 1929–1930).

DARWIN, JOHN, *Britain, Egypt and the Middle East: Imperial Policy in the Aftermath of War 1918–1922* (1981).

DAWSON, W. H., *Germany under the Treaty* (1933).

DEAK, F., *Hungary and the Paris Peace Conference: The Diplomatic History of the Treaty of Trianon* (New York, 1942).

DOCKRILL, M. L. and GOOLD, J. D., *Peace Without Promise: Britain and the Paris Peace Conferences, 1919–1923* (1981).

DOCKRILL, M. L. and STEINER, Z., 'The Foreign Office at the Paris Peace Conference of 1919', *International History Review* (January 1980), 55–96.

DROZ, J., *Les Causes de la Première Guerre Mondiale* (Paris, 1973).

DUGDALE, BLANCHE E. C., *Arthur James Balfour* (2 vols, 1936).

DUROSELLE, J. B., *Histoire diplomatique de 1918 à nos jours* (4th edn, Paris, 1966).

EGERTON, GEORGE, W., *Great Britain and the Creation of the League of Nations: Strategy, Politics, and International Organization, 1914–1919* (1979).

——, 'Britain and the "Great Betrayal": Anglo-American Relations and the Struggle for United States Ratification of the Treaty of Versailles; 1919–1920', *HJ*, 21, no. 4 (1978), 885–911.

——, 'The Lloyd George Government and the Creation of the League of Nations', *AHR*, 72, no. 2 (1974), 419–44.

ELCOCK, H., *Portrait of a Decision: The Council of Four and the Treaty of Versailles* (1972).

EMSLEY, CLIVE, *Conflict and Stability* (1979).

EYCK, ERICH, *A History of the Weimar Republic: Volume 1, From the Collapse of the Empire to Hindenburg's Election* (New York, 1972).

FEST, W., *Peace or Partition: The Habsburg Empire and British Policy, 1914–1918* (New York, 1978).

FISCHER, FRITZ, *Germany's War Aims in the First World War* (1967 translation of 1961 original).

——, *The War of Illusions* (1973 translation of 1969 original).

FLOTO, I., *Colonel House in Paris: A Study of American Policy at the Paris Peace Conference, 1919* (Aarhus, 1973).

FOCH, F., *The Memoirs of Marshal Foch* (1931 translation).

FRIEDMAN, ISAIAH, 'The McMahon–Hussein Correspondence', *JCH*, 5, no. 2 (1970), 83–122.

GATHORNE-HARDY, G. M., *The Fourteen Points and the Treaty of Versailles* (Oxford, 1939).

GELFAND, LAWRENCE E., *The Inquiry* (Yale, 1963).

GILBERT, MARTIN, *Sir Horace Rumbold: Portrait of a Diplomat 1869–1941* (1973).
——, *The Roots of Appeasement* (1966).
——, *Winston S. Churchill: Volume 4, 1917–1922* (1975).
GOLDSTEIN, ERIK, 'British Peace Aims and the Eastern Question: The P.I.D. and the Eastern Question 1918', *Middle Eastern Studies*, 23, no. 4 (1987), 419–36.
——, 'New Diplomacy and the New Europe at the Paris Peace Conference: The A.W.A. Leeper Papers', *East European Quarterly*, 21, no. 4 (1988), 393–400.
——, 'The Foreign Office and political intelligence 1918–1920', *Review of International Studies*, 14, no. 4 (1988), 275–88.
——, 'Great Britain and Greater Greece 1917–1920', *HJ*, 32, no. 2 (1989), 339–56.
GRENVILLE, J. A. S., *Lord Salisbury and Foreign Policy: The Close of the Nineteenth Century* (1964, 1970 paperback).
HANKEY, LORD, *The Supreme Control at the Paris Peace Conference 1919* (1963).
HARDINGE, LORD, *Old Diplomacy: The Reminiscences of Lord Hardinge of Penshurst* (1947).
HARRIS, H. W., *The Peace in the Making* (1919).
HEADLAM-MORLEY, AGNES (ed.), *Sir James Headlam-Morley: A Memoir of the Paris Peace Conference 1919* (1972).
HEADLAM-MORLEY, J. W., *Studies in Diplomatic History* (1930).
HELMREICH, PAUL, *From Paris to Sèvres: The Partition of the Ottoman Empire and the Paris Peace Conference of 1919–1920* (Ohio, 1974).
HENIG, RUTH (ed.), *The League of Nations* (1973).
——, *The Origins of the First World War* (1989).
——, *The Origins of the Second World War 1933–1939* (1985).
——, *Versailles and After 1919–1933* (1984).
HEPBURN, A. C. (ed.), *Minorities in History* (1978).
HIDEN, J., *The Baltic States and Weimar Ostpolitik* (1985).
HOUSE, E. and SEYMOUR, C., *What Really Happened at Paris* (1921).
HOWARD, MICHAEL, *The Continental Commitment: The Dilemma of British Defence Policy in the Era of Two World Wars* (1972 paperback).
JAFFE, LORNA S., *The Decision to Disarm Germany* (New York, 1985).
JEFFERY, KEITH (ed.), *The Military Correspondence of Field Marshal Sir Henry Wilson 1918–1922* (1985).
JELAVICH, BARBARA, *History of the Balkans* (2 vols, Cambridge, 1983).
JESSOP, T. E., *The Treaty of Versailles: Was it Just?* (1942).
JOLL, JAMES, *1914: The Unspoken Assumptions* (1961).
——, *The Origins of the First World War* (1984).
JORDAN, W. M., *Great Britain, France, and the German Problem 1918–1939* (1943, 1971 edn).
KEDOURIE, E., *In the Anglo–Arab Labyrinth: The McMahon–Husayn Correspondence and its Interpretations 1914–1939* (Cambridge, 1976).
KEIGER, JOHN, *France and the Origins of the First World War* (1983).
KENNEDY, A. L., *Britain Faces Germany* (1937).
——, *Old Diplomacy and New* (1922).
KENNEDY, PAUL, *The Rise and Fall of the Great Powers: Economic Change and Military Conflict from 1500 to 2000* (1989 paperback).
KENT, BRUCE, *The Spoils of War: The Politics, Economics and Diplomacy of Reparations 1918–1932* (Oxford, 1989).

KENT, MARION, *Oil and Empire: British Policy and Mesopotamian Oil, 1900–1920* (1976).

——, (ed.), *The Great Powers and the End of the Ottoman Empire* (1984).

KEYNES, J. M., *The Economic Consequences of the Peace* (1919).

——, *A Revision of the Treaty* (1922).

——, *Essays in Biography* (second edn, 1951).

KING, J. C., *Foch versus Clemenceau: France and German Dismemberment, 1918–1919* (Harvard, 1960).

KITCHEN, MARTIN, *Europe between the Wars: A Political History* (1988).

KLOTZ, L.-L., *De la Guerre à la paix* (Paris, 1924).

KOCH, H. W., *The Origins of the First World War: Great Power Rivalry and German War Aims* (1972 and 1984 second edn with variations).

LAMBERT, MARGARET, *The Saar* (1934).

LANSING, ROBERT, *The Big Four and Others of the Paris Peace Conference* (1922).

——, *The Peace Negotiations: A Personal Narrative* (New York, 1921).

LAROCHE, J., *Au Quai d'Orsay avec Briand et Poincaré* (Paris, 1957).

LEDERER, I. J., *Yugoslavia at the Paris Peace Conference: A Study in Frontiermaking* (Yale, 1963).

LENTIN, A., *Guilt at Versailles: Lloyd George and the Pre-History of Appeasement* (1984 paperback).

——, *The Versailles Peace Settlement 1919* (forthcoming).

LEVIN, N. G., *Woodrow Wilson and World Politics* (New York, 1968).

LIEVEN, D. C. B., *Russia and the Origins of the First World War* (1983).

LLOYD GEORGE, D., *The Truth about Reparations and War Debts* (1932).

——, *The Truth about the Peace Treaties* (2 vols, 1938).

——, *War Memoirs* (2 vol. edn 1938).

LLOYD GEORGE, FRANCES, *The Years that are Past* (1967).

LOUCHEUR, LOUIS, *Carnets Secrets de Louis Loucheur* (Brussels, 1962).

LOUIS, W. ROGER, *British Strategy in the Far East 1919–1939* (Oxford, 1971).

——, *Great Britain and Germany's Lost Colonies 1914–1919* (Oxford, 1967).

LOWE, C. J. and DOCKRILL, M. L., *The Mirage of Power: British Foreign Policy 1902–1922* (3 vols, 1972).

LOWE, C. J. and MAZARI, F., *Italian Foreign Policy 1870–1940* (1975).

LUCKAU, A., *The German Delegation at the Paris Peace Conference* (New York, 1941).

LUNDGREEN-NIELSEN, K., *The Polish Problem at the Paris Peace Conference: A Study of the Policies of the Great Powers and the Poles, 1918–1919* (Odense, 1979).

MACARTNEY, C. A., *National States and National Minorities* (Oxford, 1934).

MACARTNEY, C. A. and PALMER, A. W., *Independent Eastern Europe: A History* (1962).

McCRUM, R., 'French Rhineland Policy at the Paris Peace Conference, 1919', *HJ*, 21, no. 3 (1978), 623–48.

MACDOUGALL, WALTER, A., *France's Rhineland Diplomacy, 1914–1924: The Last Bid for a Balance of Power in Europe* (Princeton, 1978).

——, 'Political Economy versus National Sovereignty: French Structures for German Economic Integration after Versailles', *JMH*, 51 (March 1979), 4–23, 78–80.

MAIER, CHARLES S., *Recasting Bourgeois Europe: Stabilization in France, Germany, and Italy in the Decade after World War 1* (Princeton, 1975).

——, 'The Truth about the Treaties?' *JMH*, 51 (March 1979), 56–67.

MANTOUX, ETIENNE, *The Carthaginian Peace* (Oxford, 1946).

MARDER, ARTHUR J., *From the Dreadnought to Scapa Flow: The Royal Navy in the Fisher Era: 1904–1919*. Vol. 5, *Victory and Aftermath, January 1918–June 1919* (1970).

MARKS, SALLY, 'Behind the Scenes at the Paris Peace Conference of 1919', *Journal of British Studies*, 9, no. 2 (1970), 154–80.

——, *Innocent Abroad: Belgium and the Paris Peace Conference of 1919* (Chapel Hill, 1981).

——, *The Illusion of Peace: International Relations in Europe 1918–1933* (1976).

MARSTON, F. S., *The Peace Conference of 1919: Organisation and Procedure* (Oxford, 1944).

MARTEL, G. (ed.), *The Origins of the Second World War Reconsidered: The A. J. P. Taylor Debate After Twenty-Five Years* (1986).

MAYER, ARNO J., *Political Origins of the New Diplomacy, 1917–1918* (New Haven, 1959).

——, *Politics and Diplomacy of Peacemaking: Containment and Counter-Revolution at Versailles 1918–1919* (1968 edn).

MEDDLICOT, W. N. (ed.), *From Metternich to Hitler* (1963).

MILLER, DAVID HUNTER, *The Drafting of the Covenant* (2 vols, New York, 1928, 1969 reprint).

MIQUEL, PIERRE, *Poincaré* (Paris, 1961).

——, *La Paix de Versailles et l'opinion publique française* (Paris, 1972).

MONGER, GEORGE W., *The End of Isolation: British Foreign Policy 1900–1907* (1963).

MONROE, ELIZABETH, *Britain's Moment in the Middle East 1914–1956* (1963, 1965 paperback).

MORGAN, J. H., *Assize of Arms* (vol. 1 1945, vol. 2 not printed).

MORGAN, KENNETH O., *Consensus and Disunity: The Lloyd George Coalition Government 1918–1922* (Oxford, 1979).

NÉRÉ, J., *The Foreign Policy of France from 1919 to 1945* (1975).

NICOLSON, HAROLD, *Curzon: The Last Phase, 1919–1925. A Study in Post-War Diplomacy* (1934).

——, *Peacemaking 1919* (1933).

NISH, I. H., *Alliance in Decline: A Study in Anglo–Japanese Relations, 1908–23* (1972).

NELSON, H. I., *Land and Power: British and Allied Policy on Germany's Frontiers, 1916–1919* (1963).

NEVAKIVI, J., *Britain, France and the Arab Middle East 1914–1920* (1969).

NEWMAN, K. J., *European Democracy between the Wars* (1970).

NORTHEDGE, F. S., *The Troubled Giant: Britain among the Great Powers 1916–1939* (1966).

PARKER, R. A. C., *Europe 1919–1945* (1969).

PEARSON, RAYMOND, *National Minorities in Eastern Europe 1848–1945* (1983).

PERCY, LORD, *Some Memories* (1958).

PERMAN, D., *The Shaping of the Czechoslovak State* (Leiden, 1962).

PETSALIS-DIOMIDIS, N., *Greece and the Paris Peace Conference, 1919* (Thessalonika, 1978).

POINCARÉ, R., *Au Service de la France* (11 vols, Paris, 1928–1974).

PORTER, BERNARD, *The Lion's Share* (1975).

PSOMIADES, HARRY J., *The Eastern Question: The Last Phase* (Salonika, 1968).

PUGH, MARTIN, *Lloyd George* (1988).

RAFFO, P., 'The Anglo-American Preliminary Negotiations for a League of Nations', *JCH*, 9 (1974), 153–76.

——, 'The League of Nations Philosophy of Lord Robert Cecil', *AJPH*, 20, no. 2 (1974), 186–96.

REMAK, J., '1914 – The Third Balkan War: Origins Reconsidered', *JMH*, 43, no. 3 (1971), 353–66. Reprinted in Koch (second edn), pp. 86–100.

RENOUVIN, P., *L'Armistice de Rethondes* (Paris, 1968).

——, *Histoire des rélations internationales; les crises du XXe siècle: 1 de 1914 à 1929* (Paris, 1969).

RIBOT, A. (ed.), *Journal d'Alexandre Ribot et correspondances inédites, 1914–1922* (Paris, 1936).

RIDDELL, LORD, *Intimate Diary of the Peace Conference and After, 1918–1923* (1933).

ROBERTS, J. M., *Europe 1880–1945* (1967).

RONALDSHAY, EARL of, *The Life of Lord Curzon, Being the Authorized Biography* (3 vols, 1928).

ROSKILL, S., *Hankey: Man of Secrets* (3 vols, 1970–1974).

——, *Naval Policy between the Wars: Volume 1, The Period of Anglo-American Antagonism, 1919–1929* (2 vols, 1968 and 1976).

ROTHWELL, V. H., *British War Aims and Peace Diplomacy 1914–1918* (Oxford, 1971).

RUDIN, H., *Armistice, 1918* (Yale, 1944).

SAUVY, A., *Histoire economique de la France* (2 vols, Paris, 1965).

SCHMIDT, ROYAL J., *Versailles and the Ruhr: Seedbed of World War II* (The Hague, 1968).

SCHUKER, S., *The End of French Predominance in Europe: The Financial Crisis of 1924 and the Adoption of the Dawes Plan* (North Carolina, 1976).

SCHULZ, GERHARD, *Revolutions and Peace Treaties, 1917–1920* (1972 translation of 1967 original).

SCHWABE, KLAUS, *Woodrow Wilson, Revolutionary Germany, and Peacemaking 1918–1919: Missionary Diplomacy and the Realities of Power*, translated by R. and R. Kimber (North Carolina, 1985).

SETON-WATSON, H. and C., *The Making of the New Europe: R. W. Seton-Watson and the last years of Austria–Hungary* (1981).

SEYMOUR, C. (ed.), *The Intimate Papers of Colonel House* (4 vols, 1928).

SHARP, ALAN, 'Britain and the Channel Tunnel 1919–1920', *AJPH*, 25, no. 2 (1979), 210–15.

——, '"Quelqu'un nous écoute": French Interception of German Telegraphic and Telephonic Communications during the Paris Peace Conference, 1919', *Intelligence and National Security*, 3, no. 4 (1988), 124–7.

——, 'Britain and the protection of minorities at the Paris Peace Conference, 1919', in A. C. Hepburn (ed.), *Minorities in History* (1978), 170–88.

——, 'Some Relevant Historians – The Political Intelligence Department of the Foreign Office, 1918–1920', *AJPH*, 34, no. 3 (1989), 359–68.

SMITH, M. L., *Ionian Vision: Greece in Asia Minor 1919–1922* (1973).

SONYEL, S. R., *Turkish Diplomacy 1918–1923: Mustafa Kemal and the Nationalist Movement* (Beverley Hills, 1975).

SPECTOR, S. D., *Rumania at the Paris Peace Conference: A Study of the Diplomacy of Ioan I. C. Bratianu* (New York, 1962).

STADLER, KARL S., *The Birth of the Austrian Republic 1918–1921* (Leiden, 1968).

STEINBERG, J., *Tirpitz and the Birth of the German Battle Fleet* (1965).

STEINER, ZARA, *Britain and the Origins of the First World War* (1977).

STEVENSON, DAVID, 'French War Aims and the American Challenge, 1914–1918', *HJ*, 22, no. 4 (1979), 877–94.

——, *French War Aims against Germany, 1914–1919* (Oxford, 1982).

STEVENSON, FRANCES (ed. A. J. P. Taylor), *Lloyd George: A Diary* (1971).

TARDIEU, A., *The Truth about the Treaty* (1921 translation).

TAYLOR, A. J. P., *The Origins of the Second World War* (1961, 1964 paperback).

TEMPERLEY, H. W. V., *A History of the Peace Conference of Paris* (6 vols, 1920, 1969 reprint).

THOMPSON, JOHN M., *Russia, Bolshevism and the Versailles Peace* (Princeton, 1966).

TILLMAN, SETH P., *Anglo-American Relations at the Paris Peace Conference of 1919* (Princeton, 1961).

TIRARD, PAUL, *La France sur le Rhin: douze années d'occupation rhénan* (Paris, 1930).

TOYNBEE, A. J., *The World after the Peace Conference* (Oxford, 1926).

TRACHTENBERG, MARC, 'Reparation at the Paris Peace Conference', *JMH*, 51 (March 1979), 24–55, 81–5.

——, *Reparation in World Politics: France and European Economic Diplomacy 1916–1923* (New York, 1980).

——, 'Versailles after Sixty Years', *JCH*, 17 (1982), 487–506.

ULLMAN, R. H., *Anglo-Soviet Relations 1917–1921* (3 vols, 1968 onwards).

VANSITTART, ROBERT, *The Mist Procession* (1958).

VINCENT, JOHN (ed.), *The Crawford Papers: The Journals of David Lindsay, twenty seventh Earl of Crawford and tenth Earl of Balcarres, 1871–1940, during the years 1892 to 1940* (Manchester, 1984).

WALDER, DAVID, *The Chanak Affair* (1969).

WALTERS, F. P., *A History of the League of Nations* (Oxford, 1952, 1967 reprint).

WALTZ, K. N., *Man, the State and War: A Theoretical Analysis* (Columbia, 1959).

WALWORTH, A., *Wilson and his Peacemakers: American Diplomacy at the Paris Peace Conference, 1919* (1986).

WANDYCZ, P., *France and her Eastern Allies 1919–1925* (Minneapolis, 1962).

WARD, KEN, *Mass Communications and the Modern World* (1989).

WATSON, D. R., *Georges Clemenceau: A Political Biography* (1974).

WATT, RICHARD M., *The Kings Depart: The Tragedy of Germany: Versailles and the German Revolution* (1968).

WEILL-RAYNAL, ETIENNE, *Les Réparations allemandes et la France* (3 vols, Paris, 1947).

WEINTRAUB, S., *A Stillness Heard Around the World* (New York, 1985).

WHITE, S., *Britain and the Bolshevik Revolution: A Study in the Politics of Diplomacy* (1979).

WICKHAM-STEED, H., *Through Thirty Years, 1892–1922, A Personal Narrative* (2 vols, 1924).

WILLIS, J. F., *Prologue to Nuremberg: The Politics and Diplomacy of Punishing War Criminals of the First World War* (Connecticut, 1982).

WOLFERS, ARNOLD, *Britain and France between two World Wars* (New York, 1940).

WRIGHT, GORDON, 'Comment', *JMH*, 51 (March 1979), 74–7.

YAPP, M. E., *The Making of the Modern Near East 1792–1923* (1987).

YEARWOOD, PETER, '"On the Safe and Right Lines": The Lloyd George Government and the Origins of the League of Nations 1916–1918', *HJ*, 32, no. 1 (1989), 131–55.

ZEMAN, Z. A. B., *A Diplomatic History of the First World War* (1971).

ZIMMERN, A., *The League of Nations and the Rule of Law 1918–1935* (1939).

Index

and eastern and central Europe,
146–55: and Hungary,
147–8; and Czechoslovakia,
148–51; and Austria, 151–2;
and the Baltic Provinces,
152–3; and Russia, 153–5
and the colonial settlement,
159–65
and the Near East, 165–75
and the Middle East, 175–84
and the settlement, 188–96
Greece,
joins *Entente*, 11
and the conference, 26, 27
and the Near East, 36, 167,
169–74
on League commission and
council, 55, 61
on Reparations commission,
85–6
and the Balkans, 134–5, 142–3,
146
Grey, Sir Edward (Viscount Grey
of Falloden), 8, 39, 43, 44, 46

Hague conference (1899), 43
Haig, Field Marshal Sir Douglas
(Earl Haig of Bemersyde),
124, 128
Hama, 176
Hankey, Sir Maurice, 29, 31, 46,
59, 161
Hardinge, Sir Charles (Baron
Hardinge of Penshurst), 138,
156, 173
Haskins, Dr Charles H., 30, 33,
35, 114–15, 122
Headlam-Morley, Sir James, 30,
33, 64, 112, 113, 114–15,
116–17, 121, 122, 193
Herzegovina, 136
Hindenburg, Field Marshal, 127
Hitler, Adolf, 151, 165, 196
Holland,
and Belgium, 102, 116–18
refuses to surrender the Kaiser,
126–7

Holy Alliance, 42, 56, 57
Homs, 176
Hoover, Herbert, 194
House, Colonel Edward Mandell,
comes to Europe, 13, 15
and armistice, 16–17, 80
and the organisation of the
conference, 20–3, 28–9
attempts to pass the treaty in
the USA, 39–40
and the League, 44, 47–8, 50,
53, 56, 60
and reparations, 80, 92
and the Rhineland, 108
and the American guarantee to
France, 113
and Fiume, 139
and the Sudetenland, 149
Hughes, William Morris,
and the League, 59, 161
and reparations, 81–3, 86
and mandates, 161–2
Hungary,
Treaty of Trianon (4.6.20), 39
and the conference, 147–8, 195
separate treaty with the USA, 40
revolution in, 130, 145
and the Banat, 136–7
and Czechoslovakia, 151
Hurst, Cecil, 26, 45, 53, 64
Hurst–Miller draft of the League
Covenant, 25–6, 53–5, 56,
57, 58
Hussein (Sherif of Mecca, king of
the Hijaz), 176, 178, 179–83
Hymans, Paul, 56, 57, 58

Imperialism, 3, 6–7, 159–83
Indemnity, *see* Reparations
India, 52, 167, 191
Inquiry, The, 50, 114
Inter-Allied debts, 78, 99, 194
International Labour Organisation
(ILO), 24, 25, 62
Ionescu, Take, 137
Iraq, 174, 175, 178, 183, 184
Ireland, 190